Women, We're Only Old Once!

Keep What You Can
Let Go of What You Can't
Enjoy What You Have!

Bertha D. Cooper

**written over ten years of growing into
an old woman with the help of her friends**

For information, contact
MSI Press
1760-F Airline Highway, #203
Hollister, CA 95023

Photos ©Laura Brown Photography

Back cover author photogaph by Michael Dashiell, Editor, Sequim Gazette

Cover design and layout by Carl Leaver

Cover graphic: Elymas/Shutterstock

Copyediting by Betty Lou Leaver

Permission received and greatfully acknowledged for use of copyrighted/ adapted material from Alzheimer's Association and Dr. Fiona McPherson

LCCN: 2020902163

ISBN: 978-1-950328-26-0

To Paul

who gave and gives unending love and support during all our ages together

Bertha D. Cooper

"I know that the actions of body, speech and mind are my only true belongings. I know I cannot escape the consequences of my actions of body, speech and mind."

Thich Nhat Hanh

Bertha D. Cooper

Contents

Acknowledgements ix

Expert Resources xi

Introduction 1

Part One
Navigating Instead of Denying the Aging Process 7

   1 We're Only Old Once 9

   2 The Bold Impermanence of Aging 21

   3 Reflection, Reconciliation, Reward 29

Part Two
Stepping Onto and Staying on the Path to Healthy Aging 39

   4 Aging is Not a Disease 41

   5 Face Up to It and Other Issues of the Skin 53

   6 Renewable Energy Is Not So Renewable 65

   7 An Aging System Delivers 81

   8 Aging Women and Weight 91

   9 Word Finding and Mental Fitness 107

  10 For Better or Worse In Health Planning 123

Part Three
Living as an Older Woman In America 137

  11 Making Appearances 139

  12 Relationships are What Women Do 153

  13 Old and New Partners In Love 163

  14 Aging Women and Sexuality 173

Part Four
Aging Women Becoming What They Are 185

  15 A Woman's Work (And Play) Is Never Done 187

  16 Losses That Matter 199

  17 Aging Women and Spirituality 211

  18 Coming of Old Age 219

   Notes for Quick Study or Contemplation 227

   References 231

Bertha D. Cooper

Acknowledgements

Writing a book on aging over a period of ten-years has the advantage of living and sharing the experience with many people. The most constant person is my husband Paul who proved to be my role model and who never gave up on encouraging his wife to write her first book.

Earlier on, I was fortunate to be in touch with an expanding group of women who shared my curiosity and questions about aging as a woman. Nearly 50 women participated in either interviews or conversations about aging; each one was an inspiration for my purpose and research. They are this book.

I am grateful to experts in their fields who gave of their time and expertise: Claire Haycox, Paul Cunningham, Carol Kalahar, Cheryl Bell and Pat Mortati all gave substance and credibility to the content.

Three women, all good and smart friends, read the book in its various developing drafts and provided suggestions that help shaped the narrative. For that, I am grateful to Bonnie Svardal, Susan Molin, and Pat Coate. Many other friends never gave up on me or the book.

Then, after many failed efforts to interest an agent or publisher in my book, I was fortunate to find Betty Lou Leaver, co-founder of MSI Press and San Juan books, who was willing to risk time and effort on an unproven old writer whose only platform was a network of professionals and friends. Thus started the journey of becoming an author, led, pushed, and challenged by a woman who will only publish a quality book. Betty Lou copyedited and helped me through a steep learning curve to end with the book I wanted to be read and savored by women. I am grateful to this amazing woman who happens to be in the book's cohort and serves as an example of a woman engaged in life and aging well.

Expert Resources

Paul Cunningham

Paul Cunningham MD, Board Certification in Family Medicine, Geriatrics, and Hospice/Palliative Care, is a Clinical Professor of Medicine at the University of Washington School of Medicine providing administrative and clinical leadership in the provision of care to a spectrum of medically complex patients. He also currently serves as the Chief Medical Officer of Jamestown Health Clinic in Sequim, Washington.

Through interviews with me, Dr. Cunningham provided me with general information, as well as specific information for Chapter 4, "Aging Is Not a Disease" and Chapter 9 "Word Finding and Mental Fitness."

Claire Haycox

Claire Haycox MD, Ph.D., a board-certified in medicine and dermatology, who holds a Ph.D in bio-engineering, has been honored with awards and fellowships: the 2016 Leadership Development Program, College of Medicine-Jacksonville, Florida; 1997 Women's Dermatologic Society Mentorship Award to study for one month with Dr. Vera Price at University of California-San Francisco; 1996 Scottish Dermatologist Society Visiting Fellowship; and N.I.H. Medical Scientist in Training Program Scholarship. Dr. Haycox has practiced over 20 years in the Pacific Northwest and is a former clinical associate professor at the University of Washington School of Medicine. Through interviews with me, Dr. Haycox provided me with general information as well as specific information for Chapter 5, "Face Up to It and Issues of the Skin."

Pat Mortati

Pat Mortati is an exercise physiologist who earned a Master of Science degree in exercise physiology from the University of Nevada, Las Vegas. Mortati served as coordinator of the Cardiac Rehabilitation Program at Olympic Medical Center in Port Angeles, Washington for 17 years and as a member of the editorial board of the American College of Sports Medicine Health-Fitness Journal from 2001-2005. In addition, Ms. Mortati is a nationally certified yoga instructor. Through interviews with me, Ms. Mortati provided general information as well as information specific to Chapter 6, "Renewable Energy Not So Renewable."

Cheryl Bell

Cheryl Bell is an American Council on Exercise (ACE) certified personal trainer, experienced yoga teacher, and Ayurvedic Wellness Counselor. Working in the fitness industry for more than a decade, Ms. Bell has focused on blending Western science with Eastern practices to extend our years of wellness. Through interviews with me. Ms. Bell provided general information as well as information specific to Chapter 6, "Renewable Energy Not So Renewable," and Chapter 10, "Making Appearances."

Carole Kalahar

Carole Kalahar, NP, is an Advanced Nurse Practitioner in Obstetrics and Gynecology. Certified by the North American Menopause Society as a Menopause Practitioner. With over 40 years of diverse experience in nursing, she currently practices as a member of the provider staff of Jamestown Family Health Clinic in Sequim, Washington. Through interviews with me, Ms. Kalahar provided general information as well as information specific to Chapter 14. "Aging Women and Sexuality."

Introduction

I stood at the door to my old age, somewhat reluctant to enter. Since I was only partially committed to the inevitable, I took a cautious first look at this new territory and came up with more questions than answers. What should I wear? What must I plan? What must I pack? What do I leave behind? What does it matter?

I embarked on writing Women, We're Only Old Once!: Keep What You Can, Let Go of What You Can't, Enjoy What You Have when I was 66 years old and found myself asking even more questions. I knew that I was not alone. I would write from a woman's point of view. Women, We're Only Old Once! would be a book for women. I knew that I wanted to share my journey with other women and that I wanted to invite women to share their journeys with me.

Aging doesn't start at 50, 55, 60, or 65. It starts at birth. Aging doesn't get a bad name until accompanied by wrinkles, arthritic bumps, and the certain knowledge that we have fewer years left to live than we have lived. Denial takes over, especially in a culture that markets anti-aging products. All my experience has shown me that aging into old age, like any other transition, is a natural process. I knew that Women, We're Only Old Once! had to inform and empower with understanding, choice, and control.

For more than 50 years, I worked with, around, and for older people as a nurse and health care administrator. I went into management early in my career, mostly due to the incredible growth of services brought on by Medicare and the few experienced administrators available for the work. I am forever grateful for the opportunity to experience and work in settings like hospitals, skilled nursing facilities, home health, rehabilitation centers, outpatient services, and hospice programs. As a team, other health care professionals and I worked to provide services that would allow older and old-aged people to restore their health and function with dignity and purpose or, if that were not possible, end their lives in dignity and comfort. We did our best as we helped them to mobilize their resources. I witnessed incredible resolve of those recovering from injury, surgery, or long illness that had left them exhausted and in pain. I marveled at the will that brought back their spirits and put them back into their homes. I loved all those old people, and I am wiser because of them.

In all settings, most aging people strive to maintain their independence and control just as they have at any other time in their lives. I felt we were at our best when we helped them achieve their goals and our worst when we stood in the way of their goals. Because of these individuals, I grew to respect and admire old age. What's not to love about enduring resilience, frisky obstinacy, honest observations, and personal histories of success and failure? I know as a witness what aging does and can bring. Thus, Women, We're Only Old Once! had to be about choices we make that will or will not lead to living well into and in our old age.

Despite, or maybe because of my considerable background and knowledge, I had many questions about why certain things happen when we grow old and wondered if these things are truly part of aging. Having worked in an industry that saw people with medical problems, I didn't necessarily know what natural aging was. Recognizing healthy aging was not as programmed into me since my knowledge and experience was primarily around pathological aging.

I started Women, We're Only Old Once! by interviewing younger and older women friends. I discovered they had the same interest, even a longing, to talk about what it means to get old. They soon referred me to other women, and my circle of women expanded. Most of the women I spoke with were between the ages of 55 and 75 and had a variety of experiences and backgrounds. I collected stories that brought new insights as well as confirming the sense of being together on an important journey. I have included several of their stories in this book. Although I haven't used their real names or in some cases, even disguised identifying information, the stories are true as they told them. Several of their quotes are included in the book and referenced as "Aging women survey."

I relied on professional colleagues including a dermatologist and geriatrician well-respected in their fields, along with nurses, an experienced dietitian, a personal trainer, yoga instructors, a hair stylist, and an exercise physiologist. I explored popular women's magazines and scientific journals. I delved into the wealth of leads and information available on the Internet that led to multiple resources for trends and data. I have included them in a reference list that can serve as a resource for additional information.

My husband of 48 years provided important motivation for my journey and writing just as he has during our all years together. This time was a bit different in that he became a laboratory of sorts for me as he transitioned into late middle age and old age. He is now a remarkable 93 years old, fully 16 years older than I am. I have watched and lived his aging. I learned the natural processes of aging are in many aspects common to men and women. I knew I wanted to age as well as he. I wanted everyone to have the experience of aging well.

The process of discovery brought me to Women, We're Only Old Once!, a guide to aging for women ages 55 to 80 who seek answers to questions about what to expect, what to question, what to influence, and what to simply accept from their aging selves. This book is a tool for wonder, empowerment, and getting the most out of this important phase of life.

Women, We're Only Old Once! is not intended to be an encyclopedia of all things related to aging. Instead, it focuses on aging as a natural process and answers questions that give us an informed understanding of the transition we are in and a greater ability to make informed choices. Women, We're Only Old Once! is not intended to replace individual medical supervision or recommendations; in fact, the importance of professional health care is emphasized in assessing and managing the effects of aging whether resulting from natural or disease processes.

Women, We're Only Old Once! is thoughtful reflection, informed perspective, and fact-based useful information about the physical, psychological, mental, and social processes of aging and suggestions for women to effectively manage their aging world. Women, We're Only Old Once! is a book about choices and control of our lives. It's the joie de vivre of drooping chins, aches, and pains that last longer than a day, hugging grandchildren, expanding waistlines, living the dream, unbearable losses, losing words in the middle of a sentence, living on a fixed income, and coming to peace. It's the joie de vivre of waking each morning and seeing the sun or the rain as if it were the first time.

Part One, "Navigating Instead of Denying the Aging Process" opens Women, We're Only Old Once! with the frank observation that we are only old once and begins to set out a positive vision of aging, one we can choose.

Most of us happen to live in a culture that prefers not to talk about getting old and its inevitable outcome of death so we don't always get the chance to define what we mean by "aging with grace," "young for her age," or "come along with me, the best is yet to come." Yet, we know the inevitability of the transition.

We've experienced the sense of time flying by and things shifting out of our control but never as much as when we reach our mid-50s and early 60s. We begin to experience an unnerving sense of accelerating change, characterizing our lives whether it is a new ache, technology innovations, or the death of a friend.

Such wonderings begin on the day we feel bonds loosening and experience concern that we no longer will be known for what we were. It is the beginning of contemplations, recapitulations, and resolutions that allow us to move forward into the transition, a process not unlike the other transitions in our lives. We are tasked to learn the art of grieving, acceptance, and renewal in the face of accelerating loss.

Part Two, "Stepping onto and Staying on the Path to Healthy Aging," focuses on the physical and organic changes that forever change our abilities, our appearance, and our futures. The changes are dramatic and seem life altering mainly because we live in a society that sees beauty only in the young woman and not possible in the aging woman.

Physical changes related to normal aging are presented in a factual way to help us understand what to expect and what precautions we can take to mitigate any dysfunction that could result from those changes.

Aging does make us more vulnerable to disease, but we have power and can make choices that achieve and maintain our health. Skin, energy or lack thereof, weight, expanding waists, symptoms of health problems, and mental fitness are put into the framework of our aging journey. Options are given for managing the changes with an emphasis on managing weight, relieving unnecessary anxieties, and making informed choices.

Part Three, "Living as an Older Woman in America," speaks to the many ways we live as an older person and the importance of defining and making plans for what's important for each of us. We always have known that women are more likely to live longer than male partners. How odd it is that for all of women's caring about family, security, friendship, and fulfillment, many of us enter old age as if we thought we never would. Many of us have done little planning or have no plans at all.

Many of the themes of physical impermanence, less energy, and less time also apply to our daily habits and relationships. We may have to change habits in order to maintain the appearance we wish to present. Our declining capacity for managing stress forces us to make these kinds of changes.

We continue to care about friendship and family relationships; some grow stronger, some are reconciled, and some are let go as we plan around less energy and time. We may still be in love, fall in love, or not. The desire for partnering is highly individual. We learn sometimes to our surprise that we still are sensual, sexual human beings. Most important, we learn our sexuality is not lost unless we have chosen to lose it and may just require a spark for ignition.

Part Four, "Aging Women Becoming What They Are," can be thought of as the soul of Women, We're Only Old Once!. Our purpose, obligations, limitations, and potential are explored. Some of us discover that we have new purpose, that indeed a woman's work is never done. We explore coming to terms with the lessons and meaning of this phase of life and the end of this life. How well do we embrace losses, especially those that matter? And does it matter?

Spirituality enters our thoughts at a different level as we wrap our minds more closely around the end of this life and what it means to us. Some of us emerge with deepened spirituality, which may be a strong connection with place or a sustained sense of religious faith or a simple connection with all things living, past, and present.

Women, We're Only Old Once! tells women how to take on the rightful essence of aging, not by denying age but by understanding the process of aging and making choices in a physically, emotionally, spiritually, and mindfully healthy way.

The fearful journey to the inevitable turns into challenge, then excitement through sharing, learning, and understanding that aging is not instant death of our personalities, our bodies, or our relevance to the world. Rather, we see ourselves in the reflections of other women, role models, and ever-newly-appearing realizations of the power underlying the years we've lived and the power yet to come. We come alive.

This book intends to illuminate the strength, beauty and potential of an aging woman, often hidden or unrealized. This woman is the role model of living well, and she can be found all around us. She is in our neighborhood, our church, our volunteer organizations, our work settings, and our homes. She is in you and me. She is us.

My intent is that women join me in these pages and embrace their own journey on the pathway to living well in this most interesting phase of life.

Bertha D. Cooper

Part One
Navigating Instead of
Denying the Aging Process

Women in America arrive at the door to old age that opens to a confusing environment of attitudes, biases, services, and products intended to stave off this inevitable phase of life. Buying into the narrative of anti-aging risks denial of our very selves. Part One begins the conversation around our first awareness of our aging world with optimistic and pragmatic vision.

Bertha D. Cooper

1

We're Only Old Once

"I think, like many women, I was judgmental toward women as they aged. Women, in our society are compartmentalized so that we start to feel like we're cut flowers and after a while we will wilt. I realize now that's not the case—we can celebrate every age."

—*Charlize Theron, W Magazine, May 2015*

I've come a long way and a few years from my first experience as an invisible old woman. Most women I talk with remember the first time they were ignored by a young woman behind the cosmetics counter or a barista who turned to serve the more interesting person closer to his or her own age. The shock has worn off, and I am well into the adjustments and adaptations unique to this experience of getting older. I can even say that I've made friends with my older self now that I'm no longer in a state of denial about how the world sees me. That acceptance opened to me an expansive, more positive vision of aging.

This vision begins with a realistic understanding of what aging looks and feels like, especially for women. We can prepare for this transition with grace and energy by seeking out role models and benefiting from others' experience with successful aging, but before we can look clearly at aging, we'll need to break the silence about what aging is often seen to mean in American society.

Growing Old in a Culture of Denial

As I began my journey of discovery into what being an older woman might mean in America, I learned that I wasn't the only one who had questions and fears, nor was I the only one who craved conversation about aging well but didn't know how to begin it. Most of us are at least curious about the experience of others and how it compares to ours. Yet, inexplicably we women, even those of us who tend to overshare, don't always engage in substantial discussions about what it means to grow old and how to do it with dignity and self-kindness. We live in a culture in the United States that celebrates youth and hopes to postpone aging as long as possible. As women, we've all experienced the message throughout our lives that to be socially acceptable and desirable it's necessary to be beautiful as in slender but curvaceous, with unlined, made-up faces, and gleaming hair. We have been expected, no matter what our age or ethnicity, to conform to standards of beauty and to spare no expense in achieving that level of conventional loveliness. There is always a product or program to help.

Even though in the past 40-plus years many women, from feminists to African-American activists, have challenged the stereotypes of female beauty and succeeded in enlarging our vision of the many ways a woman can be both attractive and interesting, barriers remain. The most attractive of women eventually will grow old and look it despite all the creams and treatments in the world.

With the rise of women in politics, the arts, and the business world, we now have more role models of women who are celebrated for their achievements and talents as well as for having interesting, lived-in faces. One only has to think of Hillary Clinton, Toni Morrison, Madeline Albright, Cicely Tyson, Helen Mirren, Judy Dench, Janet Yellen, Barbara Streisand, and a host of lesser-known women to realize that we live in a world where the voices of older women are increasingly heard and age is not a barrier.

On the other hand, most of us are not Nobel Prize winners, movie stars, singers, or past Secretaries of State and presidential candidates. We live ordinary lives in a world where women, especially older women, are still too often sidelined and treated as invisible. No wonder many of us buy creams and cosmetics, dye our hair, and deny that we are getting older. We contribute to the billion-dollar industries promising youth through anti-aging products and services. We live in the world of America that worships the beauty and vitality of youth and completely misses the beauty and vitality of aging.

We who are aging or aged must contend with the forces of perception played out in the market that tells us aging is a bad thing and to be avoided at all costs. After all, what could be good about aching bones, sagging bodies, low energy, and difficulty sleeping? Since I have worked with and often adored some of our oldest people, I know that isn't all there is. In addition to the wisdom of years, older people have a certain beauty. One of the most beautiful women I knew spent her day dressed and sitting by the door of the nursing home. She made herself the official greeter for this "hotel." No one entered without being warmed by her wide smile and brilliant eyes that twinkled at her own mischievous undertaking.

Pretending to be anything but what we are makes little sense even if the idea of age pride has yet to catch on despite the efforts of the Gray Panthers and AARP. In fact, being and accepting what we are may be the finest gift of aging we can give ourself. No doubt it is the finest gift we can give to generations of women following us. We just need to remember "we're only old once" and the best plan is to make the most of it just like we would of childhood, youth, or middle age. Be old and wise!

Old Age is Another Life Transition

Entering old age is, like other transitions we've made in our lives, full of mental, physical, and social upheavals. It has its own unique challenges. Life transitions, if done well, result in growth. The same is true of old age. The difference is that our old age is marked by unavoidable physical decline and accelerating losses, and we realize this age will end in our death. One of our tasks is to come to terms with that finality, but it isn't the only feature of old age.

By now, we have figured out that we are not going to fulfill some of those youthful ambitions like being a billionaire or Broadway star. We still have dreams and things we want to accomplish whether it's a bucket list of adventures or assuring that our grandchildren go to college. We balance our expectations with the knowledge of limits to our bodies, endurance, relationships, finances, and time.

Yet, most of us also know that old age will have its share of surprises, often unwelcome. We may have complications due to physical changes. We can't see, taste, or hear as well. We may develop a chronic disease or injure our bodies in a disabling way. In some cases, like someone who carries a gene for diabetes, we are destined to develop the disease. Others have choices and can prevent the development of diabetes or other diseases.

Complications or not, there are common features among our age transitions. All involve physical, mental, emotional, and social adjustments. The challenges and adjustments require, and in some cases demand, our participation. We are faced with choices in all our transitions, including old age. We start by beginning the exploration of our own experience of aging. We start by listening to our own thoughts about aging—and our questions and fears.

Our thoughts, insights, values and emotions mature as we grow older, but we don't think of them as old. We don't see them as wrinkled and deteriorating. We wonder how we can be old when our minds have the same resilience, curiosity, and capacity, in some cases greater than in our youth. We are acutely aware of the cognitive dissidence of an active energetic mind in an aging body. We hear it often, "I am not old in my head" or "I feel young in my thinking."

We feel physical limitations and hear expressions such as "the spirit is willing but the flesh isn't" or "youth is wasted on the young." So, why do we label our thinking and feelings as young or feeling young and not our bodies? Could it be our own prejudice about aging that expects decline; expects us to become sour and confused? Why not expect vitality in our thinking, feeling, and loving? Does society expect so little of us? Do we expect so little of ourselves? It's a thought to keep while we explore the experience of aging.

A near-60-year-old woman friend I see occasionally told me her story of having hip surgery and recovery that involved walking with a walker. The walker and the looks of others caused her to feel like "an old lady," a very new experience for her and premature at her age of 59.

Her impression was validated in one of her first outings with friends. One companion commented with an attitude of disgust and/or pity that she "seemed old." Although my friend knew her "oldness" was temporary, she couldn't help feeling that she might have crossed over some imaginary line into another era of her life.

My friend recovered but not before facing physical vulnerability and attitudes about being old, including those of her closest friends. Our health—fatigue, pain and other conditions—certainly has an impact on our mental outlook. In general, though, if we are healthy and not bonded by or preoccupied with a set of symptoms, our minds feel as young as ever.

We often equate our feelings when sick with what it must be like to be old. "I feel old and tired." It's true that we do have declining energy and endurance the older we get, but we also have many moments of positive feelings and experiences unencumbered by "feeling old." The risk in not recognizing the realistic potential of this stage in our lives is that we will decide that being old is being unable to do what we want to do or used to do, and being weak, tired, unhappy, and alone that turns into poor choices and a self-fulfilling prophecy.

Successful Aging

At the same time, if we think about it, we're surrounded by people growing old in a positive, life-affirming, and graceful way. Does successful aging depend on genes, or does it also consist of qualities and habits that can be cultivated, no matter what our age? To consider this question, I asked several women what they considered features of successful aging.

Role Models

One of the questions I posed to women I interviewed was "Who were your role models for successful aging?" which I qualified to be someone they knew, or knew of, living or dead, and why. Their responses were along the lines of

- my mom (died at 94) was active, aware, interested, not self-absorbed, accepted aging;
- my 95-year-old neighbor was stable, alert, had a positive attitude, was not judgmental; and
- my maternal grandmother was very alert, active, and proud of her age.

The women most often mentioned someone they knew personally. Some women, like I, had to ponder the question whereas others responded quickly and confidently and named their grandmother, mother, or aged friend as a successful ager. Some mentioned public figures known to all of us. All agreed that their role models were active, involved in life and with others, and optimistic and did not dwell on their infirmities, even those that killed them. They expressed near unanimous consensus on the characteristics of aging successfully. That congruity tells me that we know what successful aging is: it isn't a wrinkle-free face or the strength to climb a mountain.

A Passion for Life

Many judged the success of aging as viewed at the end of life after the final years were lived. In many cases those final years were lived as part of a continuum of the passion of their lives. One of the unusually interesting women I met was definite about her life and death. She threatened to sue anyone who revived her with CPR. When she's done, she's done, she stated in no uncertain terms. In the meantime, she was going to experience everything she could about other countries, including riding a yak in Mongolia.

An Abiding Interest in Others

Barbara Walters is one of our better-known examples. She seems to have insatiable curiosity about people, evidenced by having made a career of intently interviewing as many people as possible. She was hosting television interviews well into her 80s. The women I interviewed most often mentioned women who reflected a joy in learning and talking about others and rarely about themselves.

Curiosity about Life

Curiosity, intellectual or otherwise, gives meaning and purpose to life. One cited example of intellectual curiosity was Elizabeth Kubler-Ross, who spent her life studying death and dying. She defined the stages of grief to help us understand our own humanity[1]. I spoke with a lesser-known woman who is on a lifelong study to answer the question of our cosmic origins.

Involved in Life

Women who stayed active, like the well-known Gloria Steinem or the many lesser-known older women who keep their churches functioning from Sunday to Sunday, were seen as being involved in life. They maintained close ties with their interests. Many held active roles in their churches or political affiliations over a long period of time or took on new roles, like interacting with grandchildren or supporting emerging causes.

Overcoming or Accepting Limitations in Life

It was with near awe that women spoke of older women who had disabilities, living in pain or with a terminal diagnosis and never speaking of it as a burden. Some admired women who were caring for aging and infirmed partners as an ultimate labor of love.

---

1   Elizabeth Kubler-Ross (2014) proposed five stages of grief: denial, anger, bargaining, depression, and acceptance.

Positive Attitude toward Life

"Zest for life" is how one woman described her friend who just turned 70. These are the old women we want to share a room with because they are hopeful and encouraging. Their own not-insignificant hardships become insignificant in the presence of their uplifting attitude. These positive role models see the future as bright even though the future is not theirs. Betty White, 98 in 2020, still living and poking fun at others, lives out her passions for animals, humor, and acting every day. Being around her is like being around fun.

Making Right Choices for Our Well-Being

Although it was rarely mentioned by the women, I added making right choices because women who choose to care for their bodies and prevent, to the extent possible, chronic disease and disability are more likely to be active and in control of their lives. They are aware daily of the need to make lifestyle choices that support their minds and bodies. They don't obsess; they just do it. They go silently about their good choices for the health of body, mind, and spirit, and they support others in doing the same.

An Aging Role Model in Brief

Thanks to my interviews, I've come to understand the model of a successfully aging woman. It isn't her interests as much as her comfort in her own body and mind. She honors her life by knowing her strengths and accepting her limitations. In other words, she cherishes her life and greets each day with honesty and frankness. She has overcome her fears and apprehensions by learning what she can about aging, what to accept as part of aging, and what she can do to age well. She has pride in her age and doesn't strive to look anything but her age, whether 70, 80, 90 or older.

Negative Habits of Aging

For every positive face of successful aging, there is its opposite. When asked about role models for unsuccessful aging, the mood of the room darkened, and women spoke of people who lived as if their infirmities and disabilities, minor or major, had become them. The center of their lives had narrowed to a circle around themselves, and they only invited others in to talk about what was happening to them.

They spoke of women being "picky," negative, passive, blaming, and unwilling to change." They spoke of these women as people they did not want to be around even though in some cases they felt they had no other choice. Women are often the caregivers of elder members in a family, usually mothers who live into old age with disabilities, some sadly clothed in bitterness.

One woman related the story of taking care of her husband's disabled mother during the day and how her mother-in-law complained to her son about her when he returned from work. Her husband said nothing to support her even in the quiet of their bedroom. Years later and into her old age, his failure to recognize the work she did haunted her and remained an open wound in their relationship.

We do not easily forget those people who are difficult to be around and challenge our natures to look under the bitterness for fear and loneliness and muster compassion for them. We hope to rise above ourselves but often don't. What we can do is set our goals to be different, to be aware. and even under the worst of circumstances to rise above our tendency for self-absorption.

Our Worst Fears

Losing Mental Acuity

Part of what adds to our denial of aging and our negativity toward it are the many fears of what life will look like for us as we grow old and then older.

The women I spoke with whose mothers developed Alzheimer's disease or other forms of dementia were the most outspoken about their fear that aging for them meant becoming mindless. They had watched as their mothers left piece by piece until they no longer knew their daughters or any life lived before that moment.

"(I fear) becoming feeble and less mobile."
"I don't want to go to a nursing home."

Losing the Ability for Self-Care

Nursing home residents represent the most haunting role model of aging. The most common fear the women mentioned, whether 55 or 78, was losing the ability to care for themselves. We have all seen women and men who came to live in nursing homes at the end of their lives. We have visited family and seen people, mostly women, sunken and asleep in wheelchairs. We have smelled the odors of aging, incontinence, and decay, and we have heard random cries for help. No one wants to be there, yet there some of us must go.

I saw many during my career as a nursing home administrator. People end their lives in nursing homes because they have either become so physically or mentally debilitated that they can no longer care for themselves or because they lack the support system or resources that can keep them in their home and provide the level of care they need. I saw resignation in some with functioning minds but failing bodies who came to live permanently in nursing homes, but in most I also saw resilience as they exercised the personalities that had sustained them through their lives. They carved their territories and learned the ways to have some control in an environment in which they had lost almost all control.

A friend admitted to a nursing home for rehabilitation would feign cries for help just as someone tried to help her move because it was her way of assuring that she would be moved with gentleness and therefore have less pain. In later chapters, I will discuss ways to waylay losing control physically, none of which are magical and all of which involve discipline.

Overall, it is important to remember that the odds of ending life in a nursing home are small. Statistics should comfort us. Less than 5 percent of people over the age of 65 reside in nursing home and most of those are 80 years or older.[2] There are countless more who move in and out of nursing homes for short-term rehabilitation, convalescence, and, in some cases, hospice care. Living in anticipation of residing permanently in a nursing home is an unfounded fear; it's simply not a typical fate of aging.

Preparing to Be Old: "It's Never Too Late"

I expect confronting the reality of diminishing time is a common experience. When young we don't think about getting older, sick or dying. We are comforted by what seems like endless years. It wasn't until my early 60s that I became more acutely aware that the future contained far fewer years than the past. This, if not before, is the time of reflection about what we think our aging world will be and what we want it to be.

I don't propose that the young begin dwelling on getting old but I do encourage establishing lifestyle habits that will lead to a healthier old age. We all should listen to the reformed smoker with lung cancer or diabetic without an amputated leg who wisely tells us to be more caring of our bodies. The earlier in life the better it is to establish lifelong habits of caring for our bodies, minds, emotions and spirit. I am not alone in my belief as you will read throughout this book that it is never too late. We can turn back

---

2   US Bureau of Census (2016) reports that 4.2% of population 65+ years of age are in nursing homes at any one time. Slightly over 5% live in nursing homes, congregate care, assisted living and board/care homes.

our descent into chronic life-robbing disease. Late-in-life effort requires the hard work of learning and establishing new habits but as studies have shown, our disease can be reversed.

I never have been as aware of my age as I am now and probably will be for the rest of my life. I had some vague notion when I turned 50 and experienced some peri-menopausal discomforts (the first time the rewind button was pushed) and wasn't particularly aware of any aimlessness let alone body deterioration.

Now my body reminds me daily and I plot the passage to old age. I take comfort sometimes that I'm now joined in aging by the baby boomers (those born from 1946-1964). That generation, diverse as it is, as a group managed to shift society's prejudices. Although that demographic is no healthier in their lifestyle than the rest of us (and may have a greater risk of disease. See Chapter 10), they tended in their youth to be greater risk-takers than those of us born earlier, whose primary concern was long-term security.

Many boomers have seen the future of limited coverage and Medicare doctors and already have made changes to their lifestyles. Who brought us yoga, running, Tai Chai, fitness centers and home exercise equipment? Who was the first to count calories and read food labels? They are the boomers, who caught on to the joy of being fit and rewards of being healthy. Many of this age group are actively involved in their own health and likely will change the course of aging in America.

While activism and knowledge are crucial when it comes to getting older, it's worth acknowledging that physical aging isn't a movement any more than it is a disease. Aging is the natural course of life. Unfortunately, a variety of unhealthy behaviors are resulting in serious disruption of the natural course of aging and subsequently in disease. The aging phase of a boomer's life will require attention unlike any other they've experienced, deliberate and focused attention to all the securities: financial, physical, mental, emotional, spiritual, relevance, relationships and place.

We start preparing for the journey into our old age by living a healthy life now and if we are not, changing our direction so we don't carry the discomfort, the dissatisfaction, the negative world view and/or poor health into our old years when there is much less that we can do about it. We are surrounded by possibilities.

Never Before Have We Been So Many

Boomers may change the face of aging, but so will women, through sheer numbers. According to the latest statistics (Infoplease, 2020), life expectancy in the United States at birth in the early 20th century was 51years for a white woman and 35 years for all other females, with a steady increase in each passing decade such that my generation of mid-World War II white babies born in the early 1940s could expect to live to age 67 and all other women of the same generation could expect to live to 55. Centenarians have been a rarity and celebrated in papers with photos of uncomprehending faces startled at their own longevity but comfortable in their skin.

The 21st century ushered in an unprecedented average life expectancy of 80 years for white women and 75 years for all other women. Far more people can expect to live beyond 80, longer if they live in Japan, which ranks second, or in Canada, which ranks 16th in order of anticipated longevity. (By comparison, the United States ranks 46rd.) (Worldometer, 2020).

Some states in our United States do better than others. According to a study released by the Centers for Communicable Disease and Prevention, life expectancy for a person reaching 65 and living in Mississippi will be about 17.5 more years with at least seven being lived in poor health (2013). According to the same study, a person living in Hawaii can expect to live 21 more years with only five years in poor health.

Never have so many been this old at the same time for this long. I have yet to meet a man or woman who says he or she wants to live a long time in poor health. We want to live our old age with quality of life. Additional years have been granted us through technology. We now have safer water, vaccinations, open-heart surgery, and a marvelous opportunity to enjoy a long life and live as the role model for successful aging in this new age. We have an opportunity to live those years to their fullest.

We start by getting used to the experience of aging.

Bertha D. Cooper

2

The Bold Impermanence of Aging

"I never thought about mortality (mine) before. I have less [sic] years in front of me than behind me."

—*Aging women survey*

Aging brings an accelerated sense of impermanency that ranges from small fissures in our complexion to deaths of those close to us. By the time we reach 60, we've moved from home to home, watched our children leave home, had a few jobs or careers, experienced health problems, and perhaps have been married or partnered one or more times. We may think we know impermanency until we realize that now we wake each morning and discover a new drooping in our face or thighs or a new ache in a part of the body we didn't know we had. If we are lucky that day, these are the worst losses.

We cannot begin to talk about aging without talking about changes that occur daily, many, if not most, representing loss of some part of ourselves. Physical losses become more noticeable and seem to exaggerate after aging 55 or 60 years. We know that they didn't just start, but none were as apparent as they are now.

At first, we call them temporary until we gradually come to know with certainty that the losses are permanent. Some changes interfere with functioning, hearing and vision being good examples. Health seems more at risk, causing us to lose confidence in something on which we thoughtlessly depended. We are beginning the transition to the young days of old age.

Beginning Awareness

The process of our personal recognition of aging starts for real in our 50s. Menopause signals the end of our reproductive life. Turning 60 signals the beginning awareness of our old age and triggers fears and denials. Physical malfunctions and disease take on greater importance. Recovery seems less certain and takes longer.

Most of us have not reached a state that allows us to deal seamlessly with the body, mind, and life changes that seem to accelerate as we approach our 60s. Changes and losses begin to be framed by the certain knowledge that they may not be replaced by new relationships, new jobs, new organs, or new adventures.

Bold impermanence is impossible to ignore in our aging lives. Sometimes, change is small, like seeing lines develop around our eyes; other times, it is huge and important, like death of those our own age.

In 2005, I lost my dearest woman friend to the sudden burst of a blood vessel in her brain that bled her life from her. Our relationship had developed over 20 years of common values, experiences, interests, and affection for each other. Next to my husband, she was the one who cared the most about me and all my successes, challenges and hurts. The relationship was irreplaceable: not only did I not have that many years left to live but also most of the experiences I shared with her would never come again.

Obituaries take on new meaning as we share the birth years of those passing. Unlike the deaths of older friends in earlier years, we feel deep pain when peers disappear; we miss them terribly and long to see them again. We know the stark reality that it could easily be us; our time is arriving.

Are We Ever Good at Losing?

At one time in my life, I thought I was good at losses because I experienced them early and often. I discovered, though, as most do, it gets harder as the years pass. Another loss brings back all the others to be relived. Grieving comes in predictable waves of despair alternating with hopes that the loss won't matter.

The loss of spouses, family, friends and lovers affect us the most deeply, rivaled by our pending death or dementia, which robs us of our essence and buries our souls. In all cases, we encounter separation without the chance of reconnection.

As long as we have some capacity to think and feel, we grieve both physical and symbolic losses. For some, the latter might be the invisibility in the working world that comes with aging through retirement from long-held careers, and for others, it might take the form of no longer being needed by children or parents.

Aging steals into our lives as early as our 20s, when our faces begin to take the shape of knowing adults and our bodies achieve adult form only to begin the process of subtle decline. We notice these changes in our 40s and see them accelerating in our 50s. Some of us require reading glasses, and most discover that maintaining muscular strength requires focused effort. Unless one is an ardent fitness practitioner, waists, hips, and chests expand. We realize that the same pace and amount of eating results in more storing of fat. So, we begin to realize that we must learn to manage impermanence and loss in a new or different way.

The Art of Letting Go

In our 60s, changes and losses take on a different meaning. They touch us with the sense of no return and the certain knowledge that this time is different. It is then we must learn, if we haven't yet, the skill of letting go in order to move on. Our purpose, our health, and our bodies are changing. It becomes our life's job to keep up with accelerating changes and losses. It may indeed involve more art than skill, but if ever there was a time to learn to let go, it is now.

Many of us already have had some experience with loss such as losing a promotion to a younger person, a partner to a younger partner or to a burgeoning career. Truthfully, these losses have less to do with aging than with life. Yet, such experiences cannot help but point out that we are simply not as young as we used to be.

Sometimes, we greet our losses with frustration rather than grieving and blame it on our busy lives, which in America, is frequently the reality. We strove to have enough money for now and the future, raise children who make good decisions in a world that sometimes encourages bad decisions, maintain functional relationships in marriage, partnerships, and friendships, and achieve enough fulfillment of self to feel on track. We can't help, then, but feel an element of unfairness that we have worked hard and still have more to do. We always will be letting go. We need to believe it is all part of the passage to the personal freedom to live life fully.

Breaking through Aging Denial

The obvious and accelerating physical changes make it harder to deny the realities of aging. I think I experienced an existential terror the first time I caught a glimpse of my face in one of those magnifying cosmetic mirrors at the fragrance counter. My sense of loss was for things greater than any beauty I had; it was the undeniable fact I was changing in an unimaginable and unwanted way. I quickly recovered, realizing that this was the important moment of breaking through aging denial.

We begin to learn that our aging changes represent losses of important symbols, functions, parts, and self-images. The exaggerated mirror image of my face left me no room for pretense. The gradual maturing of our skin transforms our once seamlessly smooth faces into ones with deepening wrinkles, creping skin, and dropping jawlines. We realize our youth is receding and feel a nagging sense of loss of self.

The women I interviewed were very surprised at the loss of stamina they were experiencing as they aged, the loss of a body that could keep up from early morning to late at night. All continued to be functional even with the loss of strength and endurance, but now they had the undeniable understanding that they could well lose more in the coming years. There comments included the following:

- "I have less energy, I never thought about it. I thought it would (always) be at the same level."
- "I can't stay up as long. I need breaks during the day. I can't overdo like I used to do."
- "I never want to be dependent."
- "Could I cope with being in a wheelchair?"
- "Who would care for the animals?"

Most of us have developed more than one health problem by the time we reach 60, some more serious than others but all a loss of any idea that we still wear the protective shield of youth. Muscles and joints are more painful after activity and take longer to recover. We do not bend or unbend as easily as we once did. We give up those marathon plans, not that they cannot be fulfilled, but we decide that we will not be the 75-year-old woman who completes the marathon in record time. Some women do, but most don't.

We are losing dreams of youth. In our moments of complete honesty with ourselves we experience a sense of loss, lost opportunity. We know our dreams are not realistic because we don't have the time to realize them. We still can take college courses, do some runs or neighborhood walks with friends, get a part-time job, or travel to Africa for a wildlife safari if we are fortunate enough to have money and health. Yet, they are only pieces that will not weave into a whole new dream. It isn't that dreams aren't necessary or possible; it is more that we must give up some dreams for which we no longer have time or to which we no longer want to devote the necessary effort for realization of those dreams. Even though some of us still are engaged in careers into our 70s and 80s and a lucky few break through to success or find recognition for earlier work, no one can escape the knowledge that even the most sustained career eventually will come to an end without some dreams realized.

Letting Go of the Dream of an Infinite Future

Truly understanding and accepting that we have lived most of the life we have on this planet and applying that understanding to priorities and choices we make during our coming years may be the most important work we have. In our early 60s, if not sooner, we are struck enough by the notion of our own mortality that we either will come to terms with its meaning for us or, if not ready, we will linger in the rationales that tell us we are different and that our aging will be different and thereby preserve our denial.

The women I interviewed who were under 60 focused less on mortality when identifying what they missed the most about being young and more on missing the fun of being with their children when they were small and giggly and the ability or willingness to take off spontaneously on an adventure for the day.

The women who reached 60 and beyond missed some of the same things but spoke more of some esoteric aspects of getting old. Among other things, they told me:

- "I miss (having) time in front of me, being able to project into the far future;"
- "I miss the anticipation of life lasting;" and
- "I never thought about mortality (mine) before. I have less years in front of me than behind me."

They struggled to articulate the narrowing of options presented by the simple absence of years. Less able to ignore the view of life as unending, they were not quite ready for an examination of dreams, priorities, purpose and meaning.

For What Is This Life and What Will It Matter?

I noted in my own aging and in the words of the older women I interviewed the greatest difficulty in navigating the transition to a shift in or loss of purpose and roles. Retirement from a long career, a condition that limits mobility, living on a limited income, losing a partner through death, or having adult children living too far away to be meaningfully involved with their families often triggers a sense of loss.

Like at every other time in our life, in old age, we seek relevance. We all need purpose. These changes often feel like we've jack-knifed in the road despite our best-laid plans and can no longer move forward or backward. Of course, we can and do move but not without careful work, such as the hard work of grieving losses and moving on. We learn to let go.

"I feel lucky to be this age and only compare myself to myself and not an earlier version of myself." (This was said by a woman who has arrived in the moment and let go of denial and illusions of what matters.)

Most of us haven't quite gotten there yet. We are just beginning to understand what feels like uncontrollable change physically and the way others see us—our own declining endurance or being ignored at the cosmetic counter. Change occurs in unexpected ways and places. Suddenly, it seems we start napping in the afternoon.

We begin to realize that there are no real fixes because we are living in a world of accelerating impermanence. Soon, our fixes will need fixes. It is not in the spirit of aging naturally to strive to stay young or deny the inevitable in implausible ways. It is in the spirit of aging naturally to let go of with grace that which we cannot possibly keep.

Take Time, Don't Rush, and Don't Be Hard on Yourself

Having arrived at an honest understanding that we have less time in front of us than behind us, taking the time to visualize and plan our futures is important. We need to use our time well but also need time to experiment. Included in our plans must be some practical actions

If we haven't prepared a will, both a living will and a leaving will, and told someone what we want done with our remains by the time we are 70, we are likely still in denial. Our kids probably are wondering, too, and don't know how to approach the subject. We just need to do it. Once finished, it's done until something in your living situation changes that may require an adjustment.

Once we've planned for death, we can go on and plan for life in these remaining years. How much we've thought about our future as an old person will determine how long we will experiment with our emerging self. Developing the purpose that would replace losses in career and relationships took me four years.

Unlike women who knew they would care for grandchildren or turn their art hobby into a vocation or business, I had not pre-planned what I would do. I gave myself the gift of time and freedom from self-criticism so I wouldn't be drawn back into time-consuming activities that left me no time to learn about myself. For example, I took my health care background and planning skills into schools to assist in the development of a wellness program for children. I applied my interest in the wellbeing of people and my communication skills to community forums, group work and writing this book.

Purposes are highly individual things. No one size fits all, but each of us cherishes having a reason for being. Living out a purpose feels better than wondering what the purpose is although we are rewarded by self-discovery throughout the journey. It is in our 60th decade that we disassemble, honor, discard. and reboot to become the older version of ourselves. Through the rebooting process, we finally, in a positive way, overcome the confusion associated with turning old.

I have been frankly humbled by this experience of entering the last phase of my life. I, so far, have humble thoughts, the most important include being honest about my grief and, in the end, letting go of it. I try to honor the important losses of friends, accept the devaluation of my work, shrug off the newest arthritic finger bump, and pay attention to new thoughts and aspirations that never before had room in my life.

Quite important, as you will see in later chapters, I encourage investment in well-being. Among my hopes in sharing this journey with you is that we will honor our bodies, which are changing daily, by taking care of them and will cherish our remaining relationships. We can anticipate that new thoughts and aspirations will begin entering from unexpected places as we clear out denial and grieving. Welcoming new thoughts along with letting go of old ones are important tasks of aging. It's right next to trying, and occasionally succeeding, in living out each moment of today.

The Awakening

We begin our journey by recalling and piecing together our own story. We already know how to transition from one stage of life to another, to evolve, to cope with losses—and we each learn to navigate the aging terrain in our own way. We succeed the most when we recognize that we are in a whirlwind of bold impermanence and breathe with it instead of holding our breaths. Aging is a lifelong journey, one that will end someday. In the meantime, we keep on learning and living each instance of our life differently from all the other instances. This is an age of discovery like none other when we realize that in letting go, we make room for so much more.

"It's a mystery. I am getting smarter! My mind is on fire to learn," said one of the women I interviewed.

Our own life teaches us that we know how to let go without fear. We have been moving forward, then a little backward, and then forward again for years.

Knowing the Path to Who We Are Becoming

The path to successful aging begins with embracing our own life story.

3

Reflection, Reconciliation, Reward

"I feel lucky to be this age and only compare myself to myself and not an earlier version of myself."

—*Aging women survey*

Growing older with grace and integrity requires learning to accept and value who we have come to be. Aging, just like every other phase of life, is accompanied by changes; among them are changes in our physical being, relationships, work, and sense of purpose. All these and more are part of the normal process of aging and nature's reality that nothing stays the same. What seems like a smooth passage to some seems like an abrupt ending to what we have been or what we thought we could become to others.

Many women grieve for the roles they no longer have and in which they have felt valued. Their children have their own children and no longer need or want Mom-the-decision-maker, but the unending love of grandchildren serves as compensation. Some of us grieve because our life takes an unexpected turn when we find ourselves caring for our elderly parents or a disabled partner while others fit right into the caretaker role.

No matter what our circumstances, most of us will face, at least at times, feelings of loss, irrelevancy, and uncertainty about the future. One woman may find it surprisingly hurtful to no longer be asked to chair a meeting believing that others think she is no longer up on issues. Another may lack purpose after finally retiring from a demanding job and having no replacement activity, while some peers seem to incorporate new activities instantly and say, "I was never this busy before." Yet, even many of these latter women wonder if they are doing the right thing or just replacing one kind of busyness with another.

Feelings of irrelevancy and loss often diminish as we settle into this new phase of living although these feelings may overwhelm some women who will require counseling for perspective. For all of us, they are a part of transitioning into an older self.

In this chapter I offer suggestions for acknowledging, understanding, and coping with the transition; making meaning from our life; and developing strategies to navigate the aging process while continuing to grow as a person.

Recapitulation

As we age, we can find this sense of loss and feeling of irrelevancy curious, coming at a time that should call for looking back on achievement. Joys, sorrows, successes, and failures consumed our middle years, but we navigated them.

Spent youth and becoming moving targets of deteriorating health, fitness, financial security, and relevance can cause sadness, as can the sense of finality in the changes we now experience. So many joys, especially first-time joys, have passed, never to be known again.

The questions, the limitations, the role changes, and a sense of being adrift can unsettle us, provoking us to search for new meaning in our life. I, as well as some of my friends, have consequently experienced the need to put their lives in order.

A 60-year-old close friend of mine confided one day that she was spending a lot of time on Facebook contacting old friends. Most of these were friends from 30 years earlier, when she was young, free, and adventuresome. Most were men.

She was thrilled when they responded and shared details of their lives. Their expressions of interest in her life brought a sense of emotional warmth. She was saddened to learn that one with whom she had spent an exhilarating year sailing up and down coasts had died three years earlier. She said she grieved.

I knew she grieved not only for him but for that time in her life. Yet, I also heard in her stories a reaffirmation and excitement of what she was then and now.

Nostalgia

We all recall events from our lives. The authors of a study reported in 2006 take us deeper into nostalgic memories (Wildschut et al., 2006). We generally describe the feeling of nostalgia as warm, melancholy, and special. These researchers concluded that nostalgia had a function at times of transition in our lives, especially those times that lead to changes in our social setting.

Our transition away from our middle years into our older years qualifies as one such period and may in part explain our tendency to review our life as we transition. Our roles, work environment, and physical abilities change, often resulting in a sense of dislocation. Nostalgia has proved a valuable mechanism to bring meaning to one's life and confirm one's value as a person.

Nostalgia centers around self and often results in what is described as "redemption" or positive reconciliation of key events of one's life. The above-mentioned study further reports that nostalgia usually results in a positive feeling about one's self and one's life.

Clay Routledge, one of the authors of the Wildschut et al. (2006) study has done other studies as well. He is cited by Tierney (2013) as saying:

> Nostalgia serves a crucial existential function. It brings
> to mind cherished experiences that assure us we are
> valued people who have meaningful lives. Some of
> our research shows that people who regularly engage
> in nostalgia are better at coping with concerns about
> death (p. D1).

How Have We Become Who We Are?

As mentioned above, we are drawn to reflecting upon events of our lives at important times. The value of such introspection is under study.

We seem to need our lives to flow before us so we can touch each part. We want to identify the talents that sustained us and aim to keep them in this phase of life. We want to know the needs still to be met and potentials still to be realized.

Our task is to learn that we are the combination of all the things we have become and all the experiences we have had. Leaving them behind does not signal the end of our being; it only leads us to the next purpose however small, however large.

Intentional contemplation to examine and recall ourselves is a necessary step to resolution and reconciliation for many of us. To do otherwise is to risk unattended grief, a vague feeling of loss, emptiness and longing that locks us in place.

Understanding our story through nostalgic review and frank confrontation of unresolved issues in our journals, our heads or talking with a trusted friend will result in a cherished understanding of what we have become.

One important task as we enter old age is to make sense and meaning of our lives before this transition. If we don't, we risk carrying around nagging remnants of unresolved events or experiences that impede our freedom to move forward. If we do, we are rewarded with the perspective of our own story, our own evolution to what we are today.

Here is a thoughtful way to begin the task which can't help but result in nostalgic reveries. I always have been fascinated by which events or experiences people consider having had the greatest influence in shaping them. I asked the women I interviewed to tell me the three experiences or events that led them to being what they are today. My intent in asking the question was to hear about their lives in their own words and to learn what was important in their lives. Their careful consideration of the answers became an opportunity to define meaning, nostalgic or otherwise.

You will find that many experiences immediately come to mind especially after 60 or more years of living. The revelations will come from narrowing down the list to three or four. My own short list were the events that strengthened, supported, and moved me out of what could have been lifelong despair based on the first 20 years of my life. One of my answers was my education that promised me a path to independence. Another was recognition I received early in my career that helped me recognize my abilities.

Strong themes came through in the answers I heard from the women I interviewed. Those of us who mentioned the partners in our lives as one of our greatest influences—I was one of them—reflected mostly on the growth brought about by the relationship. Often mentioned was the shared secure love with another being that provided emotional shelter and built confidence, especially in difficult times. Special praise was given to mates who recognized talents and skills and supported growth in those areas.

For others, growth was hard-won through disappointment and pain brought on by partners that betrayed them in some unexpected way. There were partners who philandered, spent money unwisely, or withheld too much. Many women who left their mates found other partners with whom they have had satisfying lives and can say they now are a positive influence. From the distance of time, these women carry their lessons of resilience and recovery from wounds of betrayal.

In many interviews, I heard responses about experiences that showed strength, resilience, and independence. Perhaps that should not be surprising for women of my generation. We grew up believing we were born to create happiness in others and to be taken care of by a fine man. Some admitted to not knowing at the time that the trade-offs of that promise meant a loss of control over their own fulfillment.

A number of women cited experiences in which their marriages ended and they were left to care for their children as a mother and a breadwinner. They discovered they could be self-sufficient, that they were stronger and more competent than they thought possible.

One woman relived her joy and sense of confidence when she won an endurance race against her male competitors. That single event pointed her in the direction of a career in physical fitness that evolved into serious study of the mind-body connection. Like me, some marveled at achieving a college degree in an environment that saw little relevance to a woman's life beyond being a wife and mother.

The women who were taken out of their comfort zones by moving to another state or country described the personal growth they experienced having to get along without close family and friends. They learned the customs of different cultures that taught them there were many ways to live, not necessarily one right way. Several of these women related how much their marriages grew in closeness when neither wife nor husband had someone else to whom to turn.

Another woman cited overcoming alcohol addiction and continuing recovery as the most profoundly spiritual experience of her life and the core of what she is today. She endured a painful discovery of self to eventually become comfortable in her own skin.

The event of birthing children frequently was mentioned as the turning point not for its lifelong commitment but for experiencing the miracle of life. Sadly, one woman followed her story of the miracle of life with the story of her son's untimely death from cancer and her consequent loss of faith.

Unexpected deaths were a theme for others as well. Loss of a parent or sibling early in life changed living situations and expectations in irreconcilable ways and left holes that could not be filled.

Several women identified childhood abuse, both physical and sexual, as setting into motion protective behaviors of vigilance and mistrust. Still, these women succeeded by society's measures of meaningful work and responsibility. They experienced no feelings of nostalgia; rather, the work of reconciliation with that part of their life was difficult.

Achieving self-sufficiency and independence dominated as themes. In great measure, strength, resiliencies and, a shared sense of the sisterhood of women who, against considerable odds, discovered their own self-worth grew out of these kinds of experiences.

Much more lies behind the experiences and events these women described. We are much more complicated than any single statement or simple interview can measure.

We move past difficulties, dropping some things and letting others drift off. As we age, though, we can expect one particular day in which we sense a seismic shift that leaves us strangely becalmed. We drift, feeling that our main reason for being has left us. What happened to our life?

Exploring the Dark Side of the Moon

Erik Erikson, well-known psychologist (1902-1994), proposed eight stages of human personality development (1993), each having a significant development task to complete in order to successfully go on to the next stage. The eighth and last stage he called maturity and identified it as beginning at age 65. The conflict experienced in maturity he described as ego integrity versus despair and the task as reflection on and acceptance of one's life. Success, he suggested, is measured by feeling a true sense of oneself and having a fulfilled or fulfilling life.

Reflection is a way to strengthen our confidence in transitioning to an aging woman with a sense of self and purpose. Some of the past is occurring in the moment. One of the women I interviewed would be 70 that year and is just now giving up working. "I haven't had a summer off since I was 14 years old," she said in a way that caused me to believe that she was astonished by this fact. That's over 55 years of working.

This woman had just entered the first stage of deep numbness to the reality that she doesn't have to do it anymore. I was just a few steps ahead of her in the process and knew that I, too, was experimenting with adjusting to life without my long-held work identity and importance.

Fortunate enough not to have to struggle to make ends meet on Social Security, I thought that I could put into motion all those retirement plans that felt so good to think about from the vantage point of a long day at work, work politics, and family pressure.

At least, I thought as much until I retired from a long career. I planned on using retirement time to write a book of management wisdom for women based on nearly 40 years of experience during a time of tremendous change in social values, technology, and wealth (in one direction or the other).

Instead, although I woke in the morning with good intentions, I had yet to find the rhythm of my life, let alone a voice to pass along wisdom. I thought I was going about this right though I had no prior experience having the luxury of time. Others told me that they were busier than at any other time of their lives and didn't know where the time was going. I suspected they were maintaining the same rhythm they had before they retired, something I decidedly didn't want to do because I was tired of the pressure and pace.

There I was an incredible 65 years beyond my first successful effort to stand on my own two feet and deliberately, if not desperately, trying to gear down after a career of long days of pressure and responsibility. I liked being able to sleep in. I liked exercising or walking with friends in the morning. I liked reading the newspaper—that would be the kind you hold in your hands while you sit with your feet up with a cup of coffee nearby. I loved being with my husband, chatting about family, our latest ache, our travel plans, or world events in the evening while enjoying a glass of wine.

It was the time between the morning exercise and evening wind downs that my rhythm acted like a bad heart without medication: mindless staring coupled with bursts of activity which may or may not have been productive depending on the definition. For example, I felt little sense of accomplishment when I cleared my emails, and yet I felt slightly lonely when my only emails were from my Internet service telling me I had junk mail accumulating.

I could and did plan times for writing or painting watercolors. When the time came, I was uninspired or, perhaps, simply not up to the challenge. There were the times tuning out kicked in. There were times I fell asleep. Time clicked by. I became increasingly and acutely aware that time moved quickly, and I was entering the dark side of the moon of my life for which I had no concept, no vision, no plan and no rhythm. I spent far too much time ruminating about daily changes that startled me and couldn't seem to apply my previous well-developed natural planning ability.

It isn't a huge surprise given my background that I would have some difficulty in adjusting to a life without a career. When I looked around, I realized that I could not see a place for me anymore. All that work, all that drive, all those first experiences, all that struggle, all that learning to become better, and all the spontaneity that led to being able to say I survived, I made it, we made it—mission accomplished, vision realized, and pressure lifted.

Suddenly, there was time to think about something else. Those pressures of success and failure were over. I breathed a sigh of relief, yet knew I was entering a deep period of grieving for the relevant person I had been. I reached out for the woman who had brought me here and began the search for the one I would become.

Setting the Stage for the Rest of Our Lives

I noted in my own life and the lives of other women that the more we remember the past and create meaning from it, the more we have the chance to honor the years we lived and move into the young years of old age. For me, that process allowed me to grieve and bid a proper goodbye to the woman of my youth and middle years.

The process of reconciling what we were and what we are now is as natural as the process that moved us from school years to adult responsibilities. We begin to orient ourselves to a new environment, one that recognizes all that we have been, done, hoped, and despaired. This stage of our life's work demands our attention and our complete honesty. The measure of our success will be acceptance and a sense of freedom to be who we are. We prepare to live fully in this important phase of life. We are setting the stage for the rest of our lives.

Pulling our story out, looking at it, touching it and putting it to rest is one part. There is no need to linger unless it gives you pleasure, and you always can return to your story. Be sure to spend the needed time to savor the richness of yourself before moving forward.

What will start floating into your vision are opportunities. Now is the opportunity to experiment, whether it means reading more books, learning to paint, writing poetry, pursuing new causes, or all the above. Aging is our opportunity to develop a renewed perspective on our potentials and our limitations.

Ironically, when we most think we will slow down, our lives seem to gear up and run at an accelerated pace of change. It is not exactly the busyness we imagined, and we will get better at it once armed with the solace of newly found identities and purpose. Until then, we must work to stabilize ourselves in the roots of our past and our dreams of our near future in a whirlwind of impermanence.

The Gift of Our Story

Several women I spoke with felt keenly the importance of leaving the legacy of their story for their children and grandchildren. They relayed their own regrets of not talking more with their parents and grandparents. For some of us, our story feels too private or unimportant for others to read. All stories are unique; there is never a perfect copy. Tell your perfect story to yourself if no one else.

The greatest gift of telling our story is to experience the joy of what we are and what has made us, the strengths that will stay with us, the weakness we must live with, and those we can leave behind. With all our blessings and all our regrets, we still will move forward as we are.

Most of us worked hard to be what we are and where we are. It is not easy to know that when we die, so will the story, but that makes it no less an important story. Our stories are rich and full of the details of life, the excitement of living, and the profound drama in and around us.

Part Two
Stepping Onto and Staying
on the Path to Healthy Aging

Section Two arms women with information about the changes they can expect from the aging process: what is natural and what isn't, what can be prevented and what can't, and what is important and what isn't. Informed choices empower women to achieve aspirations in their new life.

4

Aging is Not a Disease

"My Mom said he died of old age. That's scary. I'm around old people a lot. I hope I don't catch it."

—Young boy says to his young friend in PICKLES Comic by Brian Crane (Seattle Times, 6/27/11)

We can't prevent aging, but we can prevent disease and live a better quality of life while aging. Aging and the process of aging is not a disease. A disease is characterized by a pathology, something abnormal occurring in the body. Infections or illnesses such as pneumonia, diabetes, or cardiovascular disease are good examples of disease. By that or any other definition, aging is not a disease. It is its own distinct natural process called getting older.

Aging is expected. We have been aging since the day we were born. Early years are characterized by growth and development of our bodies and maturation of our minds. In later decades, we experience accelerated physical decline, but the maturation of our minds will continue despite some stumbles over finding words.

Peak years of physical maturation occur early in our lives. For example:

- Most girls reach their adult height by age 15 (Marcin, 2019).
- Maximum range of motion occurs in the late 20s (Mazzeo et al., 1998).

- Peak muscle mass occurs sometime in our 30s (Mazzeo et al,, 1998).

- The peak output of the heart decreases steadily from the age of 30 (Gawande, 2007).,

- The ability of the eyes to focus declines in our 40s (Giorgi, 2016).

No doubt we can influence some of those peaks either through focused or declining efforts, but in part we follow a track laid down by our genetics and, to some extent, environment influences such as excessive sun exposure.

Our bodies are continuously breaking down and dismantling as they have done all our years only to renew themselves, but sometime during the accumulation of many years of life, the renewal becomes slower and less efficient. The slowed renewal with all its discomforts is a natural process. Those discomforts are generally not present in youth and may be why we come to think of aging as "dis-ease."

Aging bodies are more vulnerable to diseases. The aged are more likely to get a disease than younger people and more likely to die with the disease still present even if it isn't the cause of death. Our lifestyle choices as we age will either increase or diminish our vulnerability. We do have some control, and the earlier we decide to maximize our body's potential the greater our choice and control.

Navigating the Process of Aging

Navigating into old age reminds me of navigating to a college degree. As a freshman, I was nervous and wondered if I could be successful—until I reached my senior year, during which I became confident and satisfied I had done well and could move on. Seventy is like the freshman of old age except by now we have developed much more self-awareness. Of course, it is also different in that we navigate physical decline through fewer years. The challenge of learning and adjusting, though, remains the same. Meeting that challenge well will result in a renewed sense of purpose and an enhanced quality of life.

Becoming old is one of the final life transitions we navigate, the next being old-old age and then death. Unlike in earlier transitions, our bodies will no longer be ignored. Subtle and not-so-subtle signs tell us our bodies are fed up and can't take it anymore. No more taking this body, its endurance, and its flexibility for granted.

Transitions used to focus on emotional and mental struggles that resulted in varying degrees of increased maturity. Transitioning into and through aging requires paying attention to the demands of the body as well as of the mind and heart. From these positions of wisdom, we could alert the young to care of their bodies early so their bodies will carry them with as much strength as possible into old age. We could, but it will most likely be perceived as the sour grapes or whining of old age, which it is. We've been there, we know.

Taking Control of Our Bodies

We start by learning to listen better to our bodies. The aging body asks us to pay attention. The choices we make as a result of listening will influence the health of our bodies. As we learn about the process of aging and our bodies, we will discover that many of our fears are unfounded and may not be realized for one or more decades, if ever. The sense of inevitability of what feels like creeping decay can rob us of our belief in the power of our choices and control over our own being, an attitude that can become self-fulfilling.

If a physician or other health care provider explains discomfort with the words "it's just aging" or "you are getting older, you know," find another provider. Aging may be the description, but it isn't the entire explanation. Resignation and inaction may be the single most important reason that people allow themselves to fall into a slow decline until their death. Our health care providers should explain the choices we can make for our health and function. Our bodies need our intelligent attention and wise care.

Routine Maintenance

My husband has complained for years about the increasing maintenance demands of his body: ointment here, cream there, eye drops, ear oil, toe stuff that smells bad, added to the usual shaving and brushing of teeth, removable or not. If you're a woman, add to that list lotion for dry skin, lots of hair conditioner, vaginal lubricant, and lots more moisturizer. Then, add special hand cream the day after you feel the pain of a crack in your finger used to transport a salty French fry into your mouth. Add daily psyllium powder or some other bulk-forming method for, shall we say, more regular elimination. Body has our attention now.

I am not certain how good an example I am at this transition since even now I am frustrated by having to clean my eyeglasses. I am especially annoyed by those "floaters" that don't disappear with lens cleaning and are said to be normal spots or amoeba-like-looking images that live somewhere in my eyeball and interfere with my views of white walls or blue skies.

Years ago, I developed ridges in my fingernails that cause micro canals to form that collect polish in the recesses and scuffs on the ridge edge creating a strange stripped affect. Maybe it is the fingernail's version of "creping" reinforcing the body's message that everything about you eventually will wrinkle.

Most aging people don't complain about ridges on their fingernails. Instead you will first hear most voice their distress over the growing intolerance of their bodies for activity, let alone exercise. What ever happened to the days in which you could work hard, wake up with muscle pain, work again, and soon you were conditioned with strength and endurance instead of becoming a physical wreck of a human being? Nowadays the pain lasts well into the second day, and resulting conditioning disappears after a few days of inactivity.

Choosing Preventive Maintenance

If we refuse to accept the wreckage as an inevitable part of aging, we can minimize it in some ways. Chapter 7, "Renewable Energy Not So Renewable," discusses what is happening to our bodies, what we can prevent or delay and what we must accept. We begin with the recognition that we have a choice to either improve strength in the face of deterioration or give into it. Early limits in mobility and subsequent early dysfunction may be part of a disease process, but those limits and dysfunction are not a consequence of the aging process. Rather, they are the result of the disease or of our own choices. It is within our power to accelerate or slow the aging process. The consequence of not taking preventative action is to enter a cycle of increasing immobility and increasing inactivity, a precursor to developing disease and dysfunction. Our health care system is designed to focus on treatment not prevention. Fortunately, the trend is in the direction of prevention; legislation under the Affordable Care Act is providing more preventive services without copayments to encourage our participation in our own preventive maintenance.

So, What Makes It So Hard?

Our hard-won maturity as a person with confirmed values, settled anxieties, and established coping skills doesn't mean we pay less attention to the emotional upheavals of aging. Hardly! We've all noticed that some things never get easier and often get harder. My story of compounded grief is an example. The first time I lost someone through early death, my mother, I thought it was the most confusing and painful experience I had ever had—that is, until the next death, my father's, when not only did I grieve his loss but also experienced an instant replay of grieving for my mother.

My compounded grief wasn't neurosis due to a regrettable childhood. No, it was a normal occurrence. Studies have shown that grief accumulates, and we are destined to relive every loss (Potter, 2020). Our bodies, our losses, and the presence of our young married grandchildren tell us that we are passing into a time when just about everything seems harder and we will be challenged to stay vital.

In our 60s, we can no longer deny that this transition is different from previous transitions. We see it; we feel it; and society doesn't expect much from us anymore. I was nearly traumatized when, at 65, I asked my stepson's help in designing a home for a sloping piece of property we liked. He agreed initially, but by the time we talked, his advice to me was to buy a small house on a flat piece of property.

This was his version of putting me out to pasture! I can forgive but can't forget that upon reflection he decided that I was too old to have a dream. Of course, he can't stop me from achieving new dreams any more than my traditional father stopped me decades earlier from getting a college education. I don't need his support, but I wish he could have seen the same 20 years ahead of me that I did.

Incidences like mine or the views of my stepson, however caring, tell us those around us are lowering their expectations of our future. After all, we are getting old. We know that part of our world denies the fact of aging and another part believes that aging is sickness and death. We fear loss of control even though we are in control.

If we share any one dream, it is to be an old person who is in control of his or her life: able to walk with minimal aid, drive without running into curbs, carry on conversations that make sense, leave the room when we want to, live independently, love and be loved fully, and then, suddenly, one day die.

Paul Cunningham, MD, advises his patients that it is possible to avoid slow decline to death. It is possible to keep healthy and then simply die. "If you have dodged the genetic bullet and the metro bus, you can make it this way," he tells them (personal interview, July 15, 2011).

Dr. Cunningham is a geriatrician, board-certified in the care of the older adult. He practices in a small town that attracts many retirees.[3]

Dr. Cunningham's motivation and interest was built on exposure to "old" people early in his life. He speaks with genuine fondness for his patients and wants them to have the quality of life that allows them to be involved, be positive, and have meaning in the remaining days of their lives. Sometimes, that means treatment, sometimes prevention, and sometimes end-of-life discussions—and always control and choice to the extent possible.

Dr. Cunningham says he sees too many older people who blame their declines on aging and take no action to reverse or stabilize their ill health. "It doesn't have to be that way," he counsels his patients stuck in the belief they cannot influence their functional decline. He also says it is never too late and cites examples of people who have turned their health status around at 70, 75 and 80 years of age by changing bad health habits like eating more than they need and not moving enough. To do otherwise, he says, is to increase our vulnerability to disease which leads to decline and diminished quality of life.

Common Disease of Aging Women

Because it is so prevalent and so destructive to human bodies, especially aging bodies already slowing in renewal capacity, I selected the disease of diabetes to point out the difference between normal aging and pathological aging. I recall older friends of my mother saying they had diabetes and must control sugar intake. They seemed to accept the disease as part of aging so much that I included having diabetes in my aging expectations along with tree trunk legs. I still hear those sentiments and fear that

---

3   The time and effort it takes to become a geriatrician are economically thankless. Our reimbursement system for health care services does not financially value the skill necessary to treat the unique medical needs of the elderly in the way it financially values the skills of a surgeon or radiologist.

many continue to believe that diabetes is a "normal" part of aging. Unless genetically inherited, it is not!

Nearly 27 percent of Americans 65 years or older have diagnosed or undiagnosed diabetes compared to 17.5 percent in ages 45-64 and 4.2 percent in ages 18-44. Diabetes is the seventh leading cause of death in the United States (Center for Disease Control [CDC], 2020).

Diabetes is a major cause of heart disease and strokes (the first and third leading cause of death, respectively, for those age 85 years and older) (Herron 2019). As these numbers tell us, the aging of our bodies sets forth an environment that makes it easier for diabetes to take hold. (Although it needs to be said that the epidemic of obesity in our younger people is increasing the incidence of Type 2 diabetes in young age groups.)

Type 2 diabetes accounts for 90-95 percent of all diagnosed cases of diabetes in adults and is characterized by insulin resistance developed for a variety of reasons, old age and obesity being two major factors (NIDDK, 2017). During aging, we lose muscle and gain fat. We gain fat if obese. Both processes have the potential of increasing our insulin resistance which means we are not processing sugar in our body and putting it to good use. To be both aging and obese compounds the risk (Gambert & Pinkstaff, 2006).

Type 2 diabetes, unless genetically determined, develops as a result of a likely combination of poor eating habits, sedentary lifestyle, and obesity. Aging adds an additional predictor in that muscle mass is reduced. Having less muscle can result in insulin resistance and higher than normal fasting blood sugar, one of the three risk factors define in metabolic syndrome.[4]

The person, man or woman, with metabolic syndrome has greater risk of developing cardiovascular disease and Type 2 diabetes.

Health care providers will recommend lifestyle changes to correct the risk factors. If lifestyle changes aren't done or sufficient to bring measures into a healthy range, the provider may suggest medications(s). Medical Supervision is important in monitoring measures that uncontrolled can cause serious medical conditions.

---

4   Metabolic syndrome is defined as having a combination of high blood pressure (135/80 or above), high fasting blood sugar (100 mg/dL or above), large waist circumference (for women, 35 inches or more), low HDL (good) cholesterol (under 50 for women), and high triglycerides (150 mg/dL or above). (Mayo Clinic, 2020)

Diabetes Accelerates Aging

The disease of diabetes accelerates the aging process and may lead to a nightmare of declining function and increasing discomfort (Gambert & Pinkstaff, 2006).The known medical consequences of diabetes come from impaired circulation due to blood having extra sugar or glucose (medically called hyperglycemia) that attaches to proteins in the blood; resulting in blood vessels becoming thicker and less elastic Diabetes thus narrows the blood vessels, progressively diminishing the blood flow throughout the body. Feet begin to feel painful from lack of blood supply. Amputations occur from a cut on a foot that refuses to heal because the blood cannot carry healing nutrients to the wound and the foot begins to die. Kidneys stop functioning for lack of blood, and eyes go blind. Diabetes Type 2, unless genetic, in the end is a horrible inhumane disease caused by humans' failure to care for their bodies.

Diabetes Is Not a Consequence of Aging

Diabetes is not a consequence of aging even though aging can sow the seeds in a person who is not vigilant in maintaining health. For the older person diagnosed with diabetes, the hope rests in vigilance in controlling the disease, i.e. in controlling blood sugar, which is possible. In some cases, diabetes has been reversed for the obese person by a significant loss of weight. In all cases, diabetes and weight loss require careful monitoring and medical supervision.

When Disease Occurs in Aging

I chose to highlight the disease process of diabetes because it is a pathological process that is increasing in incidence and severity among the aging population today and is for the most part preventable. There are other pathologies such as heart disease and stroke that also often result in declining function and quality of life. They, too, are preventable and not a natural outcome of aging until very old age.

The second leading cause of death is cancer, which may or may not be preventable. We know smoking is a cause of lung cancer, and obesity can be a factor in the development of some estrogen-based breast cancers. However, there is much we don't know, and we live in a rapidly changing environment that is likely out of our control. We can, though, control our lifestyle choices.

Disease once in the body results in damage. We all marvel at the survival rate of people whose heart stopped and were given CPR (cardiopulmonary resuscitation). Often, those people are left with damage to their heart which seriously affects their ability to function physically. Medicine and surgery have given us miracles of longer lives. In some cases, the remaining life is a struggle. Heart disease, diabetes, and most cancers are not the result of the normal and natural wear and tear of aging.

The wonder is in the knowledge that we can extend our lives and its quality through the choices we make even while we experience the normal wear and tear of the aging process.

Normal Wear and Tear in the Aging Process

So, what is normal wear and tear, and what is going to occur whether we work on it or not? There are several good resources that discuss the so-called inevitable. One is "The Way We Age Now" by Atul Gawande (2007). The article is an excellent and readable description of the unavoidable wear-and-tear on various systems of our body.

Gawande points to the complexity of the human body and the vast biological variability in the life spans of people even in the face of similar attributes. He extols the amazing ability of our bodies to depend on backup systems when primary systems fail, that we have unused cells able to take over. He tells us of the marvel of redundancies that replace and repair but warns us that backups eventually run out. Then, we die.

Another good resource is How and Why We Age by Leonard Hayflick, Ph.D. This book includes details of the aging body along with insights that arm us with inside knowledge of our insides. The more we know, the more power we have to make good choices.

Most of us hope for a life that ends in death for age-related causes, a death at the end of a life that has relatively good quality and avoids the steady decline and misery of chronic disease. Recent obituaries listed the deaths of 58- and 69-year-olds as due to age-related causes. Really, it's almost scary to think we have so little understanding of aging. I do not know what these departed souls died from, but I am pretty sure it wasn't from the process of aging.

Today, the grinding down of teeth and joints, signs of normal wear and tear, is more apparent as we enter our 80s or 90s, not our 60s and 70s. The deaths of 85-, 90- or 100-year-old people said to be from age-related causes are undoubtedly correct unless they were hit by a metro bus. Being hit by a bus and being very old gives them that much less chance for recovery and subsequent survival.

We have all read or heard the claims that 25-30 percent of Medicare health dollars are spent in the last year of life with a significant portion occurring the last month. I am a health care professional and do not find that statistic shocking. After all, that is when we are at our sickest and need the most resources. Some of us cannot be saved. Some of us can be.

There are instances in which costly care has been provided in order to extend life such as the woman who finally decided to have surgery to repair an aortic aneurysm, a life-threatening bulge in her main aortic artery leading from her heart. The surgery was a success, but she died in a state of confusion unable to understand the sad goodbyes of her family. Poor and/or uninformed choices or delayed choices can result in what I call "Hail Mary" passes for life where odds are clearly against them. The older and more diseased we are, the greater the risks.

More health care professionals are adopting practices of frank and detailed discussion with patients and families, thereby giving them the opportunity to decide their course of treatment. Often the choice is between spending somewhat longer remaining time in painful treatments and spending shorter remaining time in a hospice-like environment. Those who care for cancer patients have been having these discussions for a long time and are experienced in compassionate and straightforward exchanges with patients. They see it as part of their roles and view the patient as the final decision maker.

We Have Choice

Generations are more aware today. The women I interviewed did not want their lives prolonged if they had no chance of quality of life. We've all heard of or known people who have declined chemotherapy that sickened them and only promised a few more months of life. Nearly 100 percent of the women had living wills and instructions for what they wished done with their remains.

Dr. Cunningham talks with his patients about their end of life wishes and says most want the choice of whether to continue treatment unless their diseases have left them without the mental competence to decide. He urges his patients and others in frequent talks to the community to have discussions early and leave others with a clear understanding of their wishes should they be unable to make the decision.

Death is the end of a lifetime of the aging process. It is as natural as the process of becoming a physically independent adult and then an old person. I believe there is a sense of timing and desire to rest from this life that we will hear if we listen to our bodies. Natural processes and our choices to maintain them in a healthy way is the path to quality and health of life and a natural death.

Bertha D. Cooper

5

Face Up to It and Other Issues of the Skin

*"There is always something to be thankful for if you take the time
to look for it. For example, I am sitting here thinking how nice it is that
wrinkles don't hurt."*

—*Restaurant Table Trivia, McCleary, Washington*

The mirrors on our walls and the mirrors in the eyes of people we know but haven't seen for years show us the aging changes of our appearance, especially our faces. I look at pictures of me in my youth and see a young, line-less, and firm face and wonder how the picture could show me so much prettier than I ever thought I was. Regardless, I more easily recognize my young self than I recognize the face I see today in the mirror. The face that seems to be changing at an ever-accelerating pace. In my case, turning 65 seemed to be the tipping point; the point at which the changes were more than I could keep up with and certainly more than I could hide.

We each have a tipping point as a result of variables such as our genes, health, race, and maintenance, all of which play a role in how our skin looks as we age. The surface skin of an older black woman may be less wrinkled than that of a white woman, but we're all pretty much subject to the reality of human physiology. The inherent factors present in the process of aging are increasingly noticeable as we age. We sport fewer lines in our 60s than 70s. The progressive sag of jawlines, skin, and eyelids conspires to reshape our face until in our 70s we take on an unintentional sullen disinterested look. Without a smile on our face or an animating expression in our eyes, we can look unhappy to the average stranger or even to someone who loves us.

How does it happen that our once-expressive faces along with the rest of our skin change so much as we age? To help me get started on answering the question and what is the inevitable aging of skin, I spoke with Dr. Claire Haycox, a dermatologist with a doctorate in bio-engineering and a former clinical associate professor at the University of Washington School of Medicine. I was not disappointed.

What's Really Happening to Our Face and Skin?

"Everything is just breaking down ... it just is," Dr. Haycox told me matter-of-factly in her captivating English accent.(personal interview 11/04/10)

Skin is the largest organ of our body and the first to show the signs of aging. Just like our vital internal organs, skin is regenerating at a slower pace; unlike our internal organs, we can see it. Of course, a life without skin is unimaginable, but it is lost on most of us that the skin is a complex organ without which we would not have protection, body temperature control, pain or pleasure sensations, hair, and padding. We also wouldn't have the body contours and structure that shape our faces, our expressions, and bodies.

Skin is flexible and accommodating of thin figures and obese figures, although once skin is stretched over an obese build for a long period, skin never can return to hug a thin build.

Understanding the anatomy of the skin helps us understand what happens in aging. Skin has three primary layers, the epidermis, the dermis, and the hypodermis, more commonly known as subcutaneous tissue. Each layer has layers or cells within it, all with specialized functions. We have most familiarity with the epidermis, in which skin cells are developed and pushed to the top only to slough off as dead cells. Our skin completely sheds about every two weeks.

The epidermis is thinnest on the eyelids and thickest on the palms of hands and soles of the feet. The dermis also varies in thickness; again, the thinnest dermis is on our eyelids and the thickest is on our back. The dermis has collagen, elastic tissue, and reticular fibers (a type of connective tissue) which holds together hair follicles, oil glands, and sweat glands. Blood vessels and nerves running through the dermis are responsible for transmitting sensations of pain, itch, and temperature. Specialized nerve cells transmit the sensation of touch and pressure.

Finally, subcutaneous tissue is a layer of fat and connective tissue and is important to the regulation of temperature of the skin and body. The layer also houses blood vessels and nerves. Subcutaneous fat is important to padding our bodies to give us soft landings, contouring our bodies to give us plump cheeks and insulating us to keep us warm.

Elastic Bands Wearing Out

Dr. Haycox explains that elastin, a substance in the dermis or second layer of skin, starts to break down as we age, and our skin no longer has the recoil of our younger years. "Snap the back of your hand, and it doesn't immediately snap back," she directed. So, I did, and it didn't. Instead the pinched fold stayed intact for at least a second and then began to slowly return to cover my hand. "Pinch the back of a baby's or child's hand and the skin snaps back like a rubber band."

I envisioned miles upon miles of elastic bands covering our bodies that are simply wearing out like the waistbands of underwear. These are the bands that keep us firm and hold up our features. These are the bands that tuck our chin under our jaw, point our breasts out instead of down, and keep our eyelids from falling over our eyes. Unfortunately, we can't replace the elastin of our dermis like we can replace the elastic in our underwear.

Losing Fat Cells Not a Good Thing

The breakdown of elastin is but one accomplice in our falling features and figures. Surprisingly, loss of fat cells is another, surprising because most of us think of loss of fat cells as a good thing.

"Loss of volume," Dr. Haycox continued in her professional matter-of-fact way, "is another problem. The skin starts to lose the fat within its layers and everything caves in and droops down. Not only are fat cells decreased, those that replenish are smaller and provide little or no lift to the heavier layers of skin."

"Now, wait a minute," I protested, "most women have been fighting with fat cells all their lives and would love to have fewer and smaller fat cells."

Dr. Haycox asked me to think of people who have lost a great deal of weight and explained that their skin doesn't bounce back, especially as they get older, and the fat, whether too much or not enough, no longer holds their skin in place.

As we age, we no longer have the resilience of elastin or sturdy natural fat. Gravity begins to rule, and our skin begins to droop. Gravity pulls our chins, breasts, and butts down. The structure of our contours tumbles for lack of girders, and substance falls away for lack of walls.

Our bodies no longer have the rapid replacement capacity necessary to keep up with the rate of losing elasticity and supportive fat cells. Slowing replacement and renewal is the fact of aging skin just as it is for all organs of the body.

Loss of volume from fewer and smaller fat cells also means the loss of the insulation or padding of our hands, feet, arms, and legs that helps keep us warm. Our fat may collect in certain and most unwanted places, but it isn't enough to ward off chills and explains why I bought an "old lady's sweater" several years ago.

Natural and Unnatural Images of Aging Women

Before jumping into the care of aging skin and remedies for common conditions, as well as what we can do to keep our expressions livelier and more animated, it's worth pausing here to look at what we think an aging woman's face and skin should look like and why. As noted in the introductory chapter, the advertised face of older women is young, usually women with attractive white hair and relatively unlined faces. You need only check your recent AARP Magazine or Town and Country for examples.

Television and big screen images, usually unforgiving in close-ups, show women who've grown old with us over the years without the wrinkles we have. Exceptions can be found in movies about older folks finding their groove, e.g., The Best Exotic Marigold Hotel. In contrast to few roles for older American women, British actors like Judi Dench, Maggie Smith, and Vanessa Redgrave are sought after for roles in which they play characters their age. Few have had the extensive cosmetic work that freezes the faces of some in the aging Hollywood set and, as a result, their faces are more mobile, fuller of expression, and readily express the range of human emotion.

Working actors over 50 tend to gravitate to the theater where there are more varied parts for older women and age isn't an impediment. (Cicely Tyson, age 95, won a Tony in 2013 for her role in A Trip to Bountiful at age 89.)

Still, in America, we have solid examples of strong and interesting women's faces on the national stage. They belong to successful women in all walks of life: Hillary Clinton (72), Senators Diane Feinstein (87), and

Barbara Milkulski (84), Gloria Steinem (86), and Supreme Court Justice Ruth Bader Ginsberg (87) to name a few.

These national leaders are joined by hundreds of state and locally elected women officials, artists, writers, and activists. When we see photographs of all these women, we see intelligence, wisdom, humor, and resolve in addition to their wrinkles and sagging jowls.

My guess is that all these women use one if not several skin care products, and some may well have had cosmetic surgery, but few are in service of the beauty industry or dependent on their looks for their success and recognition. This is worth remembering as we explore the twin aspects of caring for our faces: paying attention to both skin and expression.

Care and Remedies for Aging Skin

Since most of us get our scientific skin information from beauty aids and cosmetics counters, I thought it necessary to go to the practitioners of skin medicine, those who diagnose and treat, dermatologists, and those who comfort, moisturize, and touch, aestheticians, to learn the care and remedies for aging skin.

Earlier, I noted the pressures on women to stay young and beautiful along with our own desire to stay visible and relevant. Remembering that aging is a natural process and one that cannot be prevented, each of us need to carefully think about what is important to us in the care of our skin and what is feasible in time and money. We have it within our power to make the decision that is best for our well-being and not to be influenced by expectations and attitudes of others.

To some of us, it is important to maintain as youthful an appearance as possible. This could be due to careers that require a certain look. It could be due to our own desire to forestall the slippage into old age. It could be that we want an appearance that matches the vibrancy we continue to feel as we age. How often we hear our voice or the voice of other women saying, "I don't feel old in my head." Today, we aging women have options that women before us never had or even dreamed.

There is no true antidote for aging skin. However, there are measures we can take to prevent premature damage, repair damage, and simply look better because we do proper skin care and hygiene. Many remedies are covered in more detail in the chapters on energy and weight (exercise, nutrition and hydration). Overall good health and health practices means healthier skin.

The first, foremost, and most critical action is to stop smoking immediately or never start. Smoking constricts blood vessels; therefore, circulation and the amount of restorative blood that can reach the skin. I am happy to report that I stopped smoking 30 years ago. One of the first things one of my friends said was that my skin was beginning to look pinker. That would be the blood reaching all the cells of my skin.

The next important action is the diligent application of sunscreen. Exposure to too much sun damages our skin. Sunscreen is particularly important for fair-skinned women who are more susceptible to sunburns. All you need to do is look at areas of your body exposed to the sun and areas not. You will see that unexposed skin continues to be softer even though it, too, is going through the aging process.

Sun isn't the only environmental concern. We face pollution, wind, dust, and cold. Exposed skin loses the natural protective moisture sooner and results in dryness, making the skin more prone to flakiness and, in worse cases, open areas, such as cracks, splits, chafing, and infection. Those of us who live in colder climates and stay indoors more during the winter have the additional problem of heated air drying out our skin. We are not as aware of the drying when we are young, but as we age, we feel the dryness because our body is losing its natural ability to restore moisture to our skin. The good news is that we can replace moisture by putting a pot of water on the wood stove, using a humidifier to replace moisture in the air, and applying moisturizer as part of our skin care hygiene.

The dry skin problem is not lost on the makers of cosmetics who know that the best remedy for skin that loses its protective moisture is to replace it. The manufacturers vie for our attention in marketing their products, a remarkable number of them within a wide price range. Replacing moisture is what counts and should be a part of every woman's regime starting in their 30s if not sooner.

I have a beloved female relative in her early 50s who enjoys all things outdoors. She has a natural zest and desire for challenging her body. She runs, she climbs, she bikes, she swims, she competes, and she gets down in the mud. She is attractive and healthy except now in her late 50s her face is showing what I think are serious signs of damage. I pointed out to her that the skin on her face had as many if not more wrinkles and dryness than mine which is well into the aging process.

Hers is not natural; mine is. Hers is damage. She listened patiently as I explained that her skin only would get worse and is losing the ability to restore itself. She even agreed to use sunscreen and moisturizer. I sent her a starter kit—along with a stern warning about skin cancer—which she promised to use. We live far enough apart that I won't know what she will do. I will not make it an ongoing part of our relationship. I love her too much for that. I think she may be like many women who see skin care as either vanity or a waste of time rather than seeing it as protective and caring for the largest organ of their body.

For the rest of us, many if not most manufacturers of skin care products tie moisturizing to "anti-aging" remedies like reducing fine lines. I really don't know what "reducing fine lines" means and don't know of any meaningful studies. What I think it means it that the product can't reduce big lines.

Another product claim is that the product when applied will improve elasticity or result in a minor skin lift. I do think there are products that tighten skin temporarily. Eventually, our skin will droop again as Dr. Haycox tells us. We only are helped by our genetics and our physical fitness; that is, unless we turn to special remedies which include surgical intervention.

Facials as a Remedy

Aestheticians are trained practitioners of skin care and typically provide services around the care and keeping of the skin of our face. Most are credentialed through training and in some states are licensed for their expertise. In my opinion, a woman should have at least one facial during her life. Not only is she treated to an hour of total attention to caring for her face in an environment of comfort and relaxation, she learns from her aesthetician how to care for her own skin. Aestheticians will advise a woman on the condition of her skin especially as it relates to dryness and hydration. No doubt she also will be introduced to products sold by the aesthetician, but there is no obligation to buy.

A good aesthetician will interview her client before she starts the service to determine what her client is looking for and if there are any medical issues that might influence treatment. Rosacea, a skin condition often present in older women, is characterized by varying degrees of sensitivity to heat. Clients with rosacea or other types of heat sensitivity are not candidates for steamy towels on their faces but can enjoy other aspects of having a facial.

Aestheticians generally exfoliate which means a treatment that removes dry skin from the face, then deep cleans the skin, sometimes picking out those tiny whiteheads encased in membrane, and finally moisturizes with wonderful facial massage. Many will include massages of hands and feet, too. The experience is truly beneficial to the skin, and most women leave relaxed and slightly red, a condition that soon disappears. There are products a woman can purchase inexpensively or expensively that will exfoliate and moisturize their skin, face, and body. Products are available for exfoliation that do not use microbeads which are known water pollutants and harmful to sea life.

The cost for facials varies depending on area and the salon. The most reasonable are around $75-$100 an hour. Of course, they are only reasonable if a woman can afford the service. A woman seeking the service of an aesthetician will want to get references from those she trusts.

Whether done by an aesthetician or at home, establishing a skin care routine of hygiene, moisturizing, and hydration becomes more important as we age. Good skin care is as much, if not more, about maintaining the good health of the largest organ of the body as appearance.

Drooping Lids and Disappearing Lips

Our eyelids are the thinnest skin area of our bodies so we should not be surprised that eyelids often are the first noticeable casualties of lost volume and elasticity. In youth, our eyelids stay up and away from covering the top of the eye. If we choose, we can apply eye shadow on the lid over the top of the eye and liner at the eyelash line to create a more defined deep-set eye look. For many, this makeup trick brings out sparkle and color of their eyes.

As we age, our eyelids lose their elastic capacity to stay in place, and the eyelid progressively covers more of the eye. Eye makeup gets lost in the folds and is absorbed into the creping skin and may never be seen again until it appears on the makeup remover pad. Our eyes appear smaller as eyelids encroach on eyes. In more advanced cases of eyelid droop, the lids fall over the eye enough to affect vision and may require surgery to lift the eyelid.

Many women choose the same eyelid surgery called blepharoplasty, the procedure for taking out excess skin from eyelids for cosmetic reasons. If eyelid drooping is significant enough to impair vision, Medicare covers the cost of the surgery for Medicare beneficiaries up to the benefit limit; supplemental insurance will cover deductibles and co-payments depending on the plan.

Another mark of an aging face is thinning lips which start to disappear as winkles appear. Lips also are losing volume and will appear thin especially when our mouths are closed. Lip plumping is a remedy for thin lips. Certain products such as lip gels and exfoliation promise lip plumping.

The most effective temporary remedy for thin lips is through injections of products such as Restylane or Juvéderm administered directly into the lips by a dermatologist. The resulting lip plumpness is reported to last up to six months.

From Peels, Injections, and Lasers to Facelifts

Several procedures have evolved to help women who are looking for remedies for damaged skin or simply want a younger look. Nearly every procedure mentioned here should be done only by a trained and experienced professional because if done by inexperienced hands, permanent damage can result. The color and tone of your skin is a prominent consideration in whether you are a candidate for any of the treatments because the procedure could result in uneven color on darker tones.

Most results are temporary, lasting weeks to months and occasionally years. I gave myself the gift of a laser treatment on my face for my 60th birthday. Lasers work through application of pulsating light that penetrates the skin. I was looking for something that would refresh my skin down a few layers and get rid of blue veins that had popped up on my chin. The procedure was performed by a dermatologist in a clinical setting. I was pleased by the result even though she warned me the veins would reappear in the future. I treated myself again for my 65th birthday. This time the procedure was done as effectively by a trained physician assistant who worked under the direction of a dermatologist.

Dermabrasion, also performed by a dermatologist or plastic surgeon, is much like having your face "sanded" or a more extreme form of the exfoliating scrub you do at home. The upper layer of the skin with some of its imperfections is removed. This may be a procedure suitable for women with more color tone; however, careful consultation with an experienced practitioner is strongly advised.

Chemical peels are applied and blister, causing the skin to peel off. What results in what seems like a bad sunburn is performed by a physician in a controlled setting and results in smoother less-lined skin.

These procedures involve working with and to some extent through the top layers of skin, causing disruption and using the body's own healing mechanisms with noticeable smoother skin as a result.

Botox injections temporarily lessen the appearance of wrinkles work by blocking the nerves that contract muscles. Since the injected muscle doesn't voluntarily or involuntarily move, the injected skin area is smooth and wrinkle-free. The resulting unresponsive skin area explains the common perception that those who have had Botox injections are expression-less.

The more commonly known of all the procedures is the facelift. Face-lifts are surgical procedures with all the potential risks of surgical procedures: anesthesia, infection, and pain. Plastic surgeons go to great lengths to explain the risks and establish reasonable expectations. Like all surgical procedures, a recovery period is necessary for healing. Unlike several of the above procedures, healing doesn't cause the transformation; rather, surgical shaping of the face takes place during the facelift.

Facelifts do exactly what they say: pull, lift, shape, and tighten the skin and tissue of the face and neck. The face and neck are relieved of excess unnecessary skin, and, voila! bone structure is once again seen surrounded by smooth-appearing skin.

Facelifts will make a woman look five to ten years younger, but, of course, she will continue to age. The woman with a facelift always will have a face that appears five or ten years younger than her actual age. That is, as long as she continues to make healthy choices for her skin like wearing sunscreen, not smoking, using moisturizer, and staying hydrated.

The average cost of a facelift and neck lift varies according to the region, surgeon, how much is done, and where it is done. The best I can find on what one can expect to pay is anywhere from $10,000 to $12,000. The cost is in part explained by remembering that these are surgical procedures that involve a sterile environment, anesthesia, post-op medicines, and aftercare.

"I can tell that (she) had a facelift because her face looks young but the back of her hands look old. You can't fool anyone," announced my favorite mother-in-law. I decided she was correct; the thinning and creping skin of our hands exposes our aging, often accompanied by age spots. Moisturizers and sunscreens are as important to our hand skin health but won't correct thinning and creping.

Creping hands are only a problem if your motive is to hide your age. For many, hiding age is less the point of cosmetic surgery than just wanting to look good and feel good about how we look. It does help to use moisturizer.

Not everyone is a candidate for elective cosmetic surgery. If you smoke or stopped recently following a long period of smoking, the surgeon may advise you that you will not heal properly. Once again. remember that smoking constricts blood vessels, reducing circulation and the amount of healing blood that can reach the surgical area.

Our Aging Face May Not Display Our True Feelings

As we age, faces no longer reflect the automatic expression of what we are feeling, which may explain why we tend to see older folks as unhappy. When the skin tissue and remaining muscles of an older person's face relaxes as in his or her most contemplative moods, the folds seem to fall into the sad face of the clown with the downturned lips. The elasticity and volume that kept us looking alert no longer holds the tension of our expressions. The same look may occur when we are listening intently, causing the speaker to think we are uninterested or disapproving.

The single most effective antidote to a sullen aging expression is a simple smile. All those slackened facial muscles lift up, eyes brighten, and noses lose their prominence. Every one of the women I interviewed appeared younger when they were animated with thought and expressing themselves—and never more so than when they were smiling.

Smiling for the sake of smiling is not always easy, of course. A forced smile may feel unnatural or too reminiscent of being told to smile to be pretty. As girls and young women, we may have been encouraged to smile because we were much more attractive when we smiled. On the other hand, a genuine smile of appreciation, interest, or friendship is almost always is appreciated.

Either way, I recommend becoming more aware of what our faces are doing and recognizing that after a certain age the default tends to be a downturned mouth, conveying the opposite of what you are intending. Improving your awareness increases your opportunity to use your face to express what is no longer automatic. Engage your face to reflect your engagement in the moment with another person.

Observation of others tells me that curious minds are betrayed by complacent faces. We older ladies no longer have the security of a youngish face with enough elasticity to hold our expression in place regardless of our interest. As much as we think that others should honor our age and seek to learn from us, it simply doesn't happen, especially if we appear uninterested and grumpy.

Be Aware, Be Interested, Be Engaged

Part of healthy aging is to understand why people no longer pay attention to you or ascribe characteristics to you based on those slack jowls. It takes hard work and focus to balance acceptance of natural aging with preservation of a healthy and engaged appearance. My solitary walks are often on the same path as others my age and older whom I pass on their walks. People who ignore me are rare, and eye contact with a smile brings an immediate smile and greeting.

Most of us don't feel as old and dispirited as we look. Inside, we are still the person we always have been. In fact, we are at a loss to explain the reaction of others who ignore or avoid us. The societal view of aging as a grumpy dumpy time is pretty much caused by our lack of awareness of our own presence. Practice animation so that you convey what you intend to convey.

Be aware, and be engaged.

6

Renewable Energy Is Not So Renewable

"I thought it would (stay) at the same level. I am less spontaneous; I don't have the same energy."

—*Aging women survey*

Declining energy is either equal to or a strong second to drooping chins and other body parts as the most noticed consequence of aging. For the women I interviewed and me, it also wins the prize as the most unexpected in that it didn't occur to most of us that we would not be functioning at the same level long term. It's not that we thought we wouldn't slow down a bit but, on some level, we thought we always would have adequate endurance even if at a slightly slower pace.

We still may have marathon days of weed pulling or spring house cleaning but awaken the next morning and realize we will need more than one night's sleep to recover physically and mentally. Our physical fatigue seeps into our minds, and an unenthusiastic mind aligns with an unenthusiastic body. Low energy in our bodies lowers the energy of our minds. So, our renewable energy isn't as renewable anymore.

Is declining energy and endurance a normal part of the aging process? Can we prevent the decline or hold it off in some way? The answers are yes and no to both questions. This chapter sets forth an explanation for the inevitable decline but also the hope and challenge of managing the strength and endurance of our bodies so we can maintain precious independence in our daily lives well into our old age.

It will not be the independence of our youth, but it will be enough to allow us control of our lives and the functional ability to make choices. Some of us eventually may need appliances to help us manage daily life, appliances such as walkers to maneuver in or out of our homes. Some of us may need big-handled potato peelers or long-handled tools with grasping jaws (reachers) to pull our socks on, but we will be leading our own lives. Many of us fortunate enough to escape debilitating disease or injury will continue to walk unaided with sturdy footsteps in the grocery store, across our yard, or to meals in the dining room of our retirement home.

The degree of our independence will be determined by our genes, our general health, and our efforts to maintain our strength and mobility. Other than a genetic abundance of constitutional fortitude, there is no magic solution. Alas, even enormous efforts to exercise reach a point of diminishing returns.

Untold numbers believe that the right exercise and the right diet will keep us functional and younger in form and strength at any age until the day we die. Some believe that enough hard work and daily workouts for long hours will achieve more body sculpting and stretching skin over bulging muscles.

The sad realization is that we cannot stop some decline in energy and endurance any more than we can stop drooping body parts. I have yet to hear of surgical reconstruction or plastic surgery for energy levels. I have seen ads for a regime that seems to act like energy Botox in that it promises muscles, stamina and, oh yes, unending sexual prowess by consuming a tablet of antioxidant nutrients said to increase cellular energy. I have my doubts. Still, most people could be doing more than they are right now and achieve levels of strength that will enable them to be independent for many years into their old age. We are surrounded by older people who walk with energy and spirit but also, sadly, many who don't.

What we do know is that physical activity and exercise can build and maintain the strength we need. We may not be able to do as much as we should, but any exercise is better than none. Dedicated gardeners know the value of stooping, pulling, planting, hauling, and walking around gardens. They also know that they can't quite stay bent now as long as in the past without a back twinge, but, overall, they stay in pretty good shape.

Later this chapter will explore what we can do as we age to build and maintain strength, energy and endurance. First, we are helped by understanding what's happening in our bodies that slows our walk or sends us to the couch to rest before we really want to stop.

Explaining Loss of Strength in Aging

Our muscle strength peaks sometime in our 30s or 40s and, given little or no attempt to maintain our muscles, we begin to lose lean muscle mass at a fairly predictable rate. Lean muscle mass is responsible for strength and our production of energy. A debilitating loss of lean muscle mass during aging is important enough to have its own name, Sarcopenia comes from Greek, meaning poverty of the flesh.

Women tend to think weighing less is a good thing until we remember that muscle loss generally is replaced by fat and not the good kind. Fat offers little to us in the way of strength or energy and can cause a lot of other problems. Fat uses little or no calories to maintain itself. Muscle mass increases metabolism and uses calories to maintain its mass.

Another important factor to keep in mind is that our need for protein increases as we age (Hayes, 2018). Protein is essential in our diet to maintain and renew muscle mass and our aging bodies don't process it as well. We must eat more protein to make up the difference, otherwise, our diet will contribute to the loss of muscle mass.

Muscle strength is further compromised in women following menopause when we no longer have the influence of enough estrogen to maintain our muscle mass (Epigee 2020). During menopause our levels of testosterone drop which also results in loss of muscle. We begin to be aware that we no longer have the strength and endurance we once had.

Presenters at the National Institute Aging Workshop on "Unexplained Fatigue in the Elderly" (June 2007) provided some insight but also raised questions that require additional research. They pointed out that muscle is measured by both strength and power (muscle force); leg power was more associated with gait speed and self-reported disability among the elderly than leg strength. We may have the strength to move but not the power or force to move very fast. I'm not slow but I do not walk as fast as my granddaughter.

Think of the power it takes to move us across the room, onto a curb, up from the floor. The workshop report shows that a decline in muscle power seems to occur earlier than muscle strength. Loss of strength together with loss of power results in some degree of loss of function. The sense we have, regardless of whether we know the cause, is that we can't move as fast and do as much.

Once again, the danger of disability resides in failing to act on that sense and becoming less active and more sedentary. That single decision begins the cycle that can only end in limited function and dependence. Decreased strength and stamina as we age occurs in large part because of the change in muscle mass and resulting lessening of strength and power. Loss of function is a result of our conscious decision to accept these changes as inevitable and subsequently make little effort to build and maintain our strength and endurance.

One of my most vivid memories as a young nursing home administrator was a woman in her mid- to late 70s who could not walk. She was mentally oriented, appeared strong, and did not have a diagnosis that explained her leg weakness. She also was sad and most likely in deep depression. In 1975, there were no studies that I could easily find to explain how this formerly vital woman could no longer function outside of a nursing home because she couldn't use her legs. In those days, we were just beginning to think more about the infirmities of aging, whether mental or physical, instead of just putting old disabled people into homes for care. My guess with the amazing vision of hindsight is that she stopped any exercise of her legs, which soon fell into permanent disuse.

Today, regulators insist that older people in nursing homes receive regular exercise and, in some cases, therapy. What regulators can't insist on is that people living in their own homes exercise regularly or, better yet, begin planned exercise at an earlier age.

Loss of leg strength is an inevitable consequence of disuse, not an inevitable consequence of aging. The same can be said of declining aerobic capacity that results in breathlessness due to the body's reduced ability to breathe in enough oxygen to perform an activity. Decline in function and independence is an inevitable consequence of loss of leg strength. Institutionalization or need for help with daily activities is an inevitable outcome of decline in independent functioning. We are not destined to lose the use of our legs before we see 70 years, 80 years, or 90 for that matter. It is not inevitable; it is not natural physiological aging.

It's True: Use It or Lose It

The idea struck me as so simple that I wondered why it hadn't become the most common advice given to older people. Cheryl Bell, the personal trainer I consulted for this chapter, told me she advised all her clients to lie on the floor every day and get up. Her reasoning is simple. If you can't get up, something is wrong with your body, or if you can't figure out how to get up, something is wrong with your thinking. (personal interview 07/19/11)

Her advice reminded me of the experience of a friend. I was stunned when this dear friend, who is about my age, told me she had fallen recently and was unable to get up. She and her husband live in a large home. He was fast asleep in another part of the house and couldn't hear her calls for help. Finally, their dog heard her and woke her husband but only after several hours of her lying on the floor of the storage closet.

My friend wasn't injured. Rather, she did not have the leg power to help herself up, even using her hands and arms. Here was a busy professional woman who could no longer depend on her body to lift her to her feet. Whether or not she knew it, she had real reason to worry that she could fall and not be able to get up on her own.

She explained her dilemma of being stuck on the floor was a consequence of having "worn out her body." She believed that the hard work of her life had sapped her body, and she was resigning herself to the fate of growing limitations which included lying on a cold floor possibly injured and unable to get up. Yet, the idea of wearing one of those buttons that signals need for help appalls her. She feels too young.

Declining strength and declining energy occur as we age but need not result in disability and need for assistance in our daily activities. If my friend had made a point of getting up off the floor every day or even three times a week, she would have known that her legs and arms were weak and could no longer support her. She would have recognized her loss of strength and may well have prevented the decline.

Aging women can come to understand the physical consequences related to aging and the remedies to keep us engaged in life. Maintaining as much muscle mass and strength as possible is one of the top three most important remedies if not the first requirement of maintaining an independent functional life.

Dr. Walter Bortz (1982) suggests that

> "a portion of the changes that are commonly attributed to aging is in reality caused by disuse and, as such, is subject to correction. There is no drug in current or prospective use that holds as much promise for sustained health as a lifetime program of physical exercise" (p. 1203).

The greatest fear of the women I interviewed was being unable to care for themselves and thereby becoming a burden on their families. If we could prevent dependence and loss of control, most of us would. Understanding the distinction between the effects of aging and the effects of disuse on our strength, energy, and endurance provides us with the tools to avoid losing our independence.

Serious limitations in one's ability to function result from disuse, with the greatest decline in muscle mass, strength and endurance. Other attributes like balance and agility decline as well. Aging brings with it the requirement to spend more time in maintaining function, what today is referred to as " functional fitness," something we take for granted most of our lives.

Pat Mortati, exercise physiologist, subscribes to the notion of "use it or lose it" and tells us that re-conditioning can happen at any age. However, the longer you have been inactive, the longer it will take to restore your fitness.[5] We all know this from times we have extended periods of inactivity, perhaps due to illness or injury, and had to spend longer periods regaining our health/fitness. The good news is that it can happen at any time. Re-conditioning can happen unless one gives into the myth of it being too late. It's never too late.

Explaining Loss of Energy in Aging

A more obscure explanation for our declining energy and endurance is the changes occurring in our mitochondria which are the "power plants that provide energy for all the cell's activities (Hayflick, 1994, 1996). Mitochondria are located outside of the nucleus of the human cell. As we age, they decrease in number and increase in size and abnormalities. Mitochondrial dysfunction can lead to reduced energy production, resulting in fatigue. In addition, decreased oxidative metabolism in mitochondria

---

5   Currently, there are two schools of thoughts about muscle memory. The oldest explains muscle memory is a type of procedural memory and claims the memory center actually lies in the brain, not in the muscles. When we repeat an action over and over again, it gets transferred from our short-term memory to our long-term storage (Mahak 2019). In the beginning, our brain is more actively working to perform the task, but as we practice or repeat it, over time, our brain needs to pay less attention to successfully perform that task. The second and recent school of thought is that the muscle actually experiences some type of molecular change that results in the ability of the muscle to return to its formally trained status faster than untrained muscles (Reynolds 2020) Either explanation makes a case for the value of strength training in the event, we become deconditioned for a long period of time.

leads to increased anaerobic metabolism and lactic acid production (NIA, 2007).[6]

We may experience aches in our muscles similar to aches that occur when we are breathless and keep working our muscles. Those arches are caused by the buildup of lactic acid caused by insufficient oxygen getting from lunch to muscles as energy. If mitochondria don't completely do its job of converting available oxygen to energy, an aging woman will feel fatigue and muscle aches earlier than her younger exercising self.

How important is it to remember that loss of mitochondria occurs as we age? It's probably not very important except for Trivial Pursuit. What is important is understanding that something happens to all of us as we age that in part explains why we can't totally restore our youthful energy by exercising to maintain our muscle strength. We can forgive ourselves for not functioning as a 35-year-old but resist using it as an excuse to forgo strengthening exercises.

On the other hand, the good news is that we can maintain and, in all cases, build muscle strength with the appropriate resistance training program. The right exercise regimes will result in having more energy and stamina, just not the energy and stamina of our youth.

A woman trying to maintain strength for whatever motivates her is always better than someone who doesn't try at all. Although I am skeptical about promised outcomes of youthful beauty and form and unending sex for most people over 60 and breathless at the expense, I think efforts in this direction are better than simply giving into a perceived inevitability of aging.

Risks of Giving into Low Energy

Using low energy explained by aging as a reason to stop striving for as much muscle strength as possible is a step into becoming that burden that my interviewees feared. Believing low energy is inevitable means becoming powerless in the face of aging. Yet, too many women choose to be powerless as evidenced by studies, such as this one:

---

6   Oxidative metabolism refers to process of converting oxygen into energy. If mitochondria are inefficient in oxidative metabolism, sufficient oxygen will not be available as energy and result in anaerobic metabolism instead of aerobic metabolism. In our everyday lives, we experience both aerobic and anaerobic metabolism depending on how much oxygen our lungs are delivering to our bodies. We've all experienced aches caused by a buildup of lactic acid in our leg muscles if we continue walking/running while breathless.

"Data from the Framingham (100) study indicate that 40% of the female population aged 55-64 yr, 45% of women aged 65-74 yr., and 65% of women aged 75-84 yr. were unable to lift 4.5 kg. In addition, similarly high percentages of women in this population reported that they were unable to perform some aspects of normal household work. (Mazzeo et al. 1998, p.6).

Those kg are about 10 pounds or the weight of a grandbaby in the first weeks of life. The Framingham study data documents declining strength resulting in limiting function in nearly one-half of us as we age. Women may live longer but to do what!

We may want to give up housework, but we don't want to give up lifting grandbabies. Gardening, grocery shopping, shopping-shopping, and many sports require muscle strength. More than those activities, our bodies need our strength. Staying fit is not a call for perfection; it is a call for healthy engaged living.

Admittedly, the time of aging is the most difficult time to stay fit especially when our bodies seem to set up barriers. For example, we tend to become less flexible. Bending over and kneeling to pull weeds becomes more difficult as we age. We lose flexibility as we age. Range of motion (how widely and in how many directions we can move our joints) declines significantly with age. Range of motion depends on muscle, bone and connective tissue, each of which declines due to aging (Mazzeo et al .,1998).

One of the most popular remedies for increasing flexibility is to practice yoga. The positioning and stretching of yoga challenge many women to move in ways they never thought possible. Practitioners of yoga advance through differing degrees of difficulty but it's not necessary to advance through all the degrees to receive the benefits of yoga. Many women who practice yoga at beginning levels can improve and maintain flexibility, among other benefits.

Some of us are at higher risk to declining function due to lack of exercise because we have other conditions that seem to make exercise even more difficult. Common among those conditions is arthritis.

Arthritis Hurts

One of the women I interviewed complained that she "can't dance—bad knees, bad back." She obviously suffers from osteoarthritis.

Osteoarthritis is the most common form of arthritis and occurs more frequently in the aged population and more often in women than men

(Mayo Clinic, 2020). Arthritis is caused by the chronic degeneration of the cartilages of the joints and felt as a painful tightening of joints. Wear and tear over time, injuries, and obesity are risk factors for arthritis.

Osteoarthritis is the bone pain we feel after a night of sleep in which we barely moved. The pain seems to ask us to stop moving when the reality is that we manage the pain by doing the opposite, getting our bodies to move. Not moving to avoid the pain is in fact giving into the pain and ironically produces more pain. Stretching exercises and yoga can gently move us into more activity and less pain. (See discussion on arthritis in Chapter 10.)

Poor Posture

A far more insidious condition of our bodies than the pain of arthritis is poor posture, which develops over time. I still carry my mother's voice in my head telling my teenage self to stand up straight. Truth is, I didn't really know what it meant except to lift my shoulders back. Mention posture in a roomful of people, and you will see a wave of straightening. We are in a time when hunching over computers is de rigueur.

Driving the freeway during rush hour finds us tensely hunched over the steering wheel. Eventually, what seems to be natural betrays us in how truly unnatural it is. I happen to believe that poor posture is a major factor in looking old. Among other things, it adds to the dowdy look and the perception of advanced age. However, looking fit, while important to our sense of self, isn't the primary reason to stand up straight.

The Tipping Point of Poor Posture

Cheryl Bell literally walked me through the consequences of poor posture seen as seriously rounded shoulders. In four minutes, she fast forwarded the movement that eventually leads to falling. She started by reminding me that most of our activity involves pushing, not pulling. Typically, we reach forward to get something. Typically, we push a door open. Typically, we hold our grocery bags to our chest. Pushing and not pulling results in good strong chest muscles and poor weak shoulder and back muscles. The stronger muscles are the shorter they are. The shorter your chest muscles are the longer the muscles around your shoulders are. The longer they are the weaker they are. Voila! Seriously rounded shoulders set the stage for falling.

The more out of balance upper front and back muscles are to each other, the more out of balance we are. To show me how this works—or doesn't work, Cheryl demonstrated. She stooped her normally good posture enough that she had to bend her knees to balance her body and avoid falling. While she mimicked the stooped person, she began to shuffle because it was the most secure way to move. Shuffling, or not picking up your feet when you walk, leads to imbalance and is a major risk factor for falls, not to mention simply tripping over rugs.

Fear of Falling

Moreover, once you fall, you become fearful of falling. Fear of falling often leads to progressive caution in daily activities. Inadequate mobility will reduce physical fitness with the consequence of increasing the risk of falls. Based on my experience and what I have heard other women say, I believe that as we age, we develop an intuitive sense that we need to be more careful in order to avoid falls. It is as if the body is asking us to listen to this alert. In fact, as we age, we begin to lose the sense of proprioception or where our bodies are positioned.

Proprioception has fascinated me for a long time. Imagine the sense of knowing where your feet and hands are and then imagine not knowing where your feet and hands are. The sense of placement of your hands and feet are proprioception. We begin to realize that our balance is not as certain as it has been. If we listen to this body alert, we know we must be more careful and draw on other senses to know where we are and what we might step into next. We compensate and don't fall. We shuffle and increase our risk of falling.

We generally fall the same way we did when we were younger, but if we haven't worked on muscle strength, we may not have the muscle that serves as protective padding. If enough of our body form has shifted, we may have unprotected joints. Those butt muscles that seem to fall away or down may no longer surround the hip joint.

In addition, the risk of injury from falls is increased for women who have osteoporosis, a condition in which the bone itself is weakened and becomes brittle. Regular exercise is a factor in maintaining bone strength and preventing osteoporosis.

Aging slows our reflexes, more so if we are not in activities that demand a reflexive response such as tennis or driving. Our bodies respond automatically when we fall. Many times, we stop the fall. If we can't stop, we cover our faces, try to turn our bodies or wrap our arms around our heads. If we can't respond quickly enough, we can only hope we are not walking down the stairs or on a concrete surface.

Sobering statistics from the Centers for Disease Control and Prevention remind us of the particular risk that older people have as a result of a fall (CDC, 2011, 2020).

- Nearly 30,000 people age 65 and older died as a result of a fall in 2016, an increase of 31% since 2007 (Burns & Kakara, 2018).

- 81% of deaths from falls were among people 65 and older (CDC, 2011).

- Women fall more than men. Women are more likely than men to be injured in a fall. Men are more likely to die. Women are more likely than men to suffer a nonfatal fall injury (Burns& Kakara, 2018).

- 300,000 people age 65 and older are hospitalized with hip fracture 95% of those hip fractures are caused by falling. Women experience 75% of hip fractures (Parkkari et al .,1999).

- Falls are the most common cause of brain injury (CDC, 2020, Jager et al ., 2000).

- People age 75 and older who fall are 4-5 times more likely than those age 65-74 to be admitted to a long-term care facility for a year or longer (CDC, 2011).

The bottom line is that a fall can be a life-threatening event in the life of an aging woman. Maintaining muscle mass, bone strength, good posture, and awareness of surroundings may not guarantee a fall-free life but will prevent the preventable falls and give us the strength to get up when we fall.

The Effect of Limiting Activity

Another reason we lose muscle strength and energy is inactivity due to illness or injuries causing a significant period of inability to maintain our activity. The older we are the shorter the time of inactivity before we lose strength and energy and the longer the time to recover. Eighteen days of inactivity due to a bad sinus infection turns a routine condition into a debilitating one.

Many physicians will withhold antibiotic treatment for infection in favor of relying on the body's own defenses to resolve the infection. Physicians say that the overuse of antibiotics will result in antibiotic allergies and antibiotic-resistant bugs. Both are legitimate concerns unless a woman is over 70 and will suffer serious deconditioning in the time it takes her body to fight the infection. The risks of deconditioning must be weighed against the risks of drug allergies. The importance of taking the entire course of antibiotic as ordered must be emphasized for anyone on antibiotics. Doing so kills all bugs and therefore, their ability to mutate into drug resistant bugs.

Respond to Loss of Energy with Energy

Responding to the loss of energy and endurance that comes with aging by resting more and moving less deepens a spiral of less energy, more resting, less endurance, less moving and so on. Stop, don't let it happen!

We have control. We can change the tides of normal aging by accepting, adapting and working within the changes that announce we are no longer young. We still control our destiny and can use the enduring strength and resilience that has gotten us this far.

"Our biography becomes our biology," says Caroline Myss (1996, p..40). One of the women I interviewed confirmed this, "I have more energy; I started hiking and feel better."

Pat Mortati, exercise physiologist, often uses this quote in her work with patients with chronic disease. She goes on to say that "we are the sum total of our life's experiences and habits which are directly related to the state of health we find ourselves in." According to Pat, what matters is that we understand ourselves well enough to know we have made us who we are. We can continue to do so, but if we aren't satisfied with our aging prospects, Pat says emphatically that we can make a course correction or start a new and different path. Recognizing we may have limitations; she tells us it is important to embrace our limitations with a positive attitude as we work to regain the physicality that has been lost. We can make a course correction at any time. It's never too late (personal interview, July 11, 2011).

Pat has done a lot of thinking about those course corrections in her work to improve the quality of life for those people with chronic disease that now helps define their lives. We can't say that all chronic disease is a result of lifestyle behaviors. Some people are genetically predisposed or triggered to develop disease. One of the women I interviewed has diabetes by virtue of a dominant diabetes gene. Her mother had it, and her daughter has it. She has the good sense and motivation to control her disease through medical supervision and lots of self-discipline, but she still has diabetes. She is one of the exceptions to the lifestyle disease rule. Most of us have created our own destinies when it comes to chronic conditions such as diabetes and heart disease.

Childhood Impacts

A more insidious and less self-inflicted factor may have had an impact on the development of chronic disease for some women. The Adverse Childhood Experiences (ACE) study (Felitti et al., 1998) is significant study performed by Kaiser Permanente and the Center for Disease Control retrospectively analyzed the medical records of 17,000 people, controlled for variables, and determined that adults who had significant adverse incidences in their childhoods were at greater risk for development of a chronic disease earlier in life.

Ten adverse experiences were identified as significant and included physical abuse, sexual abuse, emotional abuse, and neglect. One of the women I interviewed experienced some form of every one of these and developed Type 1 diabetes and a heart valve problem in her early 60s despite efforts to maintain healthy practices in eating and exercising.

We need to be keenly aware of our childhood histories and their impact on our health. With adverse childhood experiences, the road to good health is more complicated, and we likely require additional supports to navigate our emotional and physical trauma.

Rest and Renew (Sleep Well)

"Someone needs a nap," sings the mother to her toddler who is screeching, twisting his body, and wearing that not-so-adorable pout. The older I get, the more I am saying the same to myself without the tantrum. We know that the sure signs of not getting enough sleep for most of us are crankiness, a heavy-head feeling, less ability to concentrate, and fatigue. Not only do we feel too tired to exercise, we are hungry and want to eat more!

The need for rest and sleep may be the most underrated health issue of our day. During our sleep, our bodies are balancing hormones, replenishing cells, and sorting ideas for future use. All are essential functions for our well-being. Our bodies, our minds, and our attitudes suffer if we don't get adequate rest. Some say America is a nation of sleep-deprived people due to our schedules and technology which is allowing us, in some cases addicting us, to work or communicate into the night. Aging adults have no immunity to the pressures but are more likely to be observed falling asleep watching television than other adults.

We older adults tend to have days with naps not because we need more sleep than before but rather because we aren't sleeping as well at night. As we age, we tend to sleep more lightly and are more easily wakened. Naps help to compensate for loss of sleep if there is time and opportunity during the day. Although some researchers have proposed allowing the 15-minute nap for all ages to improve productivity, it hasn't caught on as a standard in America's hard driving work ethic.

Sleep is essential to our physical and mental well-being throughout our lives. Sleep is the time for renewal of our body which we have learned is slowing down. We can't afford to miss any opportunity for rest and renewal and in the case of our brain, the opportunity to do its work of processing the day, an important factor in retention of information. Adequate sleep results in more productive days, an inclination to be more active, and greater mental acuity.

Adults need 7-9 hours of sleep each night which is a large enough variation that we can't say for sure what any individual needs other than at least 7 hours of sleep. The test of having enough sleep is feeling alert, energetic and able to manage most things. We can learn the amount of sleep that leaves us feeling in positive control through tracking our sleep and post sleep well-being.

The common suggestion we hear or read from several experts is to establish a sleep routine. Go to bed and get up at the same time each day. They tell us exercise, alcohol, and caffeine too close to bedtime, as well as lights from computers, televisions, notepads, laptops and phones, should be avoided. Getting good sleep as we grow older may require experimentation. Don't be embarrassed by needing a nap; it really doesn't mean "old lady nods off and snores." It's your body telling you it needs more rest. Listen.

Getting a Smart Start—It's Never Too Late to Learn or Have a Course Correction on the Healthy Path to Healthy Natural Aging

Ginny was bumping close to 80 years of age when I interviewed her. Even though I did not plan to interview women of that age, I was prodded by two other women to talk with her. "She is amazing," they said.

Ginny is amazing. She lives this chapter and more. Every morning, she and her husband get up, have coffee and go to the local community gym.

She walks regularly around the neighborhood with friends. Her advice for "looking younger" is to exercise and be active in your community. Her diligence has been rewarded by good health, strength, and independence. She says, too, "I feel better now than I did at 20." I doubt she can imagine living her life in any other way.

The first step on changing longstanding habits of poor health is to accept the role we play in our own health. Most of our habits have been with us like comfortable shoes, and we somehow feel we will be somewhat lost without them. The next and most important step is making a commitment to good health in our old age by breaking the habits that either are hurting or will hurt us. Start to break those habits by getting a release from your physician that sets out the pace at which it is medically safe to work on the necessary changes. Next, seek recommendations from qualified people like Pat and Cheryl if you feel you would benefit from direct support from a professional. Seek family and friend support. Going it on your own only will work as well as it has in the past. Take a big breath and give yourself a hug.

Reminders:

- Listen to your body.
- Accept that a certain amount of decline occurs naturally with aging and that trying to keep up with 25- or 40-year-olds amounts to self-abuse.
- Stop the slide into a comfy aging process that allows muscles to turn to fat.
- Put in disciplined effort to strengthen and maintain muscle • strength.
- Move to strengthen bones and keep joints moving.
- Keep moving to build and maintain the most energy possible.
- Practice balance to compensate for loss of proprioception.
- Learn stretching, balance and flexibility. Try yoga.
- Become aware of posture, and either maintain good posture or develop a plan to strengthen muscles to build posture and walking confidence.
- Make adequate rest and sleep a priority.

- Don't give up because it seems too late to change; learn and get on the track with the natural aging process.
- And yes, get down on the floor every day and get up.

Next, we turn to what's different about nourishing our body as our digestive processes change during the aging process.

7

An Aging System Delivers

"Take care of your body. It's the only place you have to live."

—Jim Rohn, motivational speaker

Staying strong and energetic is not the only thing that gets complicated as we age. Just as our skin and our energy change as we age, so do our nutritional needs, metabolism, and digestion processes.

This chapter delineates the changes that take place in our digestive system as a result of the aging process and the importance of adapting to those changes. Not only do we want to nourish our bodies for health, we also want to continue to enjoy all the pleasures and satisfaction of eating, drinking, and dining well. This chapter focuses on the digestive system because discomforts are common and changes have a distinct impact on the nutritional health of our bodies.

We know that many adults suffer from digestive discomforts; the numbers increase with age. If we have any doubt, we need only look at the array of over-the-counter acid-reducing medications. Anyone who has experienced such digestive problems as heartburn, constipation, and frequent diarrhea wants to fix them. Often, the physician visit and follow-up tests end with reassurance that we do not have cancer or some other serious condition, but we still have the symptoms of digestive disorders.

Eat, Drink, and Be Healthy!

Just as aging-related changes occur in our skin and energy, changes also occur in our digestive systems. If we learn what to expect, we can accept and/or take action to mitigate the changes.

First, we never should forget why we drink and eat. We eat to nourish our bodies to keep them going and to keep them healthy. Our body signals us to drink and to eat, and we are rewarded by a feeling of satiety and satisfaction. No doubt signals cross when we eat to solve problems, but our primary biological reason for eating and drinking is to live.

We also eat for enjoyment. Food serves a central theme in much of our life, whether it's working to be sure there is enough food for the family, celebrating a holiday, or meeting for lunch. Facebook users, mostly women I suspect, post pictures of wonderful presentations of food, turning the appearance of food into an art.

We eat for other reasons, too. These include sociability and comfort, among others. We spend time and money on planning to eat and eating although often we just eat on the run.

One can't help but marvel at the workings of a digestive system that supports the essential function of transforming food and drink into energy. Our food enters one very long tube that moves it into the stomach where it is broken up, digested, and some nutrients absorbed. The digested food journeys into the small intestine where more nutrients are extracted and finally into the large intestine that manages the waste, allowing us to expel it from our bodies. Our liver, pancreas, and gallbladder contribute the right enzymes or chemicals at the right time during the digestive process. They are heavy lifters in processing the healthy and detoxifying the unhealthy.

Knowing the complexity of relationships and timing, we may well wonder why more doesn't go wrong with this interconnected system that needs to do its job every day. The older we are, the more work the system has done. Normally, it works without prompts save the food we put into our mouths.

Just like every other part of this human system the digestive system is affected by aging. The food and drink we've enjoyed for years may start to add extra pounds. Our digestive system may begin to take some of our enjoyment away by causing more abdominal discomfort, heartburn, burping, and passing gas. Our taste buds aren't even as sensitive. You don't have to be in your 60s to experience digestive problems, but they are more predictable the older you get.

We learn throughout our lives that there are consequences of eating certain foods. Food intolerance and allergies are highly individual. There is no one size fits all in diet advice except to eat a balanced diet in moderation. A person who has eaten hot peppers for decades tolerates spicy foods better than the person just introduced to jalapeños.

Eating and Age-Related Changes

We can avoid some of the woes of an aging digestive system by knowing what changes occur as a result of the aging process.

Mouth

Gums, saliva, and sense of taste all go through aging changes. Specifically,

- **Gums** shrink as we age, causing dentures, if we have them, to loosen and diminish our ability to chew well.
- The production of **saliva** essential to digestion decreases. Reduced saliva in our mouths impedes digestion and may contribute to swallowing difficulty.
- Our **sense of taste** diminishes.

Esophagus

The esophagus is the food pipe that extends from mouth to stomach. Changes here include the following:

- Food travels more slowly through the esophagus, and too much food can result in **choking**.
- The wall of the esophagus relaxes more and, combined with lower stomach acid, either worsens or initiates the problem of **acid backup**.

Diaphragm

- We don't usually think of the diaphragm, the thin membrane that separates the upper and lower parts of our body, as part of the digestive process but it has a role. We associate the diaphragm's function more with respiration but it also functions to increase abdominal pressure when we urinate and defecate and puts pressure on the esophagus that prevents acid reflux. Just as the muscles of the esophagus relax due to aging, the diaphragm has age-related changes that can cause relaxation of pressure on the esophagus that results in the development of a hiatal hernia, a condition in which the upper part of the stomach protrudes into the chest through the opening in the diaphragm or through the esophageal opening in the diaphragm causing heart burn, acid reflux and pain in some cases (Santos-Longhurst 2018).

Stomach

- The muscles of the stomach are more relaxed and function more slowly and food stays in our stomachs longer as we age. If we continue to eat as if our stomach is emptying as usual, we risk overfilling it, which may result in food backing up into the esophagus and mouth.

- Our bodies produce less stomach acid as we age, which is the opposite of what we expect is happening when we are burping up acid.

- The unseen consequence of less stomach acid is the **reduced absorption of vitamin B12**. Vitamin B-12 is essential to our bodies and is particularly important to the proper function of our brains. Adequate vitamin B12 is needed to support the myelin sheath around the neurons of the brain. Less myelin means less brain volume, not a good thing.

- Another important consequence of less acid is the **reduced breakdown of food in the stomach**, so it arrives in the small intestine less prepared to deliver nutrients through the wall of the small intestine.

- Ever more study is researching the impact of less acid on normal intestinal flora or bacteria. Less acid results in **fewer defenses against harmful bacteria**. Fewer good bacteria and more bad bacteria put our system off-balance and contribute to the bloating, gas pain, and discomfort. Imbalance in intestinal flora or bacteria results in bloating and excessive gas.

- The **muscle of the large intestine loses strength** and as a result moves contents more slowly, which can cause constipation.

Common and Problematic Digestive Experiences

We become more aware of changes related to the aging process as we enter our 60s. Many of us have had problems before then. One of the most unseen but most uncomfortable adjustments we make as we age is managing digestive changes. Digestive discomforts can be the alert system for all kinds of maladies. Discomfort causes could be as normal as an aging intestine that takes longer to process food or as abnormal as a malignant tumor. Knowing that some cancers of the digestive system are not only unseen but also unfelt until it may be too late is particularly concerning. We all know people who have died of stomach cancer, colon cancer or pancreatic cancer. We all are advised to seek medical assessment if we note any change in our bowel movements such as change in color of stool and difficulty emptying the bowel completely.

Certain gastrointestinal symptoms can signal serious conditions that seem unrelated to digestion. For example, a woman experiencing unexplained GI symptoms often will be referred to a gynecologist for evaluation of the possibility of ovarian cancer, in which the presenting symptom is often unexplained intestinal bloating. Since symptoms may be the result of serious conditions, we always should seek a medical evaluation. We are serving our own best interests to know as much as possible about the influence of aging versus the influence of pathology. Once cleared medically, we are then prepared to manage our condition, which includes managing those lifestyle behaviors that add to our problems.

Acid Indigestion/GERD

Acid indigestion is an older term for what we now call "heartburn" or Gastro Esophageal Reflux Disease (GERD), which refers to the backup of stomach acid and contents into the esophagus. We need only look around Walmart, Safeway, or Costco to be convinced that there are many sufferers. We see ever expanding displays and sales of acid-reducing drugs and probiotics. If products for the treatment and management of digestive problems are any indication, we are having an epidemic.

Twenty percent of Americans are affected by GERD (Fogoros, 2018). Often, the condition begins as a discomfort too vague to describe, and we simply adapt to the discomfort until it begins to interfere with our lives in some way. We often self-treat when we shouldn't and intensify the problem, missing the opportunity for early intervention in a serious medical problem. The tipping point that usually drives us to medical help is when heartburn is no longer tolerable because we wake out of a sound sleep with burning acid in our mouth.

Regardless of the cause, anyone who has experienced hot acid filling their throat and spilling into their mouths does not want to experience it again. It is particularly alarming when it occurs in the middle of the night. Sufferers of acid reflux jerk awake, sit up reflexively, and cough in a usually successful effort to prevent acid from going into the lungs. The experience is frightening and extremely painful and the sufferer is left with a burning sensation in the throat. A friend of mine sucks ice cubes to sooth the hot fire in her throat. Most people who experience nights like this search for ways to prevent it from ever happening again.

Medications are available for short-term relief, but sufferers are best advised to see their physician for direction. Overuse can result in other digestive problems and a long-term reliance on their use. Health care providers typically will advise their patients with GERD to monitor their diet to determine those foods or drinks more likely to cause reflux. Common offenders are tomato-based sauces, caffeine, alcohol, and spicy foods.

Another mitigation is to practice mindful enjoyment of eating; pay attention, chew well, swallow smaller amounts, allow time to eat and stop eating when full. We mindfully seek to reduce the amount of food we eat because our stomachs don't process food as quickly and fill faster. I know mindful eating is easier said than done. We are not used to it. It takes more time at first to establish the habit and more time than taking a pill. My husband and I often remind each other to quit "shoveling," the mindless one-handed delivery of dinner to our mouths after a busy day.

Reduced Vitamin B12 Absorption

"In older persons, food-bound (vitamin B-12) malabsorption becomes the predominant cause of deficiency, at least in part due to gastric atrophy, but it is likely most elderly can absorb from fortified food." (Allen, 2008, p. 693). Vitamin B-12 is critical to the maintenance of a healthy neurological system. Symptoms of deficiency include weakness, confusion, heart palpitations, dizziness and weight loss (West, 2017 WebMD 2020). One of the difficulties is that symptoms may show gradually because we have a large reserve of B-12 and it takes time for the deficiency to show. Imagine how these same symptoms in an older person may be manifestations of other conditions making this diagnosis more elusive.

A significant vitamin B-12 deficiency can result in dementia. Keep in mind that vitamin B12 deficiency can be caused by simply not eating foods with B-12. Either way, it is a serious deficiency with serious consequences if not treated. Treatment is uncomplicated and is accomplished by replacing and rebuilding body stores of vitamin B-12.

Foods rich in vitamin B-12 include shellfish, meat, salmon, milk, cheese, eggs, fortified cereal and fortified soy products.

Good bacteria Is Good for Us

Researchers have discovered that by transplanting fecal material from a healthy donor to someone with intestinal conditions such as Crohn's disease, an autoimmune disease that causes severe diarrhea, vomiting, and pain, the disease can be controlled. In all instances, these treatments require medical assessment, treatment, and oversight. Much remains to be studied in the complex area of intestinal bacteria (flora). Such research is especially important in view of increasing digestion problems in our modern age and aging population.

Years ago, a peptic ulcer (occurring in the stomach or duodenal lining) was thought to be caused by stress and failure to control stress. This long-held and accepted theory was debunked with the discovery of the H. pylori bacteria, the primary cause of peptic ulcers. H. pylori works in conjunction with stomach acid; the bacteria wears away the lining allowing acid to reach sensitive stomach lining tissues.

For years people with ulcers were thought to be uptight rigid individuals when they really had bacteria eating away at them. Now peptic ulcers are treated with antibiotics and short-term use of acid-reducing medications. Things we do, like drinking alcohol and eating spicy food can increase existing discomfort, but these foods do not cause peptic ulcers any more than stress does although a person with exposed sensitive stomach lining likely learns to avoid foods and drinks that cause pain. Aging persons also should be aware that certain drugs like aspirins, ibuprofens, and other NSAIDs can cause peptic ulcers by resting against the lining of the stomach.

Intestinal flora is increasingly the subject of research. More and more studies are finding links between the imbalance in the floras of the digestive system and conditions that seem unrelated to intestines. Recent studies are leading to more research in the relationship of intestinal floral imbalance to heart disease.

Flora or bacterial balance occurs when good bacteria is present in abundance enough to breakdown food waste. Some conditions such as reduced stomach acid can reduce the quantity of good bacteria and result in an imbalance in which bad bacteria causes problems such as bloating. More and more people are turning to probiotics, which contain good bacteria and are packaged to deliver good bacteria to the digestive system, particularly the small intestine that works to breakdown food.[7] I laughed the first time I heard about probiotics, thinking it was some sort of cosmic joke, but I have learned through my own mixed-up experience of bacterial imbalance that responded for the better to my taking probiotics. I also learned that the condition is more easily treated than diagnosed.

Conditions of Large Intestine

The large intestine gets more of our attention than we really want to give it. It is the source of embarrassing noise, unpleasant odors, uncomfortable turns, and painful bloating. It is the place that gets probed and examined after we've spent an afternoon on the toilet emptying it and a night not eating or drinking. Colonoscopies are recommended after age 50 and every 5-10 years after, depending on what's seen. Colonoscopies are the surest way to discover colon cancer and polyps. Although now routinely screened, any change in bowel habits calls for a visit to your physician and a thorough evaluation.

A more common condition of the large bowel is diverticulosis, in which small pockets develop in the large colon. Diverticulosis occurs in 35 percent of the population age 50 and younger and in 58 percent of people 60 and older (Peery, A et al 2016(. Less than 5 percent of people with diverticulosis develop diverticulitis, an infection resulting from something getting stuck in one of those pouches. (Shahedi et al ., 2013). Diverticulitis can have serious life-threatening consequences if not treated and is another reason anyone with abdominal pain should be medically evaluated. Diverticulitis is highly treatable if caught in time but can be fatal if it results in a rupture in the intestine, spilling bacteria into a clean part of the body.

---

7   Probiotics are produced by many manufacturers and sold at varying prices. The place to start in seeking what probiotic is best is with your primary health care provider who will assess your symptoms for other causes. When you've been cleared for probiotics, your provider may or may not have a probiotic recommendation. Health food store and friends with similar problems may have recommendations. My recommendation is to try one that is commonly sold, preferably one that does not require refrigeration (for convenience). Follow directions, some of which suggest taking two capsules if one does not work. Give the probiotic time to work before increasing.

Aging and Eating Habits

Many of our symptoms can be explained by slowing processes due to aging. The same eating behaviors we had when young now cause discomfort. Despite new knowledge that tells us our conditions are not necessarily stress-induced, we should be clear that stress or response to stress can make conditions worse or at least seem worse. For example, sleepless nights do not allow our bodies the opportunity to rest and heal.

Practice Mindful Eating

Paying attention to our eating can help alleviate or mitigate symptoms resulting from aging changes. Mindless eating is a nemesis of good nutrition and good eating experiences according to dietitians. They advise us to turn off all distractions while we eat. They are no doubt speaking to our inclinations to watch the news, do our office work, and drive our cars while we eat. Isn't that why we have fast food drive-through windows?

Not so, dietitians warn. When we eat too fast, we don't chew our food well enough before we swallow or leave enough time for our bodies to tell us we are full enough. We are asking our stomachs to do the work of our mouths and likely filling our stomachs too much in the process. Ouch! No wonder the stomach reacts and sends some of it back. Taking the time to eat and to enjoy the act of eating is especially important as we age. If we pay attention, we will chew our food and avoid swallowing too much and too fast. If we pay attention, we know when we are full. Of course, getting dentures adjusted to fit also is a good idea.

It may be that we must at least pay attention through enough meals to discover how much food we can comfortably consume at one time. Many older people manage symptoms of overeating by eating several small meals during the day.

Eating mindfully or not, eating is one of our greatest pleasures in life and too often one that puts us at odds with our own best interests, especially if we don't account for some of the issues that may be a result of the aging process.

Don't Forget to Drink!

Staying well-hydrated is essential to basic functioning and means we usually drink enough water each day. Many of us are more mindful when drinking a glass of red wine, however. Even though red wine in small quantities is seen as a health value, it's not an important drink. Water is necessary to the smooth functioning of many organs of our bodies. Older people often do not have enough fluid reserves and are sensitive to loss of fluid. Fluids lost to excess perspiration and/or diarrhea or reduced intake must be replaced. There is a reason that the alarm goes out to check on the elderly during heat waves. The young of old age are more resilient but may well notice symptoms of fatigue or mental lapses earlier on a hot day than when they were younger.

Eat to Live and Enjoy Life on the Path to Natural Aging

We don't talk out loud much about digestive complaints, especially intestinal discomforts. It's just not polite. We really have no need to make it a topic of conversation except with our health care provider. We do have a need to understand and be informed so that we can be alert and make choices that result in better quality of life.

- Listen to, be aware of your body—what's working well, what isn't.
- Seek medical help when unusual symptoms occur; don't accept them as part of aging.
- Keep in mind that nutritional requirements change as we age.
- Learn about and adapt to the digestive system changes brought on by aging; avoid overfilling your stomach.
- Adapt to aging changes by adjusting behaviors that no longer work for your body.
- Eat mindfully, and savor the taste and experience,
- Stay hydrated!

Next, we move into the area around eating that gets the most attention: our weight.

8

Aging Women and Weight

"The two greatest epidemiological trends of our times are the aging of the population and the obesity epidemic."

—*Roubenoff (2004, p. 887)*

"In June 2012 the prestigious International Journal of Eating Disorders published the results of a seminal study on the prevalence of eating disorders in midlife and beyond. Lead study author, Cynthia Bulik, Ph.D., director of the Center of Excellence for Eating Disorders at the University of North Carolina, Chapel Hill, found that 13 percent of American women 50 or older experience symptoms of an eating disorder; 60 percent report that their concerns about weight and shape negatively affect their lives; and 70 percent are trying to lose weight." (Arnold, 2013; Gage et al., 2012).

Maintaining weight and figure is much like maintaining one's youthful appearance; it gets harder with each year added to our life. Most American women have spent considerable time and effort, in some cases considerable money, trying to manage their weight during their lives. Popular culture sets standards for the female figure that essentially defy the normal body inclination of most women, especially as we age.

"Aging Woman and Weight" is about taking care of our bodies by being a healthy weight, not by dieting to lose weight to achieve the perfect form but instead to support the body in doing its work of keeping us alive and fit as we age. This chapter highlights weight changes brought on by aging and lifestyle choices and what choices women can make to manage those changes.

The right weight supported by good nutritional habits and regular exercise promises greater opportunity for a life lived long and well. We seek health and fitness, not form and figure. Weight and nutrition-related problems include obesity and morbid obesity, an epidemic of our time, as well as anorexic thinness and malnutrition at any weight.

Aging Women and Weight

Some of us smartly gave up the body perfect after the first baby, not by becoming obese or even overweight but by giving up the 24-inch waist. Then, we entered the post-menopausal years only to see the 26-inch waist grow to 28 or 30 inches and above. And, if we are paying attention, we have noticed that our body's annoying response to eating the same diet and doing the same amount of exercise is to gain weight.

Even more annoying is conspicuous weight collection around our waists and hips. Much to my dismay, I began to experience a thickening waist, softer drooping butt, and weight gain as I left menopause to enter my 60s for literally more of the same and in more parts of my body. For me and many like me, the lifelong struggle of weight control just got more complicated.

It was a revelation for a few of the women I interviewed who never had an overweight problem to realize they could no longer eat anything they wanted without gaining weight. It seems that aging women are destined to pudgy square bodies that droop. It's not unusual that an older woman appears overweight when in fact she is not.

Overweight or not, we are experiencing gravity's pull. Overweight or not, we droop. It is as if our bodies are separated into distinct segments, chins, chest, stomach, hips, and thighs. Each segment seems to give up its form to gravity and literally rolls to a stop at some unmarked border between segments. Skin and fat pile onto the borders, giving the illusion of being overweight even if our weight hasn't changed in ages. A sagging chin extends a face, drooping breasts shorten a torso, a sagging belly hides form, and a sagging butt flattens the once curvy backside.

The pull of gravity, along with the frustrating creep of pounds that many women experience during and after menopause, becomes a middle-aged wake-up call.

A Wake-up Call

Pat was petite in stature and bone structure and never had been overweight until sometime in her 50s. When I met her at age 66, I didn't think of her as overweight. Her outgoing and engaged personality was what I noticed the most. I later learned from her that she weighed 145 pounds on a 5-foot 2.75-inch frame which put her at a BMI of 25.9, barely putting her in the overweight category.

A year or so later, I realized that she was losing weight, which I hoped was not due to illness, a common reason for weight loss. When I inquired, she told me with great conviction that she didn't like what was happening to her and decided to change the trajectory of her middle-age look.

Her personal wake-up call was seeing photos of herself and wondering "who was that dumpy middle-aged woman?" Her weight, which she could have carried better as a younger woman with skin full of collagen and elasticity, appeared to her as cascading rolls and lumps. She also didn't like the way she felt. "I wasn't sure I could keep up with my partner of 19 years who is an active man who enjoys long hikes and climbing mountains." Filled with determination, she started by monitoring her eating and discovered she ate a lot, at least 500 calories a day not associated with a meal and that she didn't need.

Pat stopped eating late in the evenings, ate half instead of a whole sandwich for lunch, and consumed one cookie instead of three for dessert. "I didn't believe in diets; I knew whatever I did had to be forever," she explained. The weight started coming off easily and quickly and soon she felt more energy. She had always worked out and walked, but now she relished doing more. Pat liked this new way of feeling and living and knows she never will return to late-night snacks.

Factors That Lead to Weight Gain in Aging

A natural change in hormonal balance occurs as we age. Both women and men experience a decline in estrogen and testosterone. Recent studies have shown that the decline in estrogen is a primary factor in the accumulation of fat (Lizcano & Guzman, 2014). Testosterone decline results in reduced lean muscle and muscle tone. Together, we can expect flabby abdomens and arms among other noticeable shifts in body parts. There is some comfort in knowing we come by these changes naturally and not as a result of the dessert we had last night.

Most of us don't need to be told that our metabolism is slower. We realize that when we eat the same number of calories, we gain weight. Scientists are studying just what happens to decrease our metabolism. So far, they have confirmed that our resting metabolism rate (calories we expend while being at rest) declines with age. Studies point to smaller organs and other cellular structures that require fewer calories as an explanation. We shouldn't be surprised since we already know that muscles and skin are losing mass.

As we age, we lose less energy sitting in a chair. We learned earlier that we also are expending less energy because we do not have the same endurance and tire sooner. The result is less physical activity. "Renewable energy is not so renewable" cautioned us to beware of giving into an inclination to exercise less that may occur as we grow older.

Lack of sleep or poorer quality sleep also can add difficulty to managing weight and appetite. Sleepiness puts our body in a state of alert that signals us to be ready, a nervous kind of readiness. Sleepiness causes our bodies to release more stress hormone and raises our blood sugar. Appetite hormones (ghrelin and leptin) are disrupted (Van Cauter et al ., 2005). Our body reads all this as a signal to eat more and store fat.

Habits That Weigh on Us

We know that some of our discomforts around eating are a result of aging changes, but many are compounded by or result from long-held habits that don't adapt to our changing bodies. Pat's consumption of extra calories was a habit to which she didn't give a second thought. We might not recognize that our daily habits of eating or activity may be compounding a weight problem that will become unhealthy if we don't correct these habits. If we continue to have a midnight snack, dessert after dinner, or pancakes with sausage for breakfast and make no change in calorie expenditure, we will start to pile on weight.

For some, gaining weight is a new and unwelcome experience. It may be their first experience buying larger-sized clothes, cutting calories, or increasing trips to the gym. Many of us who gradually slip into being overweight or obese are set back by the realization that without eating more, we are getting fatter as we age. We feel betrayed, especially those of us who in good faith worked at establishing the right diet, the right exercise plan, and the right weight only to find that each age brings the need to reduce calories and increase exercise. Once again, we are made to understand that no plan is permanent in the changing world of our aging bodies.

For some, managing weight has been a lifelong struggle accompanied by lifelong cycling between dieting and gaining weight. Sadly, what every frustrated frequent dieter knows, the body wants to regain weight and will do so more quickly than before. Studies now are telling us that once overweight, our bodies adopt a new set point for weight which the body constantly strives to reach (Parker-Pope, 2012). You've heard women's stories of dieting only to gain back more than they lost.

Some of us were overweight and lost weight, leaving a residual abundance of fat cells waiting to be filled. Our relationship with food always will be one of supervising intake and managing weight. It's not hard to understand why someone would want to give up constant vigilance in eating or look for the latest miracle diet.

Far too many women (and men) are choosing to become or remain excessively overweight or obese. The consequence of adapting to the medical outcomes and physical limitations of being overweight or obese is a reduction in quality of living and likely a shortened life span.

Obesity Epidemic

As Roubenhoff (2004) noted, the two most widely spread health problems of our time are the aging of the population and obesity. Of great importance, research results support the notion that obesity worsens the age-related decline in physical function, with physical frailty in obese elderly people being common (Villareal et al . 2004).

Ironically, in spite of all the attention, services, products, and dollars devoted to healthy weights, the obesity rate never has been higher for all ages. As a result, obesity-related conditions are on the rise. It is well worth repeating as we get into fitness for successful aging that both obesity and malnutrition are factors that shorten the length and diminish the quality of aging lives.

Several years ago, I renewed an acquaintance with an old friend of mine. We had lost touch over 30 years of busy lives. I was astonished and saddened to see the amount of weight she had gained since I saw her last. By any definition, she was morbidly obese. She worked in a profession that required intelligence and people skills. In our personal chats, it was not her work or relationships about which she talked, nor was it about her weight; rather, it was her health or apparent lack of good health. Over the course of several chats, I learned she had a condition for each system of her body. Her body speaks loudly to her. She hears the cries but not the causes.

I make no attempt to judge her or second guess her motivations, but I want this 50-plus-year-old to be the exception; I don't want her to be the prototype for aging women in our future. Becoming physically fit is hard for her now and only will get worse as she grows older. The older we get, the harder it is to become and stay fit but not impossible as we will see. We start by determining our own health risks due to weight.

When Are We Overweight? Obese? Morbidly Obese?

Scientific and medical communities have defined weight in terms of risks of excess weight to health. These are important definitions for assessing and making choices related to our own risks. I think they are especially important for the aging woman who may decide she is ready to give up this battle for form as just too hard and occupying of her spirit. A more useful calculation is for her to decide the acceptable level of weight for herself based on an informed choice.

The indicators of healthy weight are weight, waist circumference, body mass Index (BMI), and percent of body fat. Ranges have been established to provide guidelines.

We have known for some time that weight by itself is a small part of the health picture. Muscle weighs more than fat and can put a fit muscular person in an overweight category on a weight chart or BMI calculation. Experts in the field advise us to use additional measurements.

Visceral fat especially located around the waist is a health problem if excessive, even though a person may not measure as overweight or obese. Visceral fat is fat close to or surrounding organs such as the liver and pancreas. Visceral fat is thought to have a role in insulin resistance and the development of Type 2 diabetes. A woman of normal weight but with a waist circumference over 35 inches (40 inches for men) is at greater risk for type 2 diabetes, hypertension, and cardiovascular disease (National Health, Lung, and Blood institute, 2020).

To measure your waist circumference, use a tape measure. Start at the top of the hip bone, then bring it all the way around level with your navel. Make sure it's not too tight and that it is parallel with the floor. Don't hold your breath while measuring it!

Body Mass Index or BMI is another method used to determine risks of disease related to weight. A BMI from 18.5 to 24.9 is considered in the healthy range; 25.99 in the overweight range; 30 and above obese; and 40 and above morbidly obese.

BMI is calculated by dividing a person's weight (in kilograms) by his or her height (in meters, squared). BMI also can be calculated by multiplying weight (in pounds) by 705, then dividing by height (in inches) twice.

Remember that a BMI above 25 and below 30 may be misleading because a muscular woman will weigh more because muscle weighs more than fat and still be fit and not at all overweight.

Measuring the percent of body fat may be more indicative of relative health or risk for disease although it is more difficult to get an accurate number. There are ways including being dunked in water for weighing, electronic scales that measure through density and certain combination of measurements. Thirty and above percent of fat is considered obese.

All these indicators are based on measuring many people and determining ranges. Those of us who are close to but not within normal ranges may obsess about getting into range but have less to worry about in terms associated health risks. Risks increase the farther away from the normal range we are.

Those of us who clearly make it into the obese or morbidly obese categories are at high risk for serious medical conditions. The epidemic of obesity in America is establishing a pattern of chronic disease, especially diabetes which increases susceptibility to heart disease and certain cancers.

We need to bid goodbye to weight obsession for the sake of image. We have spent far too much of ourselves on it. We need to embrace health to take us into old age and older. We can give up the image and stop the struggle for the unattainable, but we must not give up our capacity for life and joy as older women by limiting our ability to get around and developing chronic disease.

Obesity is not the only controllable factor in the development of chronic disease. Smoking, sedentary lifestyle, alcoholism, and unmanaged stress also contribute to chronic disease. Obesity is the one for our age. We have it within our control to avoid or at least delay the onset of chronic disease and prevent or delay disability and cheat early death by taking control. This may be the moment, the same moment that Pat experienced, to take purposeful action to maintain our best asset for quality of life—good health—and maintain the single most important criteria for quality of life, the one we fear losing the most – control.

The Personal Cost of Aging As a Very Overweight, Obese, or Morbidly Obese Woman

Women have spent enormous resources of time and money in the compassionate search for prevention, treatment, and cure for breast cancer. The stories are compelling and pull at us to reach out to the women who could be us.

We should seriously consider asking ourselves the same important questions about obesity as a primary factor in the development of diabetes and heart disease. Incidentally, too much fat is a prime factor in the development of estrogen-based breast cancer because fat is an estrogen producer which feeds these cancers.

The woman is wise who becomes just as afraid of metabolic syndromes of high blood pressure, high blood sugar, high cholesterol, and other highs as she is of breast cancer. The woman is wise who is afraid of developing diabetes, Type 1 or Type 2[8], and who keeps in mind that heart disease is the number one cause of death in women and exceeds deaths from all kinds of cancer for women (Herron, 2019). Dead is dead, and deaths from both diabetes and heart failure are particularly difficult deaths, usually preceded by considerable symptoms and disability.

Remember that diabetes is a prime factor in the development of heart disease. The detrimental effect of diabetes on the circulation of our bodies diminishes the very nourishment our hearts and kidneys need to function and our bodies need to heal. Feet are amputated when the blood no longer flows enough or holds too much sugar to heal the sore on the foot. One may not die from this co-conspirator in deaths from heart disease and kidney disease but, uncontrolled, one can expect a life ending in pain, disability, and regrets.

Obesity by itself is a burden and can overwhelm the individual who struggles with the limitations of obesity and the development of chronic disease. Very overweight or obese people experience limitations due to their excess weight even without chronic disease. Debilitating disease or weight often means stopping to rest more often. Morbidly obese persons often are seen riding the shopping scooters to shop for groceries. They run out of breath easily and tire easily. They are less likely to participate in social activities that require moving from one place to another. They are caught in a vicious cycle of doing less, resulting in being less able. They are not lazy. They really can't do it.

---

8   Type 1 diabetes is less prevalent in adults than children but does occur. Type 1 diabetes is the type in which the pancreas produces little or no insulin, the hormone necessary to regulate blood sugar whereas type 2 diabetes involves the body's growing resistance/failure to respond to insulin.

Obesity adds greater weight for our joints to support, especially our hip and knee joints, which suffer the impact of excess weight never intended to be borne by our joints. The wear and tear of aging erodes some of the cushion of our joints resulting in an increased awareness of excess pressure felt during normal walking. The resulting pain may be enough to require a walking aide or result in less walking to manage the pain.

Because we are old, we may need to be convinced that it is never too late. It is better to start early, but even if we don't, it really is never too late as demonstrated by one of the women I interviewed.

It's Never Too Late

Joy was referred for an interview by a woman I interviewed earlier. I did not know her, but I found her to be a very accomplished woman who was enjoying her retirement from a substantial professional role. Her retirement included part-time work for a chain store. She professed to me that she was happier at this time in her life than at any other time in her life. Since she was in her late 60s, her comment intrigued me, and I asked many questions to probe her newfound happiness. Her answers led me to feature her story as an excellent example of "it's never too late."

Joy is having the time of her life in discovering herself and the capacity of her formerly obese body. The trigger for her occurred after she retired from her profession and took a few days to spend on an ocean beach. She wasn't feeling particularly good about anything in her life. In fact, she felt depressed. She surveyed the food she brought to eat and was alarmed to see for the first time that it was all junk food. These staples of her diet turned unappealing and ugly, much like she felt about herself. This proved to be the turning point for her.

She returned home and began journaling about her life as it was and realized that she was dreadfully unhappy. She was worn out with feeling ugly and inadequate. She wanted something better. Then and there in her late 60s, Joy decided to correct her lifelong condition of being obese, an amazing challenge considering she had been obese since she was 22 years old.

Once Joy knew her will to change held firm, she set her new life in motion. She said she knew herself well enough after so many years to know she could be obsessive and judgmental and that, to be successful she had to set those parts of her aside. With that understanding, she began to change her way of life. Her motivation and confidence were in place before her weight loss began. She reveled in every success, never holding her breath until all the weight was lost.

When I interviewed Joy the first time, she had lost 30 pounds in a few months. She did this by cutting down on junk food. One of the more interesting patterns she changed was that instead of buying six candy bars to eat, she bought one, cut it in half, threw one half away before she left the store and ate the other half. She also started walking for exercise.

When I interviewed her one year later, she had lost another 25 pounds, said she backslid once but got back on track. She was no longer buying any candy bars and was walking much more. She walked from her place of work to town to run errands instead of driving. She gardens with passion and energy. Her next trip is to an exotic locale which will require her to ride a camel for two days. The unhappy woman of her past didn't have the energy to do these things. "I have energy; I feel good!" Joy says today.

Joy doesn't have a goal weight. "I just want to be comfortable," she says. She doesn't know what that is but says she will know it when she feels it. Joy is taking a hard road in changing her life habits. I do not know the future for Joy, but I do know that she will not easily give up this newfound joy of life. Today, she says, "I am happy. Life is wonderful. I love every day."

I asked Joy if her health ever had been a reason she had to lose weight. She said she has yet to have any obesity-related health problems. Her blood pressure and blood work are well within normal limits. Her motivation was more about her sense of self and the sorrow and poor self-image she carried along with the extra weight.

The Will

Both Joy and Pat experienced revelations about their lives and a strong desire to change. They both believed that something better would result from becoming more fit. Both are enjoying the renewed energy of being in control of their body.

Their stories cause us to reflect on the many obese women who give up the struggle to lose weight as evidenced by the rapidly increasing rate of obesity among older women. We all wonder at the individual reasons but we know losing weight is hard and takes time. Many may believe it is too late or perhaps, not possible or even necessary at their age.

Necessary?

Loss of youth, youthful figure, or the desire to seek a mate or promotion may seem to justify letting our waistbands to expand. No longer wanting to attract a mate or make a good appearance in a career are not good reasons to abandon our bodies and good sense. Giving up and letting go only to squander our good health prospects and burden our bodily systems with excess weight is another indicator that we may not understand that obesity is one entry point for chronic disease and disability.

We may be helped in the illusion by partners who buy us elegant high-calorie pastries in the name of love—not the elegant dessert following a romantic evening but the cinnamon roll bought just before lunch. One well-meaning partner was overheard telling his partner that he didn't understand why any man would want a thin woman. Partners and friends who support and encourage our excess weight, regardless of reason, are enabling our poor health. We need to enlist their support and common sense for our good health.

Making the Decision

Lifelong habits of eating, activity, and recreation are hard to change. We are helped by stories like Joy's and Pat's. We are helped by family and friends who offer nonjudgmental support. If we are fortunate enough to have a physician who alerts us when we are on a path leading to chronic debilitating disease or tells us we have arrived in poor health, we will have the medical support we need. We can learn what is best for us in adapting to the changes accompanying our aging, but we may need help in recognizing the unsustainable habits carried on since our youth. We may need even more help to change those habits.

Studies have shown that the obese woman develops psychological barriers to exercise. She is afraid of injury. She is self-conscious about exposing her body. She is afraid of failure. She believes she is in poor health and too overweight to exercise (Temple University, 2008).

People like me who spent their career years in health care are fully aware of the human capacity for resilience, resourcefulness, hope, and survival in the most difficult and frightening conditions; we see it every day. Gaining control of weight might require all the above, but it can be done. The first and most critical step is deciding that being obese and tired isn't good enough.

Then, we must seek and accept the encouragement and support which abundantly surrounds us, including medical oversight, a program that sees and advises us as the total human being we are and the love of partners and friends who want us to live long and well. Programs are available to provide the support we need. One is Wellness Works (formerly Weight Watchers) which brings women with the desire to lose weight together in a safe and comfortable environment.

Anorexia in Women over 50

On the opposite side of the weight scale from obesity are women who weigh considerably below a healthy weight. I've known women who've struggled to gain weight; they seem to have a metabolism that burns calories at a very high rate. Many describe being very thin as children and nothing their mothers fed them would put additional pounds on them. They were otherwise healthy as children and are healthy as adult women.

Other women are dangerously thin due to eating disorders and are unhealthy as a result. Thirteen percent of women over 50 have eating disorders (Arnold, 2013; Gagne et al., 2012), the most common of which is anorexia nervosa.

Women with anorexia often appear emaciated. The disorder is characterized by a debilitating loss of lean muscle mass called sarcopenia (Greek for "poverty of the flesh") that characterizes the disorder. Anorexia requires professional intervention for potentially life-threatening conditions. Laboratory findings of an anorexic woman point to a disruption in body chemistry caused by starving her body (Poppink, n.d.) and reveal abnormal readings brought on by dehydration and poor nutrition. Electrolyte, blood, and liver abnormalities are common.

Anorexia nervosa is characterized by an extreme fear of being overweight that leads to obsessive dieting. If untreated, it results in serious health problems and can lead to death. Women with the disorder are not satisfied with their appearance, exhibit feelings of self-loathing, and severely restrict their food intake. In some cases, sufferers self-induce vomiting to rid their bodies of consumed food, a condition called bulimia.

Women suffering from anorexia are malnourished from inadequate food intake. Prolonged malnutrition for whatever reason at any age is a serious health threat to all who suffer from it, but it especially endangers aging women who no longer have the reserves of youth.

Although anorexia is typically a disorder of young women, often starting in adolescence, a growing incidence has been noted in women over 50. More research needs to be done to determine the causes, but there is some reason to believe that some of these women had the disorder when they were younger and are experiencing the same distortions of body image again. However, some women develop the disorder for the first time following menopause and the body changes that make a firm figure much harder to obtain.

The cause is not known but thought to be a complex combination of genetic, psychological, and environmental factors. We do know that extreme stress is a factor in resuming anorexic behaviors as Mary's story tells us.

Mary

"I felt I was going to fly off the earth with no control what so ever, so that's when I decided the only thing I could control was what I put in my mouth," Mary, 66, told me. My interview with Mary differed from other interviews in that we spoke only about her anorexia. I admired her willingness to share her sensitive and private struggle, one she grapples with to this day.

Over the course of a number of discussions and through emails, Mary told her story. She described herself as being insecure most of her life although she was successful in her work and enjoyed a sense of belonging and friendship with her colleagues.

Mary reported classic symptoms of anorexia. In addition to appearing emaciated, she strongly resisted gaining weight. She didn't view herself as being underweight. She felt very fat at 109 pounds on a height of 5'8". As she stated, "I am at 109 now, which feels very fat. I feel like someone has stuck a valve in me and blown me up. I definitely want to get back to 100 again because it is comforting somehow. At that weight, psychologically and physically, I have felt a lightness of being that was soothing."

Mary's BMI is 15.6, well below the healthy range for someone at age 66. The weight range for her height is 119-158 pounds. She admits to a disconnect between her perceptions ("I feel so much better") and her reality ("my body is sick") that cause her to severely restrict her food intake on a daily basis.

Mary's weight sensitivity began around puberty. She recalls her father calling her fat. Later, she had periods of normal weight and eating until her 40s when, during a very stressful period, she managed her stress by eating and drinking more than she should have. Her weight topped almost 200 pounds. At that point, she decided enough!

She lost 50 pounds. Yet, her deteriorating marriage breathed its last breath. Even given the weight loss, her husband called her repulsive.

The marriage ended, and Mary began a near-fasting diet to gain control and never returned to a nutritious diet. Smoking helped her control her weight. Health problems developed, including digestive disorders and, most recently, pneumonia and chronic respiratory disease. She stopped smoking, which she thinks is causing her to obsess over food now.

Mary is not unlike the morbidly obese woman who focuses on her numerous and significant health problems but not her weight, a primary contributing factor. One difference is that the obese woman is likely not malnourished whereas Mary is severely malnourished. Mary's body lacks the resources to combat illness. She seems unconcerned about her own disconnect and her choices. She will have to work hard to overcome her powerful denial.

Malnutrition in an Age of Obesity

Aging women are at risk for malnutrition. Being overweight doesn't necessarily mean good nutrition. Malnutrition can manifest similar body chemistry changes to those experienced by the starving anorexic woman. Decreased efficiency of our digestive system mentioned in Chapter 7 is one of several factors. Dietitians tell us, too, that our hunger cues go down; we don't always know we are hungry. Our capacity to taste flavors diminishes, making food less interesting. Our nutritional requirements change.

Our aging bodies require more protein and less vitamin C, for example. Research is showing that older people (70+) require more protein than when they were younger. As we've learned, we lose muscle mass as we age and are at greater risk of developing sarcopenia.

If an older woman keeps her protein intake at about the same level or less or if she is eating less, she will be deficient in essential nutrients (amino acids) delivered to her body through protein intake. Failure to intake enough protein will accelerate loss of muscle mass and possible sarcopenia could result if prolonged (Hayes 2018).

A recommended intake of protein for adults over 65 is 1 to 1.2 grams of protein per kilogram of body weight. That's 68 to 82 grams of protein for a 150-pound person or 50-71 grams of protein for a 130-pound person. (Taylor, 2019) An important caution for protein intake is that persons with identified kidney medical problems should discuss protein intake with their health care provider since may increase burden on the kidneys (Wempen, 2016). Good sources of protein include meat, any type of bean, salmon and eggs.

If we are not getting the nutrients we need from what we eat, some deficiencies can be corrected by taking supplements such as vitamin B-12. Health providers now are checking regularly for vitamin D levels and discovering deficiencies that effect well-being.

Non-physical factors such as physical isolation, insufficient money to meet competing needs, social isolation, and cognitive decline contribute to poor nutritional intake. Family, friends, and neighbors need to be aware of changes in behavior that may indicate poor nutrition and poor health. Confusion can be a result of poor nutrition and needs to be fully evaluated as part of an assessment of mental status.

Senior or social services are available in most communities to provide coordination of available services. All of us hope that should we be in a situation of needing help, people would come to our aid.

More so, we hope that we can act responsibly and care for ourselves in our aging years. One of the ways to that end is to be fully aware of the impact of the aging process and the choices we have to maintain control of our lives. Nourishing our bodies with the right foods, drinks, and exercise is fundamental to our success.

Eat to Live and Enjoy Life on the Path to Natural Aging

Enjoying food and drink is an enormously satisfying part of our lives. Nourishing our bodies with the required nutrients is essential to the proper functioning of all parts of our bodies; there is no part—arm, leg, brain, skin, eyes, ears, fingernails, internal organs—that escapes the need for nourishment. We know that we use food to meet other needs such as socialization and emotional comfort. These uses can be at cross purposes of good health when they result in excess weight or eating disorders. Growing older requires careful attention to what we eat, our nutritional status, our weight, and our energy levels. Our body tells us what these are, and we must listen.

- Listen to be aware of your body: what's working well, what isn't!

- Seek medical help when unusual symptoms occur, don't accept them as part of aging!

- Remember to examine the health habits you are taking into aging that no longer may work for you!

- Learn about weight and its importance from a health standpoint! Know the measures of a healthy goal weight, body mass or weight circumference instead of trying to meet an unattainable standard!

- Give yourself a break if you are slightly overweight!
- Give yourself a break if you are losing unhealthy excess weight at a relaxed pace as long as you are losing!
- Keep in mind that nutritional requirements change as we age: unless medically contradicted, eat more protein!
- Eat mindfully, and savor the taste and experience!
- Stay hydrated!
- Get adequate rest and restful sleep!
- Listen to family, friends and your own body who may be telling you that you weigh too much or too little
- Seek and ask for the support you need, the group that fits with you and your goals!
- Eat to live and enjoy life on the path to natural aging!

Next, we go into the loss that worries—losing words.

9

Word Finding and Mental Fitness

"I go for a word and it's not there."

—*Aging women survey*

Staring into the refrigerator, holding the door open, and wondering what it was that brought me to that point; walking purposely into the utility room on a mission so covert I forgot what it was; these are typical experiences among the aging (Lunden, 2020). Many of the women I interviewed mentioned the same purposeful strident actions that dissolve into meandering futile efforts to recall the purpose as a worrisome sign of mental change.

Frankly, I chuckle every time it happens because it seems so absurd, too ridiculous not to be part of some slapstick comedy; that is, unless I am in a hurry, in which case I speak unmentionable words while I retrace my steps. In my finer moments of contemplation, I attempt to understand why these incidents happen. Take the example of deciding to take the dressing out of the refrigerator to warm up. We click the mental button that starts the trip to the refrigerator. On the way to the refrigerator, we still are thinking about the next activity we have planned so much that we get to the refrigerator and no longer remember the dressing.

We no longer can rely on inner knowledge of routine behaviors. It seems like the ability to multitask has been compromised by a brain too tired at the moment to manage all that we ask of it. When we realize we don't know why we are at the refrigerator or in the laundry room, we learn to retrace our steps to remember our reason for being there.

The fact that we aren't lost in our houses daily trying to remember what to do next is evidence that this isn't about mental decline or brain interruptions. Yet, something is happening.

We all remember being preoccupied to the point of forgetting whom or why we were calling when we were younger so it is not new with aging. I know that we are, in part, simply paying more attention now because we worry about developing dementia.

The fact that many of us mention losing track of what we are doing tells me it happens more frequently as we age or at least we worry more about it. Dr. Echo E. Leaver, graduate professor of cognitive neuroscience at Salisbury State University, explains it as follows:

> In healthy, normal aging (absent Alzheimer's or dementia), the kinds of forgetting that happens day to day (lost keys, forgotten phone calls) are typically due to stress and attentional demands. When you go to the store and are focused on running in to get those four items you need and getting out in time to make it to an appointment, you park, dash in, get the stuff, run out.....and only then do you realize you forgot to pay attention to where you parked the car! Worse, you have been to this store a million times and parked in a million different locations so all your memories are interrupting each other.
>
> The ability to notice and pay attention is affected by the health of your frontal lobes, which react negatively to stress. So, the mechanisms are the same for when both old and young make memory errors because of attentional/stress/distraction issues.
>
> When older people forget where they parked the car or placed they keys, they are overly concerned about Alzheimer's or dementia because of ageism bias in our society or maybe because of family history or fears about aging. Adding to the confusion is that the frontal lobes do gradually decline with age so with some peo-

ple in their 80s, memory error could be due to frontal lobe decline or could be due to Alzheimer's damaging the hippocampus[9] or both! But when you have people freaking out because they have misplaced their keys, it is usually a very tiny bit of that frontal decline and mostly life stressors and distractions overwhelming the frontal lobe's ability to organize attention (Echo E. Leaver, personal communication, April 15, 2020).

Losing Words

The women I interviewed told me things like "I go for a word, and it's not there" and "I can't remember names." As for me, I love words and the thought of losing any of them saddens me. What I am learning, though, is that in most cases they aren't lost, more likely they are misplaced somewhere around misplaced next steps. As it turns out, many of us are wondering where these words go. The most mentioned oddity in response to the question about what mental differences were noticed in the past (few) years were "I lose the word; I know what I want to say, but I can't think of the word."

Losing words has a name well known in health care circles. The term is *word finding difficulty*. We literally can't find the word and send out a search of our brain to locate this familiar word. The same thing can and often does happen with names when our brain goes blank upon seeing a familiar face, and we must deal with either embarrassment or feigning social conversation while begging our brains to remember the name.

While not sounding scientific, researchers have a scientific name for word finding difficulty behavior. The term is *TOT* or *Tip of the Tongue*, and researchers at the University of Cambridge Strategic Promotion of Ageing Research Capacity have studied the age-related causes of losing words (Shafto et al ., 2007).

The use of Magnetic Resonance Imaging (MRI) gave researchers the information they needed to pinpoint the part of the brain responsible for retrieving information: the insula, located in the cerebral cortex of the brain—to be more precise, beneath the frontal, parietal, and temporal opercula. I guarantee you these latter terms are words I will never re-

---

9   Memory errors due to Alzheimer's are actually due to damage in the hippocampus which helps us form memories and retrieve them. If someone has Alzheimer's and is forgetting where the car was parked, it's likely because that person's hippocampus is interfering with the ability to create or recall that memory.

trieve again, but I will remember *there is a particular* area of the brain that responds when you and I remember words and helps us retrieve a word when we want to use it. The study used pictures of famous people to test older and younger participants while brain activity was measured by an MRI. Each was asked to recall the name of the famous person.

When younger and older participants stated a familiar name, the insula responded normally. When participants stated the name of a more unfamiliar yet known person the insula had a stronger response. In both these instances, the insula of older persons responded the same as younger persons. However, when either knew the name but had a difficult time stating the name, the older person's insula response was significantly weaker compared to a younger person's insula response. The researchers concluded, "With respect to aging, the current findings demonstrate that region-specific gray matter atrophy is associated with a specific age-related cognitive deficit (Sharfto et al. 2007, p 2070)."

Most of us refer to being unable to recall a name as a memory problem or "senior moment." This study explains that it is specifically related to word retrieval. The word is there, we just can't get a hold of it. In other words, we are not losing our memory of words or our minds; rather it is taking longer to retrieve the word. It happens to all of us as we age and is not symptomatic of something more serious like brain atrophy, a cognitive deficit, or Alzheimer's disease.

The insula deficit is one example of changes that occur while we age. Research is continually being done to make the distinction between brain changes related to natural aging and those that occur due to pathological brain changes.[10]

The older we get, the longer it takes to process information, meaning we hold the information or think longer before we understand and respond. Many of us or those close to us think these lapses are signs of dementia, which is always a possibility but not necessarily because of these signs. Statistically, most of us should worry more about diabetes or heart disease, which can be factors in the development of dementia.

Other factors contribute to our comprehension as we age. Sometimes, an older person doesn't hear and gives what seems an unrelated response, which is not a mental or mind problem but a hearing problem. Other

---

10   Being unable to recall a new word, at any age, can simply be a matter of what psychologists call retrieval error. Essentially, it means that after the word is learned and filed away in the brain, it sometimes accidentally gets lost on its way back to the tongue or pen when a speaker or reader wants to use it. What actually happens is, of course, more complicated, but the metaphor is essentially accurate.

times, an older person is distracted by unrelated thoughts about tasks or obligations that need attention at the moment or soon thereafter. Even ambient or chronic physical pain can be a distraction to cognitive processing without being a cognitive deficit in any way though it may appear to be so to the conversational partner.

Fear of Dementia

Like many interviewees, Mary told me, *"I worry about dementia (Alzheimer's)"*[11] Don't we all!

An estimated 5.7 million people in the United States suffer from dementia, including Alzheimer's disease, 5.5 million of those are 65 years or older. The severity of dementia varies from mild cognitive dysfunction to severe disability in mental and physical functioning. The risk for developing dementia increases with age. Three percent of people age 65-74 years, 17 percent of people age 75-84 years and 32 percent of people 85 years or older have Alzheimer's (Alzheimer's Association, 2018).

A greater percentage (two-thirds) of those who develop Alzheimer's are women, mostly explained by the fact that more women live into old-old age. Research is being done to explain the difference. According to the Alzheimer's Association (2018), only 200,000 persons with Alzheimer's are younger than 65.

Contrast dementia statistics with the 25.8 million people who have diabetes of which 10.9 million are 65 years of age or older. Coronary heart disease, the leading cause of death for women in the United States, outnumbers both dementia, which ranks as the fifth cause of death, and diabetes which, ranks as the seventh cause of death (Herron, 2018). We are reminded that diabetes contributes to heart and circulatory disease and can reasonably be related to circulatory disease that leads to dementia. High blood sugar that bogs down your blood vessels to your heart will bog down blood vessels to your brain as well.

We also need to remember that the same attention to diet, exercise, and stress reduction that prevent or control cardiovascular disease and diabetes have the same benefit for dementias. The good news is that we know a lot more about the causes and consequences of dementia than we used to. We've come a long way from the time where nursing home residents simply were labeled "senile." Dementia is now the subject of intense

---

11   Dementia and Alzheimer's disease may be used as synonymous terms, but they are not. Dementia covers other kinds of mental disability beyond just Alzheimer's.

research; some answers are being found and more discreet questions are being formed to guide research.

The important lesson is that Alzheimer's or any dementia is not a normal part of aging any more than are diabetes and coronary heart disease. The risk of developing dementia does, however, increase as we age. I focus on Alzheimer's disease since it is the headline type of dementia. The incidence of Alzheimer's is increasing as the population of people 65 and older is increasing. The disease is characterized by deteriorating brain function, whose cause is still under investigation.

Alzheimer's often is described as a fading sense of self or a death of the person we knew whose remains are like a living shell. The afflicted person begins to lose function because he/she no longer remembers how to do things, simple things like driving a car, and soon loses relationships because he/she no longer recognizes the people of his/her life. People with Alzheimer's can live from two to 20 years before the disease ends their lives.

We should be comforted by statistics that say we have a better chance of dying while trying to retrieve a word from our brain in our own home than living in a secured unit wandering the halls, but we are not easily comforted when dementia strikes us or our loved one. We all know someone who is afflicted with or caring for someone with Alzheimer's. Most of the women I spoke with had at some time during their lives a close relative who had Alzheimer's or some form of dementia.

Personal Experiences with Our Mothers

One woman I interviewed has a mother who has been living in a secured area of a nursing home for over ten years. She barely recognizes her daughter who has long since reconciled herself to having inane and repetitious conversations with her mother now in her 90s. Her mother continues to be carried about in a strong resilient body, a proud vestige of a life of hard physical work and good nutrition. Her strongly spiritual daughter comforts herself with brief and increasingly infrequent times of her mother's lucidity and the knowledge that, indeed, her mother does live in the present and is not particularly unhappy.

My maternal aunt succumbed at age 80 to Alzheimer's after five years of a steady decline. Among her first signs was a growing fear, not nervousness rather more like terror, of driving in traffic coupled with mind blanks such as not knowing how to turn on the washing machine that she used for years. Her family moved quickly to get her into safer surroundings with the onset of each new level of decline. The moves could barely keep up with her mental and physical weakening.

Despite sorrow about her condition, my aunt became my role model of someone doing her best to cope with Alzheimer's. She smiled and worked to be with the people who visited even though she didn't know who they were. On our last visit with my aunt, we realized that beneath that smile she was experiencing considerable stress in being social with people she no longer knew. When she asked if we wanted to go to lunch shortly after our arrival, I realized it was her way of asking us to leave. We stopped visiting.

We all have had these experiences. We've seen an older woman rocking a baby doll and one pacing endlessly on the figure-8 path in the garden of the secure unit. We've seen confusion and fear in the eyes of people momentarily lost. I recall my aunt saying upon seeing old people in wheelchairs seemingly stuck in hallways during our visits to assisted living facilities that she didn't want to be around them, that she didn't want to be like them. In the end, she was both with them and one of them. Still and for many reasons, she continued to be a remembered role model for me.

Causes of Dementia

The leading cause of dementia is Alzheimer's (Nall 2017). The pathology of the disease continues to be a mystery although progress is being made. We know Alzheimer's may have a genetic component or risk, but scientists still are sorting through the many factors and our pharmaceutical companies are searching for effective medications.

Although we focus on Alzheimer's disease as the poster disease for dementia, other dementias are as debilitating. Cerebral vascular dementia is typically the result of mini-strokes, big strokes, or arteriosclerosis (hardening of the arteries), in which the brain didn't or doesn't receive the blood necessary to think clearly.

Cerebral vascular dementia makes more sense to us than Alzheimer's because we know that damage occurs when a body part loses blood supply. We lose function temporarily or permanently depending on the amount of damage.

Another common dementia is termed mixed dementia which is a combination of two or more types of dementias, usually Alzheimer's and a type of vascular dementia.

Mysteries surround the third-ranked dementia called Lewy body disease. It isn't new, but it is somewhat less known by the general public. The first time I heard of Lewy body disease, named after Frederic Lewy, who first identified strange protein substances in the brain in 1912, was through the story of a daughter who spent two years trying to find out what was wrong with her mother. The daughter first noticed that her mother was agitated and had uncharacteristic bouts of anger.

Lewy body disease has some similarities to Alzheimer's and can be confused with Alzheimer's in its early stage. It differs from Alzheimer's in that the afflicted person may have vivid hallucinations and significant fluctuations in cognitive understanding. These folks fall asleep easily during the day and are restless at night. They also tend to develop Parkinson-like symptoms such as shakiness and blank stares. Those protein substances, called Lewy bodies, are scattered throughout the brain and have an impact on the brain's functioning.

One family had invited me to their home to help them plan for their father's adjustment to newly diagnosed chronic obstructive pulmonary disease (COPD). During that visit, I encountered the mother for the first time. Belligerent and complaining, she did not at all exhibit the usual behavior of a mother. When asked about her anger, she shouted to all of us that we would be angry, too, if we were trying to adjust to her husband's new disability.

Good point, and we turned back to focus on her husband's needed adjustment to living with medicines, lung aerosols, and continuous oxygen delivered through a long snaking tube of plastic. Her explanation seemed perfectly understandable except it was so out of character for this independent, strong-minded, capable woman who handled more than one difficult situation in her 75 years.

The daughter subsequently took her mother to the family physician, who saw nothing wrong except for depression associated with her husband's disability. I, who saw her infrequently over the next several months, continued to witness verbal outbursts, accompanied by a blank look that did not match her angry words. Her face was a mask that gave no clues to the anguish of her words. Over the following weeks, she began to experience increasing episodes of erratic behavior and tremors in her hands. Her diligent daughter took her again and again to physicians, including a neurologist. Eventually, she was diagnosed as having Parkinson's disease, a diagnosis that explained some but not all her symptoms.

One day one of her erratic moods occurred while she was driving, and she ran into several parked cars, an event that became her last time behind the wheel. Her frustrated daughter took her mother once again for medical analysis. This time, the mother was diagnosed with Lewy body dementia. All the pieces fit sadly together at last.

I mention this case because it took this daughter's dedication to the health and welfare of her mother over the course of months and years before her mother was properly diagnosed and treated. Our persistence may not be rewarded with a cure, but it will at least be rewarded with the peace of knowing the explanation or the peace of having done the best we could in a medical system where these kinds of issues are in a continual stage of discovery.

Either a loved one or we must take any concern to our physician and to another if the answer doesn't reassure us. I turned to geriatrician Dr. Paul Cunningham to walk us through an evaluation of mental status.

Steps to Evaluating Mental Status

Dr. Cunningham says that early on it is less important to distinguish the type of dementia than to diagnose the presence or absence of dementia. He takes seriously the concerns of patients and points out that usually it is the person or close family member who tells him that his patient doesn't remember things like he/she did a year ago or five years ago.

Dr. Cunningham recognizes patients' anxiety at the prospect of becoming one of these horror stories. So, he schedules two longer appointments, during which he administers a mini-mental status exam and orders other tests such as blood laboratory values. The mini-mental status test consists of a series of questions that reveal general orientation to time, place, and general cognitive problem-solving skills. During the second appointment, he reviews the results of all the tests and his conclusions with the patient. If needed, he will refer the patient for further testing or treatment. Based on his evaluation, in many cases he tells the patients that their status is not a concern at that time but recommends returning in a year for a repeat examination.

Most family practitioners are trained to recognize dementia. Dr. Cunningham, as a geriatrician, sees a greater percentage of older patients with dementia, but the incidence is surprisingly low: 10 to 20 cases of dementia a year. He emphasizes the importance of an accurate diagnosis. Not all forgetfulness, however extreme, is a sign of dementia.

Dr. Cunningham notes that unusual forgetfulness or inability to function can come from other causes, or what is called pseudo-dementia. In pseudo-dementia, the person is having symptoms and signs of dementia, but he/she is depressed or extremely anxious. It is well known that people in an extreme state of anxiety or profound depression are unable to focus for any length of time and cannot carry on a conversation. Depression and anxiety that interfere with function require treatment and are highly treatable. Physicians and family members need to be vigilant in their observations and avoid prematurely classifying the odd behavior of an older person as demented.

The medications we take can contribute to forgetfulness or confusion. Dr. Cunningham emphasizes that we need to work closely with our health care provider in developing our medication regime. Certain medications can cause dementia-like symptoms. For example, Benadryl, commonly used for allergies, is tolerated less well as we age and can cause confusion. Some of these medications are available across the counter (OTC) and may not be easily identified as an ingredient. Many of the "pm" nighttime OTC pain relievers contain Benadryl as a sleep aid. The best plan is to review your OTC medications with your health care provider.

Certain medications for overactive bladder cause similar symptoms. At least one primary physician needs to know the entire physician-prescribed and across-the-counter medications we are taking because certain combinations can cause mental problems or other problems from unsafe drug interactions. As with all fears, the fear of dementia is worse when it lives in the shadows; it shrinks in the light as we learn from the woman I am about to introduce who was determined to ascertain whether her fate was Alzheimer's disease.

Example of Managing the Fear of Dementia

"Penny" is an intelligent and responsible woman, qualities you will recognize as you read her story. I am grateful to Penny for telling her story for this writing. Her reason for telling it was the importance she thought it might have for others. Her story begins with her growing alarm that she was experiencing too much forgetfulness.

Penny was a 75-year-old widow and lived alone in our rural community. She had one child, a daughter who lived in the same state but far enough away that she didn't visit often. Retired, she devoted her time to many church activities, including developing a program of visitation to people in need. Both her husbands were pastors although she denied any affinity to pastors other than being around them.

Penny's initial concern about her mental status began when she was constantly hunting for lost things. She couldn't remember where she put things or even when she last had them. When asked if she also had trouble remembering names of those things or going into rooms and forgetting why she did, she emphatically said, yes that's me! She reported that her daughter hadn't mentioned any issue but added she did not see her daughter very often. When asked if her friends noticed any memory issues, she said no, adding that when she told them about her forgetfulness, they waved her concern away, saying it happened to them, too.

None of this dissuaded Penny from investigating the seriousness of her symptoms. Deeply imprinted in her is the memory of her mother, who began to show signs of Alzheimer's disease at 65 years of age. She watched her mother deteriorate over the next 20 years until her death at age 85. In Penny's mind, it was entirely possible that she was experiencing the first signs of Alzheimer's at 75 years of age.

I quickly learned just how responsible this woman was. In addition to being persistent, she left home when she was 17 years old to go out on her own. She knew now as she knew then that she had one person upon whom she could depend and plan with and that was herself.

Penny embarked on an investigation of the meaning of her memory lapses. She wanted to know if she needed to plan for different living arrangements and, if she did, just when she should put a plan in motion.

Among the options available, Penny chose one of the Amen Clinics to evaluate and guide her in the investigation. You may be familiar with the Amen Clinics through the many presentations by Dr. Daniel G. Amen on PBS related to brain health. The Amen Clinics are well known for the use of brain imaging to diagnose brain function and dysfunction. Penny referred herself to the clinic and was prepared to pay the cost of planning for her future.

The evaluation lasted over the course of three days, some days more intensively than others. She had MRI tests, memory tests, and blood tests among what seemed a comprehensive assessment of her brain function. She felt the clinic did a good job.

The Amen Clinic physician gave her the results of all the tests verbally and on paper. She received a diagnosis of "temporal lobe dysfunction" and assurance that she was competent; there was no reason that she could not be independent, live alone, or drive a car. The physician advised her to take vitamin D based on her blood test. It wasn't entirely clear to Penny what the diagnosis meant for the distant future, but for the foreseeable future, she was going to manage on her own. She didn't have Alzheimer's!

I wondered whether an aspect of the diagnosis was the insula in the temporal lobe . It was not a term that Penny knew but she found it interesting. Meanwhile, her Amen Clinic physician calls her every six weeks to see how she is doing. It's a service she appreciates, and it keeps her in touch.

Penny said that currently she felt overwhelmed with the task of organizing her belongings in order to downsize and simplify her surroundings. I could hear the imprint of her mother's experience coming to life, so I tried to speak to it in telling her the truth that the task overwhelms all of us. I also told her that her older friends were telling her the truth when they said it was happening to them, too. I knew because it happened to me.[12]

Penny makes the case that we are our own best caretakers. She worked to live her life well and leave a clean uncluttered legacy for her child. Penny will leave much more than that by being a role model for aging responsibly and mindfully until she couldn't.

Normal Mental Changes As We Age

We learn from Dr. Cunningham and Penny that we can manage our fears, that resources are available to help us understand what is happening when cognitive matters worry us. We may feel surrounded by dementia as we age, but we are surrounded more by people going through the natural aging process. Table 9.1 compares Alzheimer's signs and typical aging changes (Alzheimer's Association, 2020). Review it any time fear strikes!

Table 9.1

Signs of Alzheimer's	Typical age-related changes
Poor judgment and decision making	Making a bad decision once in a while
Inability to manage a budget	Missing a monthly payment
Losing track of the date or the season	Forgetting which day it is and remembering later
Difficulty having a conversation	Sometimes forgetting which word to use
Misplacing things and being unable to retrace steps to find them	Losing things from time to time

---

12   As it turned out, enough time passed between this interview and Penny's admission to a dementia unit to confirm Penny's worst suspicions before the publication of this book.

Similarly, Dr. Fiona McPherson of the website, *Mempowered* (2020), suggests considering the following facts:

- It is normal for word-finding problems to increase as we age.

- It is normal for us to be slower in processing information as we age.

- Difficulty in retrieving words does not mean the words are lost; there is no evidence that we lose vocabulary in normal aging.

- There is little evidence for any change in semantic structure (the organization of words in memory) with age.

- Older adults probably have more trouble dealing with large amounts of information.

- Older adults may develop different strategies as they age, probably to accommodate their decline in processing speed and processing capacity.

Dementias are real, terrible to have, and terrible to experience in someone we love, but we need to be careful about bringing unnecessary fears into our lives. More than likely we will not end our lives as demented people, especially if we practice activities that preserve all our functions. One activity that becomes increasingly important as we age is managing our stress. Just as we talk about conserving physical energy, we should consider conserving mental and emotional energy as we age. We just don't have as much energy to deal with things that don't matter. We will adjust just like we have been doing all our lives.

Pick Your Stress

We can't talk about mental fitness without talking about the effects of stress and our ability to manage stress. When my husband reached his mid-70s, both he and I began to note a change in his tolerance for stress. I could see that he became unusually flustered around things, large or small, that had not bothered him before. The classic example occurred during fixing a grand meal in the kitchen while his family was congregated in the open living area, having a good time and making a lot of noise. The same scene had occurred many times in the past. This time, however, he couldn't concentrate as well and finally firmly told everyone to be quiet. He stunned everyone into silence and went on to finish preparing a great meal. He did what we were learning would be important from now on; he picked his stress.

My husband and I developed a motto of "pick your stress" which I have now begun applying to my life as an older person. Many learn that their stress tolerance changes as they age. We may be less able to manage multitasking stress. We more keenly feel the pressure or anxiety of trying to manage too much. Typically, life involves unexpected stress at unexpected times such as the illness of a family member or the death of a close friend. These are the stresses that we don't pick because they happen outside of choice and are sewn into us through love and experience. By necessity, we must conserve energy for these events. We can choose to avoid stresses that don't really matter and save our energy for those we cannot control.

Our country experienced a particularly bad time in 2009 and beyond, in which many of us lost chunks of financial security in investments or houses; most of the losses were out of our control. Some lost jobs and health insurance as well as homes. We were challenged to manage a great deal of stress.

Most of us had to find some way to continue to put one foot ahead of the other. Some of us confronted the stresses not in our control by spending less or moving to a smaller apartment. Some of us decided not to watch or listen to any talk show hosts who were angry or who angered us because it added to our sense of lack of control. Some women became involved in local politics in order to gain control. Many of the women I talked with became involved in volunteer activities from which they benefited through helping and meeting other people.

I have learned from those I interviewed and others in my life that purpose beyond oneself fills our tanks more and feels less like stress than Thanksgiving dinner with a family who is chronically tense with each other. Whatever we do, we need to be on alert for overload and step back for reflection and rest. We must regain and maintain an emotional reserve for unexpected events.

In managing our stress, we must intentionally include self in our purpose. Staying as healthy and active as possible is a noble pursuit. Being with the partner of your life and sharing joys and sorrows is a worthy goal. Being self-confident enough to manage your own life responsibly is important. All these things are good for us and for the whole of society. We may strive to be a gain not a drain during the brief time we have on this planet.

In discussing what causes stress, one interviewee told me that fast traffic bothered her. Here is where we can look to reducing activities that are becoming too stressful. Driving, especially at night, which has to do with increasing difficulty seeing at night, commonly creates anxiety. In such a case, a woman can choose to drive during less congested times. In this way, we take conscious control of managing our stress.

Another interviewee said, "I use more notes and lists to remember things." Thus, we make adjustments, and we adapt. We build systems as simple as lists to help us remember. We can seek help in order to conserve our energy, or if we can't afford help, we can move into a situation in which we have fewer chores. We form our vision of life and pursue it.

Feed Our Minds with Purpose, Laughter, and Oxygenated Blood

Our minds thrive on purpose and grow with challenge whether it's doing a crossword puzzle, writing a poem, or learning a foreign language. We do less well around people who carry so many wounds that they inflict their negativity about life on others. If we can positively help and not enable this person, then we will feel that we have done well with our energy. If not, we will be drained of our precious energy. Picking our stress is an art worth developing. In the end, it will prolong the quality of our lives.

"I want to know at what age people decide they can back out of their driveway without looking," Jerry Seinfeld once said. Laughter is the richest antioxidant for the brain and the best medicine for our sense of well-being. Some of those word-finding incidences are very funny, especially when we substitute a word like "Mixmaster" for "lawn mower." One of the benefits of getting old is that we can drop some roles like worker or boss and qualities like over-thinking, worrying what others think. We can enjoy learning about ourselves—and even laughing at ourselves.

One interview noticed this, astutely commenting, "The blessing of the aging process is things don't matter the way they used to; I'm not as hard on myself." Among these interviews, the most important mental fitness feature identified was having control, real control of our lives. We fear loss of control the most in developing cognitive problems or, worst case, debilitating dementia. We will know long before that happens, if indeed it does, and can take steps to assure our well-being.

We also have an opportunity to prevent some dementias through lifestyle changes, exercising our bodies to maintain adequate circulation to our brains, exercising our minds as well as our bodies, maintaining balanced nutrition, seeking medical attention, and working with our health care provider as a partner in our health. We can engage as long as possible by pursuing those things we truly love to be and to do and seeking support when we feel ourselves losing our will.

We gain by remembering that just like words that are on the tip of our tongue, our will is not lost; it's just temporarily misplaced.

10

For Better or Worse In Health Planning

"[W]e deprive ourselves of opportunities to change the individual experience of aging for the better."

—*Gawande (2007)*

"For better or worse, in sickness and health," common phrases in marriage vows, might be applied to our relationship with our bodies as well, especially as we age. Imagine making a commitment to truly care for our bodies with the intention of supporting them through weak times and fostering their strength and resilience throughout our lives. The physiological and organic changes occurring in the natural aging process test our resolve as we've learned in these earlier chapters. In this chapter, we look at just what it means to foster good health as well as learn to plan for our health needs in the future. If you're over 70, that future is already here; if you're younger, you can learn to prepare for what you may face regarding health care, medication, managing chronic health problems, and deciding when you need more care.

Preparing Ourselves for a Healthy Old Age

There are many things about which we can do very little as we move past late middle age into our 60s and 70s. Our vision diminishes even with glasses; our hearing becomes less acute. We may have arthritis or a host of other bone and muscular problems that make getting around and doing ordinary tasks that call for some dexterity more difficult. We are growing old and seem destined at least statistically to develop one or more chronic diseases after age 55 and more by age 65 (Center for Disease Control, 2020; National Council on Aging, 2017). For certain populations and for those who struggle with poverty and stress, the figures are even higher.

The chronic disease data of over 70 million people 55 years or older was reported in an analysis of the 2008 National Health Interview Survey (Center for Disease Control, 2020). Only chronic diseases diagnosed by a health care provider were represented in the data and included diabetes, cardiovascular disease, chronic obstructive pulmonary disease (COPD), cancer and arthritis. Cardiovascular disease was determined by the diagnosed presence of any of the following: hypertension, coronary heart disease, angina pectoris, history of heart attack, all other heart conditions and stroke.

Seventy-eight percent of the total population included in the study had at least one chronic disease, and 80 percent of women had at least one chronic disease. For ages 65 and older, the percentage rose to 85.6 for the total population and to 87.6 for women for having at least one chronic disease.

Earlier chapters make the point that practicing certain lifestyle habits supports the health of our bodies and that we can prevent the development of some conditions or mitigate some of the effects of conditions that have accompanied us into old age. The rising incidence of diabetes and obesity discussed earlier, which contribute to the development of every one of the cardiovascular diseases mentioned above, tells us that the commitment to healthy aging has yet to take hold. Recent studies of the now retiring baby boomer generation[13] report the same trend.

Despite setting trends in exercising and calorie counting, there is reason to believe that many boomers didn't really think much about the possibility of living into their 90s and what that might mean for the choices they made in younger and middle-age years. One reason is that it's only relatively recently that life spans have expanded. For another, many of this generation has grown older in a time of relative prosperity and incredible medical advancement that transplanted livers and other body parts, including faces. Innovation and technology moved ahead of and seemed to promise perpetual hope to aging bodies.

---

13 Anyone born during the years 1946 through 1964 and still living are considered baby boomers, referring to the population boom that began at the end of World War II lasting into the 1960s.

Fortunes turned in 2008, and we lived through the worst economic recession since the Great Depression, made more difficult for many boomers in that they were at an age when they needed to be saving for retirement instead of spending their retirement savings. Well-paying jobs were lost along with employer-paid health insurance. Other age groups were affected as well but had years ahead of them to recoup unlike the boomers who were close to retirement.

The cost of health care insurance has become a primary household expense. Many learned in the process of losing their job and health insurance that it wasn't easy either financially, and, in some cases, they were unable to establish medical eligibility for affordable health insurance. Medicare eligibility was as far away as age 65 unless one could document disability. The risk of depleting financial reserves and facing bankruptcy if a woman is struck with a serious condition such as cancer or heart disease was and is great without health insurance. Many managed the risk by paying monthly premiums for a catastrophic plan with high deductibles and co-pays.

The Patient Protection and Affordable Care Act (aka Affordable Care Act [ACA] or Obamacare) was passed by both houses of a Democrat-controlled Congress along party lines in 2010 and has been a source of political controversy ever since. Its fate is unknown; the essential provision of an individual mandate was eliminated by a Republican-controlled Congress in 2019.

Some of the features of the ACA remain popular. Implemented in 2014, the ACA opened the private health insurance market through a government program of coverage criteria and subsidy. A collective sigh of relief could be heard for those living in fear of losing whatever savings or business they had left due to having a pre-existing condition. The ACA forbid participating insurers to deny or charge more to individuals with pre-existing conditions.

Health Insurance before Medicare

The Affordable Care Act created a larger pool of insured made up of people who held jobs without health insurance or had small businesses that could not afford the cost of insurance. The plan is designed to supplement cost with tax credits or government subsidy. Eligibility for the Medicaid program, designed to provide health care coverage for adults and their children living in poverty, was expanded under the ACA. Additional people such as single persons gained eligibility if they met the income requirement.

The ACA allowed people between 50 and 65 who stayed in jobs in order to keep their health insurance to move into other jobs or start-up situations to follow their dreams.

As costly as it is, health care insurance is less costly than the expense of needed services. None of us want to risk our hard-earned savings and assets, but if faced with a choice, we will spend those savings and assets to save our life or the life of a loved one. We are wise to choose healthy options for health and just as wise to plan for sickness. Turning 65 brings Medicare, but it's not a perfect insurance.

Medicare and Supplemental Insurance

Medicare is a single payer insurance system overseen by the government and available to all eligible residents. Medicare has several plans: A, B, C, and D.

Plan A is the so-called hospitalization plan and is available to all for a small yearly fee and covers hospitalization as well as home health and skilled nursing care following an acute illness. The plan has a relatively small deductible and some co-pay situations.

Plan B is an optional program that covers physicians and certain out-patient diagnostic tests and services. Medicare administers the plan, sets reimbursement levels, and pays 80 percent of that reimbursement. People can opt in or out. Most 65-plus-year-old people sign up for it because it is again a relatively low cost for the benefits received. Not to sign up would mean paying charges typically higher than Medicare pays for the service.

Plan C refers to Medicare Advantage plans which are administered through insurance plans and services. Plans offer a broad range of services often including vision and drugs not covered in Plans A and B. Plan C plans are more popular in East Coast states than West Coast states because the reimbursement formula set long ago makes the more efficient West Coast delivery system unable to provide services given the formula that benefited less efficient systems. Health Maintenance Organizations (HMO)[14] such as Kaiser Permanente that provide the services and act as the insurer have successfully managed costs to make it a viable business model in urban areas; the downside to HMOs, for some patients, is the requirement to use only physicians belonging to the HMO. For this reason, some retirees retain their PPO health insurance from their days of employment as a

---

14 HMOs, with their own network of doctors, hospitals and other healthcare providers who have agreed to accept payment at the level established by the HMO for any services they provide, permits the HMO to control costs for its members.

supplement to Medicare; these private insurances typically pay the co-pays and any other unpaid costs from Medicare B, as well as dental and vision.[15]

Plan D, enacted by Congress in 2004, is the most recent plan. It covers drugs through plans administered by private insurance companies and subsidized by the government. Drugs are a significant cost in health care, and many sign up for this optional benefit. Plan D provides incentive for signing up early and penalizing those who wait until they need drugs to sign up by adding a percentage to the premium for each year not enrolled after 65 years of age.

Given limited enrollment periods and the irrevocability of some decisions, those who plan early generally end up in the best position medically and financially. Medicare Plan B, for example, must be signed up for within six months of retirement or a higher premium will be applied for the duration of the retiree's life. Late-breaking decisions may create difficulties just in ascertaining the correct procedures, and some have found that their local social security office provides quicker and more reliable assistance than their personnel offices or the Medicare 800#, especially if life exigencies create the need for a late-breaking decision.

Supplemental insurances[16] that cover Medicare deductibles and co-pays are administered through private insurance companies. People sign up for varying levels of coverage depending on what is affordable for them; some are eligible for Medicaid supplemental insurance.

Health care insurance, Medicare, supplemental insurances, and health care are expensive and a cost that eventually will occur as we age whether for diagnostic tests or treatment for a diagnosed illness. Although the U.S. lags behind most advanced countries in assuring access to health care for all its citizens, we can be encouraged by the Affordable Care Act (ACA) in spite of much being challenged or left undone. Medicare is a complex system that is being pressed to reduce costs, the burden of which frequently is placed on providers in the form of lower payments. At some point, and for some that time is now, providers such as physicians are going to limit the number of Medicare patients they will see, ask for an additional monthly

---

15 Not all employers offer this possibility, and where they do, before retiring, employees should check with the personnel office as to whether thy have only a one-time chance to continue their current health, dental, and and/or vision insurance (as in the case of federal retirees) or can add one later.

16 These differ from continued employed insurance plans, and retirees can generally sign up for them at any time after retirement. Examples include Medigap plans offered by companies like Anthem and Medicare Supplement Insurance plans offered by associations like the American Association of Retired Persons. An Internet search will reveal a number of these.

payment to secure their services (referred to as concierge medicine),[17] or stop seeing Medicare patients all together.

Over the past decade, we have seen the growth of systems that employ physicians and consolidated large private practices. The physician managing his/her own private practice is becoming history, driven out by the costs of paper management that have taken time from patient care.

Both the cost and, in some geographical areas, a shortage of physicians has driven systems to utilize health care providers such as physician assistants and nurse practitioners. While you might prefer to see the doctor, many patients have found that physician assistants and nurses handle routine follow-ups and general care quite well.

There is, though, reason to worry about physician and health provider shortages in the future, especially in rural areas. After all, we can expect we are going to need health care as we age.

Conditions of Coming of Age

Diabetes and heart disease are not inevitable to the extent we see them today, but there are some conditions that just seem to come with age no matter what we do. Arthritis, vision loss, and hearing loss are among these.

Arthritis

By the time we turn 65, we very likely have had experience with arthritis. We have the lump on a finger joint that developed after painful swelling and inflammation. That bump will not go away by itself. Another common arthritis experience is back pain that develops while leaning over the container in which we are planting summer flowers. This is the pain that makes us rise from a chair with our torsos at a 55-degree angle to our feet. Arthritis pain can be serious pain that makes us want to avoid the use of the joint producing the pain. Back, finger, hands, neck, feet and just about every other part that has a joint have, can, or will develop arthritis.

According to a CDC Morbidity and Mortality Weekly Report (Barbour et al ., 2017), three in ten adults age 65 and older had arthritis diagnosed by a health care provider with the incidence increasing with age.

There are over 100 different arthritic conditions, some of them severe and life threatening. The type we develop as we approach old age is more likely to be osteoarthritis as years of joint use have taken their toll, whether

---

17   Some physicians, seeking to lower their patient load in order to spend more time with each patient, require patients to pay an annual or monthly fee in order to remain or become their patient. Those who can afford it will need to plan for it. Many cannot afford concierge medicine and will need to see a different physician.

from prior injury or continual pressure. Obesity is a factor in the development of osteoarthritis in knees.

The CDC report goes on to say that there is a greater chance for people with arthritis to have another chronic disease such as diabetes and heart disease. The pain of arthritis can cause us to reduce our physical activity because it hurts too much to move. Arthritis becomes a primary risk factor in limiting activity, which is a primary risk factor in developing chronic disease and obesity, which, of course further limits activity.

Somewhat counter-intuitively to the pain we feel when we first move stiff joints, the treatment for arthritis is to move the joints and work through the stiffness. Most of us know that otherwise we never would lift our stiff bodies out from under a warm layer of blankets although it needs to be said that a painful back may become more sore staying in one position for any length of time.

Activity is both the prevention and the treatment. An Internet search will provide more information on programs of management. Once again though, anyone contemplating a program should seek the assessment and recommendation of a health care provider.

Common Correctable Conditions of Aging

Other conditions coming of age are more correctable; we can be proactive in correcting what might be causing some dysfunction in our lives. Our vision, hearing, taste, smell and touch become less acute. Loss of vision and hearing acuity are the senses we most often seek to correct since their loss creates more dysfunction in our daily lives.

Vision and hearing loss are common experiences for all of us as we age. Vision is an early indicator of aging when in our 40s, as many people like to say, we no longer have arms long enough to see the news on paper or eyes to focus on computer blurs. Hearing decline brought about by aging seems to hold off a bit longer. We see more hearing aids in people in their late 70s and older.

Our sight is important to nearly all our activities. We expect to have devices prescribed or procedures done to improve our declining vision. We are used to seeing people in glasses, which often are viewed as a fashion accessory. Many of us started needing glasses long before we could be considered old.

Aging also brings eye conditions such as cataracts, the clouding of our eye lens, and glaucoma, an increase in eye pressure that can lead to blindness. Macular degeneration, the gradual degeneration of the central part of the retina, results in the gradual loss of central vision.

Your eye doctor, either an optometrist or ophthalmologist, will exam your eyes and perform tests when you show signs of any of these conditions. There are remedies in medications, surgical procedures and lifestyle management that can either correct the problem or reduce the adverse outcomes. Maintaining the health of your eyes and sight require regular vision evaluations by a qualified doctor every 1-2 years as you age.

Hearing is important to our daily lives if for no other reason than the television isn't turned up so loud that neighbors are calling the police about a disturbance or worse. Hearing or lack of it significantly affects all our relationships and our understanding of the world around us. Still, we do not reach for hearing aids to help us hear as readily we do for glasses to help us see.

Delayed use of hearing aids may be explained by reluctance to accept hearing loss or use devices that seem unnatural. Hearing aids, unlike glasses, are not an accessory. We would rather that hearing aids not be seen at all. Hearing aids require manipulation in different settings and often don't seem to deliver the quality of sound we know.

The technology of hearing aids has improved, especially over the past decade, but it differs from our human hearing in that it amplifies background noises. Watching my husband struggle with putting hearing aids in his ears is difficult. His once-fine fingers are now distorted by arthritis and less able to manage the small tubes that must be inserted in an exact space in his ears. Still, I encourage him to use his hearing aids; otherwise, we have strange conversations that are both frustrating and funny.

The Uncontrollable and Sometimes Unexplained

Some conditions come from our genetic makeup, like the woman who received a gene for diabetes from her mother. The genetic trigger awaited fate to set the disease in motion. Certain lifestyle choices increase our odds of developing disease.

Other chronic disease is more insidious and incomprehensible. Two women I interviewed who practiced good health habits were unexpectedly diagnosed with Type 1 diabetes at ages 60 and 61, respectively. In both cases the disease had a sudden onset of symptoms, requiring insulin and diet management. Both experienced a profound sense of vulnerability and mortality, especially in the face of something their health care providers could not explain. Both then exerted their characteristic sense of responsibility and learned to manage their diabetes for the rest of their lives.

Another woman in her mid-60s was diagnosed with atrial fibrillation, the most common condition of irregular heartbeat. She may have had it for a long time without showing any symptoms until she began to experience light-headedness which, in some cases, led to her passing out.

These are examples that make the case for having regular checkups and building a relationship with a health care provider.

Partner with Your Health Care Provider

Women are more likely to see a doctor than men, which results in either earlier intervention or in dismissive non-intervention, the latter being a reason to find another physician. Medical evaluation works best if the physician knows us well and we can trust him or her to take our concerns seriously.

We are more likely to seek medical care when we worried about the unknown., such as unexplained pain, discomfort, or dysfunction. We must take care not to assume we know the cause or attributing it to aging because it could be a serious pathology. Aging can explain some discomforts, but we should never accept an explanation that attributes our symptoms to normal aging until the provider has listened to and evaluated the frequency and intensity of the discomfort. A provider who dismisses symptoms as aging without explaining what aspect of aging is causing the symptom has failed to support you in your job to take care of your body.

Typically, we need help to sort through symptoms and discomforts. Unseen aging changes occurring inside our bodies may require adjustments and change of personal habits just like maintaining our muscle strength requires more effort.

Since we live in a time when medical care is characterized by brief visits, a lot of testing and, in some locations, a shortage of health care providers, we can do a few things. We can become good consumers of health care. We can listen carefully and follow medical instructions. We can question what we don't understand. We can learn how to talk with our provider and advocate for our health needs. We also can establish behaviors that value good health, practice preventative care, and access medical care for those things we can't do for ourselves.

We can benefit from the access we have to incredible amounts of information about our bodies, health and illness available online. We also can become confused and unnecessarily alarmed or inappropriately reassured. We are warned to be careful about believing everything on the Internet, and we should be cautious in accepting unsubstantiated and/or unsolicited information as true. The information found on internet sites of reliable resources can be invaluable. I have used many in writing this book. I have found helpful information about conditions of mine or others I care about. Often it is the information that sends us into the physician.

In the end, the Internet cannot replace the individualized assessment we receive from our health care provider who looks at our blood values, our X-rays, and our consultative reports. Our provider helps us decide if our experience is normal for an aging self and something we can control or something that needs to be investigated further.

Some of us see more than one provider, or we have seen more in the past. Specialists often are called in to help diagnose or plan treatment for us. This is especially true of complex conditions such as cancer in which treatment may require a medical oncologist, a radiation oncologist, and/or a surgical oncologist. We will go to an orthopedic surgeon for consultation and potential surgery on a painful knee or hip. We must rely on ourselves to be the coordinator of our care. Physicians often do not talk to each other in the detail that we might think is happening. For example, we should not think that all the medications we take have been approved by all our physicians.

Medications and the Aging Body

Speaking of medications, it is important to know that the liver becomes less efficient in metabolizing medications as we age, something providers consider when prescribing medications for older people. Older adults also need to consider the fact of longer metabolism time by the liver as well. The effects of alcohol last longer. The effects of anesthesia last longer. The effects of allergy medicine last longer. Medications that build or accumulate need to be monitored, especially if there is a risk of withdrawal symptoms when discontinued.

The less medication we take the better, but obviously, certain medical conditions require medication. Diabetics need to control blood sugar when the body no longer controls blood sugar on its own. People with congestive heart failure or lung disease require medication for symptom relief. When people with lung conditions go without medication, they struggle for breath. The point is to treat medications with respect and take responsibility for following directions and monitoring the effects. Prescribed and, in some cases, over the counter medications like acid reducers should be taken only when directed and monitored by a health care provider. A medication that we have used our entire life could unexpectedly become a problem.

Aspirin was a common over the counter medicine when I was young. The drug's popularity grew when health care providers concluded Aspirin's blood thinning properties acted as prophylactic in the preventions of conditions such as heart attacks caused by clots forming in narrowed blood vessels. Health care providers began recommending daily small doses of Aspirin.

The same blood thinning property of Aspirin and other nonsteroidal anti-inflammatory medications (NSAIDS)[18] can cause complications if a woman is taking prescribed blood thinners due to slow clotting or her body's ability to stop bleeding is compromised. Frequent use of NSAIDs can irritate the lining of the stomach and result in the development of a stomach ulcer that will cause bleeding if deep into tissue with blood vessels present.

Aspirin or another NSAID could be exactly what a woman needs or the worst thing she could take for her conditions. Women should take medications she's discussed and prescribed or recommended by their health care provider especially if she has existing chronic conditions (Mayo Clinic 2019).

Since we are the advocates for our own good health, we must coordinate our medications by telling all providers what medications we are taking, prescribed or not, complementary or not. Electronic health care records are making our information more available to providers to whom we have given access. Moreover, using the same pharmacy for all our prescribed medications is extra assurance that we are not going to be taking medications that work against each other.

But it is not fail-safe. We must be the final word or, if unable, we must appoint someone to help us for our own safety in using medications. We also should be sure that we take our medications. There are several devices to help us keep track of what we take and when. A large box with smaller boxes segmented by days, usually a week, and filled with our medications helps us to remember to take our medications and, perhaps most important, tells us whether we have taken the medication.

Alternative/Complementary Care

Many women use alternative methods for their health, which include taking herbal remedies. Although these remedies may not have been scientifically tested, they work for many women. Since they can adversely interact with some prescribed medications, we must be sure our health care

---

18   Ibuprofen, Motrin Advil, Naproxen are examples of NSAIDs.

provider knows that we are taking them. It is all part of our commitment to cherish our bodies for better or worse, in sickness or health.

Alternative or complementary care and providers are an alternative or complement to traditional medical care through a physician or other licensed health care provider such as a physician assistant or nurse practitioner. Many of these services, originally avoided because of their stark difference from Western medicine and lack of scientific testing, have, in recent days, become better accepted.

Chiropractic care focuses on neuromuscular condition mostly related to the spine. Chiropractors are professionally licensed and referred to as Doctor of Chiropractic following completion of a long course of study. Medicare, Veterans Administration, and other insurance cover certain conditions that respond to chiropractic treatment involving the spine. Examples are acute back pain, lower back pain, spinal misalignment, and whiplash. Often a combination of chiropractic care and therapeutic massage are used to relieve symptoms.

Acupuncture, an ancient Chinese remedy of practice which involves placing fine needles at certain meridian points to relieve pain or other symptoms, has undergone research and shown to be effective for certain conditions. Therapeutic massage has been studied and found effective in the relief of symptoms of pain and muscle tension. Even if those studies didn't exist, we have ample testimony from individuals who have received benefit from them.

Colleges of naturopathy exist to provide extensive training for naturopaths that work with herbal remedies, acupuncture and a variety of methods. Online resources are available to determine the credentials of the various schools.

We have abundant resources, most of which we don't think about until we need them. Then we must do our research and learn our options. Most of us turn to our friends, especially those who are familiar with the providers in the community. We may have enough discomfort that we become afraid and need the help of someone we trust to be with us. The most important act of self-care is to seek help when we don't understand what is happening to us; whatever it takes is what we should do.

Choosing Better over Worse

You know by now that I worry the most about people who accept preventable pathologies of aging as a normal part of aging. They have given up too soon when they still have much more control than they utilize. Unhealthy habits are the villain in our stories of otherwise developing chronic disease. We develop habits, and we keep them. Mostly we fail to adapt when our bodies no longer respond well to our habit.

Poor health habits are defeated by the resilience of youthful bodies but gain strength and influence as we age and lose the advantage of youthful renewal. We don't plan for correction; we may not even think about it until one day we don't recover as easily or completely and just don't feel the same.

The muscles of our organs aren't necessarily turning flabby like the skin under our arms, but organ muscle is losing resilience and changes are occurring. Over-indulgence, whether exercise, food, or drink, is no longer forgiven by our aging bodies. Our aging body begins to speak to us through pain, fatigue, and lethargy and warns us that this may become permanent unless we do something.

We are complicated beings with intricate systems that support our living. For most of our lives, we can depend on those systems functioning without complaint. We have built-in alert systems that tell us when something is going haywire and are most likely to show up as we age. Our body has a lot to tell us if we listen.

Our mind and good common sense tell us the directions that only we can take. Our hope should be that we have earned enough wisdom through living a long time that we have become wise about our body's natural processes. We want to be skilled in recognizing the unnatural and pathological, recognizing what we can and can't control, and what we know and don't know. On some level, we all seek a life that ends naturally and in as much comfort as possible. Armed with knowledge and a sense of adventure, we will know what to do and when.

Part Three
Living as an Older Woman In America

Section Three explores the living situations of older women, which are as varied and individual as women themselves. Women continue to be empowered to make choices about their lives although some may have limitations that limit choices. Women still have relationships, expanding in some way and shrinking in others. Women continue to care about how they look. Women may struggle without sufficient funds to meet daily needs or be freed by financial security to pursue activities of their choosing. Women continue to want purpose, some of which is thrust upon them, some of which they choose.

Bertha D. Cooper

11

Making Appearances

Looking In the Mirror and Looking Good

The greatest vulgarity is any imitation of youth and beauty—this is vital. You must always look your best, not try to look someone else's.

—*Diana Vreeland, editor of Vogue Magazine*

Thoughts about appearance rang clear throughout the interviews I conducted with women, yet attitudes varied widely. Here are some common comments, attitudes, assumptions, and advice that I heard from these women:

- "Appearance is important throughout aging. We women are viewed and valued for appearance."

- "Looking good brings attention and respect."

- "Appearance is very important. If you feel you look okay, you feel better. Wear makeup if you want to, but don't do it for other people."

- "Appearance is always important, no matter what age. At this age, I care less about what others think."

- "I take pride in appearance but know that beauty is from the inside, the whole person."

- "Appearance is not so important to me. I prefer to look natural and be comfortable."

The women I interviewed would call anyone out who said or implied that there was no point in looking good or, indeed, impossible to look good as an old woman. They nearly unanimously felt that appearance continued to be as important throughout our older years as in younger years. The difference? They had reached a point where what others think of them matters less than what they think of themselves. For them, looking good is more than what others see; it is more about how what we feel about who we have become, about carrying oneself with confidence and a sense of self-worth.

One of the women I interviewed said "looking good" didn't matter as a woman aged. It may have been that the term "looking good" brought connotations of makeup and preening, which likely puzzled this highly scientific woman. She seemed to hold no judgment about women who cared about such things; it simply wasn't important to her. I know other women who say they do not care about appearance, yet they, like this woman, present themselves well and with dignity.

Fortunately for most of us, looking good isn't being blindingly beautiful or preternaturally young. As these wise women said, looking good is to a great extent a sense of self and being engaged. But we don't just arrive at this wisdom automatically, not after a life of being told through slick magazines and cosmetics commercials that looking good improves our options for finding work and mates. The section on "Making Appearances" stakes out yet another process of loss, choice, renewal, and coming into being while growing old. We begin this experience with our first instance of being invisible.

Becoming Background

I am not the first or only woman to describe the first signs of becoming background. I happened to be shopping at a well-known department store, and when my turn to purchase came, I was ignored in favor of a younger woman who carried on an energetic conversation about her purchases with the salesclerk.

I was first stunned, then forlorn, and finally in despair about this turn of events. I felt old, and it mattered. When the clerk finally turned to ring up my purchase, her smile disappeared, and her demeanor changed. I tried to ingratiate myself by smiling and making a small joke and was met with indifference. The decade of the aging 50s ushered in yet another transition marker on the road to middle-age oblivion. Or so I thought.

Becoming background occurs almost like a passage, a ritual meant to anoint us into middle age. Something about us has changed enough that we no longer are noticed. Response to us is different, and most of us don't like it.

One woman wistfully stated that she missed the attention of men. Yup, I noticed that, too, which further added to the definite impression that when youthful looks disappear, life as an attractive woman could be over. Again, we feel the bewildering sense of having lost the vitality of youth, the energy, whether provocative or assertive. Mentally, there are no signals until we experience for the first time that we are not noticed by either appreciative men or salesclerks.

These wake-up calls inform us that we no longer can rely on a youthful appearance to get attention or work if we ever did. For some women, the realization may bring on the first thoughts about ways in which aging can be combated whether with creams or cosmetic surgery, in order to retain a youthful pretty appearance. For most, reality sinks in, and we realize our work will stand alone as never before.

Why Not Turn Back the Clock a Little on Sagging?

When I was in my 40s, I cavalierly proclaimed I would get a facelift from vanity. Then, I never seemed to have the time, and once well past the time I had planned for a facelift, I began to question the importance of a facelift to my life. I wondered about losing the authenticity that I so admired in older people.

Cosmetic surgery is a reasonable choice if done for the right reasons, which includes doing it for oneself with self-respect and not out of fear of the appearance of getting older. The choice for cosmetic surgery should result in a palpably improved sense of self-worth.

I had often considered eyelid surgery, especially in the morning, which had a lot to do with seeing as well as seeing my eyes. I decided to have the surgery when I noticed one eyelid falling more than another, which I found distracting to my looks and vision. I was happy that I did even in spite of a couple of weeks of blood pooling in drooping blood bags in my cheeks. Gravity ruled once again.

I also could change my mind about additional cosmetic surgery given the increasingly sullen mouth or droopy chin, both totally unresponsive to muscle tightening exercise. For now, I am embracing a broader vision of "looking good" as a woman growing old.

The Vision of Looking Good As a Woman Growing Old

The anti-aging market hasn't put much effort into defining the beauty of aging. We don't see many models of women over 70 in ads for products made for them. My guess is they, along with the rest of us, haven't really thought about it much. I feel like I am venturing into this unknown territory of aging beauty.

I think of the role model we identified as successfully aging. She is the woman who continues to live in this society and wishes to be part of the foreground, not background. She has grown comfortable in her own skin, sagging or tucked up. And, yes, indeed, she is still attractive to partners if she so chooses as we learn from women in Chapter 13. Our beautiful aging woman listens to her body and her own being and resides in the spirit of natural aging.

As we continue to age, wake-up calls start coming less from the outside than from the inside. Our bodies don't ask for aging cover-ups. Instead, for all the reasons mentioned, our bodies ask for serious attention to prevention and maintenance. Our bodies are begging us to refocus our efforts and pay attention to what's happening to them.

Doing the things to keep muscle strength, maintain weight, and take care of our health also result in looking good. All the anti-aging creams or cosmetic surgery in the world won't look good on a woman who has allowed her body and energy to fall into disrepair.

I was watching people in a hotel lobby while waiting for an appointment when I was drawn to the beautiful face of a woman. Her face was smooth and lineless. Her complexion was perfect, as was her blond hair. It was when she rose to leave that I noticed her body. She was tall and stately but more like a very stiff old-old woman. Her youthful face was betrayed by the unmistakable round drooping of aging shoulders, breasts, and abdomen. She walked with a determined bent posture and used a cane for either painful arthritis or precarious balance or both. Her face and her body were sadly and fascinatingly mismatched. Here must have been a woman who only looked at her face in the mirror.

An actress I admire and who has matched her cosmetic surgery work with her age is Angela Lansbury. She has successfully continued her career into old age and matched her roles with what she is: a charming, confident, and skilled old woman. Seeing the lady of the lobby, we are struck by her artificial appearance; seeing Angela Lansbury, we are struck by her authenticity.

Sometimes the sincerest efforts at beauty result in a palpable sense of desperation. I carry an image in my memory of a woman I saw on a street in Paris. She was petite, well dressed although somewhat overdressed for a simple stroll in the 1990s. She was into her 70s, possibly close to 80. We happened to catch each other's eye. Her eyes ringed with black liner were curious and engaged, and she smiled. Her face was deeply lined. Her lips were lined well outside her mouth and filled in with deep red lipstick. Her cheeks were a bit too pink. Her hair was dyed red.

This Parisian woman had become an aging caricature of her youth. I felt sorrow that she was trapped in the life she once had. She seemed to be the utter result of a life that failed to age. I imagined that she fought being invisible and took steps to stay in place rather than move graciously into aging. I smiled back wondering what she saw in the mirror.

Looking into the Mirror...Who Is That We See?

We all know the rules of looking good, at least well enough to recognize when another woman breaks them. We don't always recognize broken rules in ourselves as we grow older. The lip liner used to enlarge thinning lips seeps into the vertical lines touching the mouth. Dyed dark black hair frames a pale face stark in contrast.

My hair cutter has more common sense than most people I know. I out-age her by 20 years, and I continue to be amazed by her insights into the behavior of people. She has cut and styled hair in my community for over 20 years, which means she has given thousands of haircuts to aging and old women. I posed the question of women making appearance mistakes as they grow older.

This wise hair cutter theorized that when women see their face in the mirror, they only see what is different from what it used to be and try to correct it. She gave eyebrows as an example, pointing out that eyebrows may thin, lighten, or gray. The woman realizes her eyebrows are not as dark, so darkens them and doesn't consider the effect of the startling contrast between her eyebrows and the rest of the face.

We've all seen it; the woman who dyes her hair the luxurious dark of her youth. Unfortunately, dye has no natural highlights, and her dark hair forms a stark frame around her face and accentuates the translucent mature skin that has little natural shine. I've known many women who gave up hair dye and went naturally gray. Women who had dark locks in their youth tend to have beautiful silvery white hair, the envy of the rest of us who tend to have more yellow than silver in our hair.

Graying hair of Caucasian women usually becomes coarser and curlier in texture and requires an adjustment in hair care in coloring, highlighting, and everyday hair care. In my practice of having blond highlights added, I found unnatural color can result from gray hair turning white and other hair turning blond, another unnatural look although not as stark in contrast. Highlighting with a dye is one solution in that gray strands take on the dye as well as other strands that have been separated, creating a look of blended strands of hair.

Rather than relying on our own perceptions that may overcorrect, women who want something different from their aging hair can consult with an experienced hair professional who can advise and provide them with options for color, style and products.

One of my friends also recommends oiling hair to maintain a shine. Moisturizing makes sense since hair has the same issues as aging skin. Dyed, bleached, or gray hair is dry, having lost the luster of natural oils. Winter and heated rooms bring out the dry look, which for some gray hair means unattractive frizz. Oiling and/or conditioning will soften hair and add shine. One last point about hair mentioned to me by women is that many choose short hair over longer hair styles because hair around the neck emphasizes drooping jowls or chins. Such an effect may not be important to women who enjoy long locks, especially if their partners value them. A woman's comfort with her choice is what shows through.

Another very common mistake is using too much foundation to cover skin imperfections. We who notice those age spots or blotches cover them with foundation and may end up with too much foundation. A strong application of foundation works well in the sepia glow of a low light restaurant but in bright daylight, especially sunlight, every line of our face is filled with foundation, making our face look like a road map to everywhere.

Lighten up! Mistakes can be corrected by lightening up on eyebrows, hair, foundation, and lip liner. My best suggestion is to find a mature woman at the cosmetics counter who knows the tricks of makeup for older women, that is, if you want to continue wearing makeup. It may be that less is better.

A common aging change that influences what we see in the mirror is our eyes; they don't see as well. A magnifying mirror helps minimize the frustration of misplaced lip or eyeliners.

Sometimes, we don't recognize when we are breaking rules and what we should hope for is that we have a husband, partner, or very good friend who will tell us when we don't look as good as we think we do.

In lieu of those helpful people, we can rely on ourselves by taking an honest and complete look in the mirror. We have changed; we have a new look. We can experiment and discover what makes us feel the best about ourselves. I still am figuring it out and trying to have a bit of fun with it while I'm at it.

Your Ambassador Face

Remember that your face is the ambassador of your good will. Chapter 5 presented the overall effect of sagging facial muscles and tone on the impression we aging folks have on others. Left to its own response to gravity, our face belies the interest we have in our exchanges or environment. We are expressionless in a culture that reads faces for responses. We might be seen as blank and on the verge of dementia or depressed and on the verge of suicide.

Engage your face if you want to be involved, taken seriously, or simply look good. If you don't care, go ahead and wear your face like you would a comfortable sweatshirt and jeans.

Otherwise, engage the muscles around your mouth. Doing so doesn't mean you have to smile inanely or hold an artificially pleasant expression; rather, you want to be natural, relaxed or, if the occasion calls for it, intent and interested.

Smiles send messages of kindness, agreeability, interest, and involvement. Not wanting or caring to make a good impression is perfectly acceptable, but this chapter is about having presence, looking good, and being aware of your impact on others. When you return to the privacy of your own home, you always can let your face go wherever it is inclined and wear it like you would an old comfortable bathrobe and slippers.

Telltale Teeth

Speaking of smiling, most people know that a nice smile usually shows teeth. We all know women who do not smile with an open mouth because they believe that their teeth are unattractive. My own mother was ashamed of her teeth and taught herself early in her youth to smile without opening her mouth. Even though she had her teeth removed when she was a young mother to correct or prevent heart problems, she continued to be reluctant to smile broadly.

Teeth replacement is expensive and unfortunately unaffordable for some. I wish it weren't so because teeth are important to our health, nutrition, and sense of self. I wish I had a solution for those who are in this predicament. Teeth are an important aspect of our health, appearance, and confidence.

Teeth yellow as we age and lose the look of health even if they are healthy. I have one suggestion for women who wish to restore their teeth to white.

I was fortunate to be genetically predisposed to natural teeth that were well formed and even. I liked going to dentists who raved about my teeth and gave me candy when I left. (Dentists don't give out candy anymore!) As a result, I always have taken care of my teeth. It wasn't always easy but was always expensive. I grew up in a metropolitan area that didn't fluoridate water until the late 1970s so fillings and crowns became a routine part of my life. I was both psychologically and financially prone to floss, brush, and get regular checkups.

All things teeth were going well until I reached my 60s and noticed that my teeth were starting to yellow. Looking around, I noticed that I wasn't the only person with yellowing teeth. Not surprisingly, people with yellowing teeth like me were all aging. My neurosis immediately kicked in, and I sought remedies. I researched whitening with dentists and products and eventually decided on over-the-counter whitening strips which seemed more convenient and less expensive. I was relieved that product worked, and by applying regularly, I could depend on it for a long time to keep my teeth bright.

Yellowing, dull teeth are a sign of aging that can be managed if it's important to a woman. There are women whom I see that I would like to advise to brighten their teeth. These are women who do other things in their dress and manner that tell me they care about how they look. Perhaps it is not as important to them like it is to me whose only hold on being attractive as a child was her teeth.

Stand Up Straight, and Walk with Relaxed Pride

Stand and sit up straight. Is that my mother I hear in my head again? Her and my reasons probably are the same: rounded shoulders don't look right. The older you get, the more rounded shoulder become. Rounded shoulders don't look right on a woman of any age. Stooping conveys a sense of insecurity. It also telegraphs the message that an old woman is present.

Observe your own posture. Watch women who walk with posture in which ears and shoulders are aligned with the side of their bodies. Watch women who tend to stoop or frankly stoop enough so their head thrusts forward and their ears are aligned with the floor about two to four inches ahead of them. Which women seem confident? Which women seem in command of their direction? Which women appear older? Which women are at greater risk for falling?

If we currently are folding our upper bodies forward walking, standing or sitting and want to change to a straighter self, it's possible, but be prepared to take the attention and time that will be required. The older we are, the more we will be challenged to straighten our bodies when we walk, stand, or sit. The older we are, the greater our tendency to fold our shoulders as a result of years of desk or computer work as well as years of leaning over children and sink loads of dirty dishes. Some of us are plagued with back pain that sharpens as we straighten our bodies. It hurts enough that we tend to stay bent. It is better to find the source of pain, which means getting a medical evaluation and recommended treatment. Don't be surprised if treatment does not include remaining bent.

As you contemplate this suggestion, just be sure those rounded shoulders are habit, not something far more difficult to change. Post-menopausal women are susceptible to osteoporosis because we have lost the protective effects of estrogen. We may learn that we are on the edge of or have signs of osteoporosis. Our bones are at risk of folding in on themselves. As we know, osteoporosis is a potentially debilitating condition in which bones become less dense, making them less structurally sound and more prone to breaking.

Osteoporosis requires the evaluation of a health care provider. Imaging testing is available to measure bone density and should be periodically done to measure change.

Whether or not a woman takes preventive medication once she learns she is on the borderline of becoming osteoporotic requires careful evaluation by her and her health care provider. Health care providers are of mixed minds on the value and long-term effects. Still borderline readings must be watched. (Reminder: Fractured hips are difficult to repair and can result in the deaths of those who suffer them within 12 months of the fracture. The percentage of deaths increases every year of age after 65.)

Standing Straight after Years of Bending Over

Happily, a woman can do something to un-round her shoulders if the rounding is the result of habits developed over time. It takes undoing some habits of a lifetime, but it can be done. Cheryl Bell, the personal trainer I consulted, pointed out that most of what we do trains our shoulder to fold in. We slump over computers; we push doors to open; we slouch in chairs to watch television; we hang over sinks to wash pots.

The consequence of repeated overuse of shoulders in this way results in shortening of the muscles of the upper chest which, yup, results in more shortening and pulling the shoulders in. Meanwhile, the muscles of the upper back related to shoulder action have become lazy. They really don't have much to do.

What we learn from physical therapists and personal trainers like Cheryl are that those muscles can be trained or retrained. I didn't fully realize that when a physical therapist gave me a 36-inch-long and 2½-inch round Styrofoam tube to lie on that this was exactly what I was doing. I was training my shoulder muscles to fall back instead of forward. I thought I was treating annoying neck pain which I was but also was learning to use my shoulders, upper back muscles, and upper front muscles in the intended way. One woman I know had a pull-up bar installed in the bedroom doorway so that she could pull up each time she went through the doorway to strengthen her upper back muscles.

An equipment-free exercise is to stand back from the closet door opening and brace arms from bent elbows to hands on either side of a door jam. Keeping body straight, step with one foot through the doorway which pulls shoulders back and continue by alternating footsteps. Exercises made me aware of just how rounded I was. Frankly, I still am working at it. I still must stay aware of the position of my body posture and remind myself to stand straighter, walk taller and while writing this book to sit straight instead of slumping over the computer.

Walking taller works to counter some of the inevitable shrinking in height that occurs as we age. We are likely to get shorter as we age and there isn't necessarily anything we can do about it. A physical therapist colleague once told me that we are taller in the morning than we are in the evening. The cushions between our spinal vertebrae begin to lose volume like everything else and are less resilient after a day of constant weight wears on.

An aligned body posture is an effective measure to manage the diminished cushioning of our spinal column and our tendency to round our shoulders causing our bodies to bend.

Aging and Hygiene

I hate to be the one that says this, but it is true: old people have an "old people odor." It's not a deal breaker like those body odors we all have if we don't keep clean, but it is present. As an example, young people have BO or body odor from playing hard and sweating. The sweat combines with bacteria and remains long enough on the body to develop BO. I remember a story I read in which the father of a toddler was lamenting how the wonderful baby smell was disappearing and other odors arriving. Recent research reports that there are distinct smells to each age, and old age is no different. The research did go on to report that the "old age smell" was considered less offensive than other ages. Now, there's a piece of good news about aging!

Still, old people can have a problem. By the time we hit 70, our skin is drying and flaking, our mouths have less saliva, our digestion can produce some unpleasant odors, and our sinuses may be slow to drain. Managing body odors is complicated by bathing less frequently as an antidote for dry skin. We simply don't need a daily shower on our thinning dry fragile skin. We may be disadvantaged by limited range of motion that makes it difficult to get to sensitive spots. Our own awareness dwindles a bit if we have lost some of our sense of smell, which means that we are not the best judge. This is yet another time when we benefit from the careful guidance of loving family and friends.

The best remedy is careful hygiene that includes at least daily mouth and teeth care and bathing those private areas that still collect perspiration and bacteria. Those of us who are overweight or simply have those ever-increasing gravity droops must pay attention to folds known to hold bacteria and odor. We may have more difficulty reaching certain areas of our body. Reacher appliances extend our reach and can hold washcloths and bath brushers to scrub our backs or feet.

Clothes hold odors longer than bodies do. Therefore, clothes need to be laundered or dry cleaned even if not worn often. Clothes take on a stale odor if held in an airless closet too long. Fragrances that mask odor such as colognes may be worse than the smell itself in this age of hypersensitivities, and we all need to be careful in application.

Bertha D. Cooper

Dress Your Age, Not Your Granddaughter's or Grandmother's

What to wear or not wear is an important question. Most of us stopped dressing like our granddaughters 1-3 decades ago. Something about those jeans with rips in the knees is unappealing. On the other hand, I was susceptible to the just-right amount of rip in a hoodie I recently purchased and enjoy wearing. My husband still shakes his head in wonderment.

The fashion world of androgynous models gives us clothes meant to accentuate small waists and flat bust lines that don't look right on expanded waists and drooping breasts. Enough of us are buying clothes now that there is a market for attractive tops loose around the waist.

Some fashions are a matter of taste. I think mid-thigh tunics look great with leggings; however, miniskirts with blouses, even with leggings, do not seem right on a 50-year-and-older woman, no matter how petite. I confess to not knowing why I hold that opinion, but I know I would be uncomfortable attired thus. However, if a woman feels fine in a miniskirt and blouse, I defend her right to wear it.

What surprised me the most about getting older was that I no longer knew what to wear. My uniform up to retirement, like that of many women, was the look of a professional. In my case, that was a classic blazer with skirt or pants or modest dresses accessorized with some jewelry. It was a sad day for me when I sorted through years of career clothes to decide what to keep and what to donate. The whole process required coming to grips with the fact that I wouldn't live long enough to wear all those outfits again. I was left with yet another loss of identity, a self without a wardrobe.

The one thing that didn't surprise me was that safety and comfort became more important than fashion. For me, it means no heels higher than two inches and no waist bands. Fortunately, the fashion trend was to what is called mid- or low-rise pants which meant I could wear pants that fit in the butt. No so for shoes with heels that were taller than the shoe is long.

Looking Good and Being Fine

None of us expects our appearance to be the same as we age but we still can look like put-together people with or without unavoidable limps and stooping. An older woman looking good is different from a younger woman looking good. Looking good and being fine as we grow old projects our comfort with our own presence. Once again, we reach a point of reconciliation during this life transition, bid a part of ourselves goodbye, and link up with a renewed sense of growth.

150

The suggestions offered here are intended to support a positive sense of self and aging. They aren't necessarily costly, but they do take awareness, time, and effort. For the most part, they are common sense and just like channeling Mom.

- Look for the real you in the mirror; look at your whole face and whole body not just parts. Look for your true reflection. Start with your largest organ, your skin, and match colors you have control over with your skin. Lighten up!
- Cosmetic surgery, the use of makeup, changing hair color are all individual and personal choices — our choice is right for us if done with understanding of realistic expectations and outcomes.
- Smile and remember your face is your ambassador of good will.
- Whiten your teeth because we tend to look at mouths and see yellow teeth as a sign of deterioration.
- Practice sensible hygiene and maintain healthy skin
- Find your own style of dress: what fits you the best and makes you feel authentic.
- Stand up straight and walk with relaxed pride. Internalize your mother's words to stand up straight because the rounder you get, the poorer your posture, the less vital you appear.
- Recognize a new good look.

Bertha D. Cooper

12

Relationships are What Women Do

"I cultivate relationships with women. Women will be my support system as I age and I will be theirs."

—*Aging women survey*

Women are hands down involved in and best at most relationships. We care, we analyze, we obsess, we observe, we nurture, we complain, and we embrace relationships with all the seriousness of life-saving matters. Of course, there is a bell curve of low and high achievers, but I believe the low end for women starts somewhere at the high middle of the bell curve of relationship dedication or involvement of men. We spend considerable time contemplating relationships from the time we enter school if not earlier when we first learn that we are not the center of the universe.

Our relationships reflect the challenges of each age and transition into another age. When we are teens, we have best friends with whom we can talk or text for hours at a time. As young women, we have one boyfriend or girlfriend, or we may date any number of people. Eventually many of us will establish intimate relationships with the man or woman with whom we believe we will spend our lives. Most of us work at one job or another and form strong relationships with our co-workers. If we become mothers, our relationships often revolve around children.

In this chapter, we explore relationships outside of our intimate love partners as we transition to and enter this age of growing old. (Love partnerships and sexuality are explored in the next two chapters.) Our life circumstances and choices as we grow into old age determine the focus of our efforts at sustaining old and establishing new relationships. By now, we have lost relationships through moves, mental decline or death. Some we have lost because we could no longer keep up with the relationship or simply chose not to stay in it.

All we have learned about aging applies here, too. We may not have the energy for all the activities required of having certain or many relationships. We may have physical or medical limitations that preclude involvement in some activities of relationships. We find ourselves making choices about relationships in order to adjust and make the most of the time and energy we have. Most of us have come to value a small number of relationships outside our family that we will nurture as long as possible.

We may have children, grandchildren and great-grandchildren. Some of us still have living parents. We may be part of a close-knit extended family or estranged from one or some of our children or siblings. We may live thousands of miles away from our children who are pressuring us to move closer, but we like the neighborhood, community, and friends that we have had for years.

Relationships determine much of who we are, who we want to be, where we live, and what we do. For all our investment over all these years, we hope that we have learned enough to make good relationships. Relationship management to a certain extent is a measure of maturity. If we still are making our parents' approval our top priority at age 45, we are seriously mired in the challenges of becoming our own person. If we still are having temper tantrums when we don't get our way at 65, we may be hopeless because we have missed hundreds of opportunities to learn a better adult way of achieving goals.

Most of us have learned and worked through many relationship issues. Every one of us has relationships that cause us pain, stress, and endless thoughts. Every one of us has relationships that bring us pleasure, joy, and endless thoughts.

Growing Older with Other Women, Young and Old

Women best friends and confidants are a constant in our lives. That is what interviewees told me. In their own words, they said

- "(Women) friend relationships are ultra-important;"
- "I protect relationships with friends;" and
- "I cultivate relationships with women. Women will be my support system as I age and I will be theirs."

I don't think that I have ever met a woman who didn't have a close and confidential relationship with another woman, even women in very close relationships with their husbands or partners. These are the friends we turn to and tell them of our pain, ask for advice, or share a joy. These are the women we trust to tell us the truth about ourselves without hurting us. These are the women who give us hope about ourselves.

Most of the women I spoke with spoke fondly about the relationships they have or had with other women. Our women friends take on even greater value if possible as we age in part because we know we are likely to spend our remaining lives helping and supporting each other through some very difficult times. We also know that we will lose our friends or they will lose us. By now, we have given up the competition of our youth and middle age for recognition, career growth, and mates although the latter is known to continue in settings where single women outnumber single men.

We know we need one, two, or three close women friends who will be there in time of need. We cultivate those relationships. We bond around mutual interests and philosophies. We belong to book clubs, political groups, volunteer groups, and church groups and participate in multiple other gatherings that bring us together. We share purpose and stories with our groups; we share intimate sorrows and joys with those confidantes who will be with us until the end.

More Time for Best and Good Relationships

By now, we know what a best relationship is for us. I will venture a single sentence definition. The best relationship is one in which we both are truly who we are without fear of losing the relationship. We are spontaneous, vulnerable, caring, honest, sometimes grumpy or snarky, expansive and glad to be together. Dust-ups are forgiven and forgotten. Achievements are shared, and sorrows are felt as our own.

Some of us no longer have a best friend; our friend has left us prematurely or, some would say, on time if our friend was very old. The loss leaves an emptiness not easy to fill because best friends evolve over time, not something of which we have much once we reach old age.

Good relationships are the same most of the time. We all have wonderful friendships in which we find ourselves being careful in certain areas. Or we may find ourselves assuming more of a mentor role. The older we get, the more we take on the mantle of an older woman who passes on her life lessons to younger women, men, and children. Personally, I find mentoring to be one of the most rewarding relationships. Done for the right reasons, it is impossible not to regain forgotten perspectives or learn new ones.

The best relationships come from bonding with casual acquaintances or family relationships that transcend assigned roles and family dynamics. They can grow out of difficult relationships if the difficulties can be resolved. If not, one of the tasks of growing older is to resolve the relationship for oneself. Unresolved difficult relationships consume precious time and energy.

Difficult Relationships That Take More of a Toll As We Age

Long-standing relationships that are chronically stressful begin to take a greater toll as we age. We know that chronic stress and mental anguish have a greater impact on our physical bodies as we age. Making a final attempt to mend difficult relationships or to let go and to stop obsessing about them becomes an essential task when you are on the cusp of old age. Mental distress robs us of valuable time and energy we need or want for other pursuits so it becomes essential to pick our stresses.

Difficult relationships are not those friendships that seem to have a natural ebb and flow and enter and leave a life. Most of us have countless relationships that we can pick up after years. Difficult relationships, on the other hand, become tiresome, unbalanced, and demanding. If resolving a difficult relationship were easy, we would have done it long ago. However, we somehow have gotten entangled in old feelings, responses, hurts, and misunderstandings.

The measure of the need to change the difficult dynamic is the degree of stress the relationship causes in our life. If we are thinking about it, reliving it, and inventing scenes with this person, then it's taking valuable time and personal resources. As we age, we begin to weigh the stress against the value and importance of the relationship. More than likely these stressful relationships involve family because they tear us between our sense of family and our inability to resolve the stress. We do not easily leave our tribe, and I believe most of us cannot walk away without first truly trying to resolve the issues.

Difficult relationships that involve family, either birth family or relatives by marriage, are packed with emotional baggage from the past. Why else would someone choose to be in a room with unspoken but detectable resentment? Why else tolerate passive or active disrespect? Why else would someone not tip the house of cards and let it fall?

Resolutions of any difficult relationship requires will and readiness on each person's part. Both or all must accept part ownership in the successes and failures of the relationship. If we find that we feel we are the victim and abused or misunderstood by the other or, more important, feel no fault for the problems, we are setting the stage for another failure. Resolution requires accepting ownership and responsibility for our actions that contribute to the problem.

We decide. We either work to reform the relationship, to leave it, or to stay in it as is for the rest of our days. If we choose the last, then we must lower our expectations and quit obsessing about it. If not, we ought to pick again. Make peace with the selected option. Remember that we always can pick our stress.

A contingent of my family, like many, struggles in the environment of starkly differing political beliefs that divide families. Americans seem to have come to a place in our society of acceptance of calling others bad names or characterizing opposing philosophies as evil. I, like many women, struggle for peace in the household. My experience is classic in that members of my family had shared joys and despairs for years but had evolved into a pattern that did not allow for meaningful communication, let alone resolution.

Tension and disrespect started to show in unrelated communication, and I found myself spending too much time and energy agitating over the turn of events. I requested that we have a frank discussion not about the politics or philosophies but about the way we treat each other and prepared myself to listen. They didn't want to talk about it, and I had to come to understand that it was a lot more important to me than them. I had to come to terms with their explanation that their lives were too busy to resolve the communication issues that since I exposed my concerns were now wedged between us like cement barriers.

I had taken the risk of losing the relationship, the reason most of us don't give words to the tension. I lost. It was more like a burden lifted out of necessity than through a Zen moment when I finally let it go. I realized how weighted down I was by the struggle to resolve a particularly difficult relationship.

As often happens when we are ready, I was given the gift of words for my decision when the following quotes appeared in column in our local paper (DeBey, 2011). The timing was perfect and I breathed the last breath I would spend on this struggling relationship.

- "It is important to surround ourselves with people who can nourish and sustain us."
- "Surround yourself with people who will sustain your very soul. Treasure every moment with them."

This simple, even obvious, message seemed like a revelation to me; clearly, I needed permission to move on. Many women do in our complicated quest for relationship peace. Our choices can become less about giving up unhappy or unfulfilling relationships and more about choosing what we want from life. Eventually, we will lose the anger and the hurt and keep our care and love in perspective and intact. We become cleared for those occasional contacts and at least mature enough to value what we do have and stop obsessing over what we don't have.

Most of us feel deep gratitude for those relationships that seem to work for both or all of us. Good relationships are what we do for each other, a gift we give each other and accept from the other. In the dimension of growing old, we are more prudent in how we use our time and energy in relationships. As my story shows, it's not easy to give up those long-held relationships, especially family, even when that final line is crossed. We are old enough to know when we are struggling against the current of a difficult relationship and although it may take us time, we will know when to stop.

We may find that we don't have to give up everything, or we may at last discover the line that we won't cross. We will be guided by our true intention to stay in the relationship and desire to find the balance that reduces an unhealthy obsession. At least, we will learn as I did whether there is interest in our relationship partners to resolve the difficult relationship. On occasion, we are rewarded when they and we return to ride the same wave.

Lost Relationships Return

Gretchen, whom I interviewed twice at a 3-year interval, related a story of her family malfunction in our first interview. A few years earlier, an event had occurred during a visit to one of her sisters that resulted in an estrangement from both her sisters. Gretchen wasn't sure what had happened and only speculated that it had to do with sister rivalry. Sisterly invitations stopped, and Gretchen gave up on ever having a relationship with her sisters although that she clearly missed them came through in her discussions with me.

Then, Gretchen's partner arranged a surprise birthday party for her 70th birthday, and in what seemed like a split second, the feelings surrounding the misunderstandings disappeared. Gretchen walked into the restaurant for the party to see both her sisters present and happy to see her. All three took the opportunity in the glow of reunion to express their desire to be together and put the past behind them, which they had done by the end of the visit. Gretchen said that none of the hurts and misunderstandings of the past made sense anymore and became unimportant compared to having a relationship until the end of their lives. Reconciliation wouldn't have happened without the surprise party, something I am sure was contemplated by Gretchen's partner in bringing these sisters back together again.

Our Parents, Our Children, and Our Grandchildren

We just seem to be getting over turning 50 only to realize that our children will turn 50 soon enough. It won't be very long until the day our children will somewhat reluctantly ask us about our plans for our old age. It is one of those difficult conversations. We just don't expect that our children should have to worry about us.

Is it that we always want to seem capable in their eyes? I have had a niece and stepdaughter both suggest that I move close to them in my old age future. As thoughtful as they were, I couldn't' help but wonder what they saw in my future that I didn't, at least not yet. I accepted their sense of affection and duty along with the realization that something was shifting in our relationships.

Most of the women I interviewed had children. The younger the woman, the closer she seemed to the lives of her children. As adult children grow more responsible, we may begin to experience more distancing geographically and technologically and, in some cases, emotionally. One woman lamented that among their blended family of five children, they never received an invitation to Thanksgiving dinner. She said she and her husband always had prepared the holiday feast, and when they stopped, the tradition stopped. The parents say it's not an estrangement but admit to being puzzled about the family distancing from them and each other that has occurred. As sad as it seems, it's not nearly as painful as an event described by another woman that resulted in a sudden break in the relationship.

This grandmother lost contact with one set of grandchildren and their parents when she took a stand on an issue that involved her, one grandchild, her money, and an offending message on her grandchild's Facebook. She was shocked at the immaturity and future implications for her grandchild. She believed—and believes to this day—that her grandchild needed an important lesson. She told her grandchild that there would be no planned trip out of the country until the message was corrected. She was further shocked when the child's parents, one of whom was her child, did not agree. All communication ceased at that point. She is saddened and disappointed at the severity of the separation but has accepted it as their decision and hers.

In a February 11, 2012 *Huffington Blog* post, Karl A. Pillemer, Ph.D., described these kinds of situations as follows:

> "I am well aware that this sounds unfair; however, in my review of the accounts of intergenerational rifts, it's usually the parent who pays the higher price if a rift occurs. Older mothers and fathers tend to invest more in the relationship as they get older and therefore stand to lose more by letting it disintegrate. Particularly acute is the separation from grandchildren that can occur as a result of the rift."

Another grandmother in my group had a tenuous relationship with an adult child's spouse that seemed to start at the point the second grandchild was born soon after the first. By then, she had learned to withhold any judgments related to just about anything in their lives so she was at a loss to understand where the tension was coming from. She had numerous explanations, most related to the stress the couple was feeling in their lives. She grew more sensitive and careful in her communication and tolerance. She knew the power of the parents and that her grandchildren could be withheld from her at any time. She would not risk the relationship with those cute little beings who just seemed to love her no matter what. She is determined to enjoy the moments she has now with her grandchildren and has accepted the fact that she must be careful in words and actions with her adult child's spouse. She let go of needing to be treated more respectfully and has never conveyed her grievances to her adult child. Her relationship with her grandchildren and the legacy of love she will leave them outweighs the slights and unpleasantness she experiences.

There is not a parent-child relationship that hasn't experienced its ups and downs, starting with the terrible twos. The difference now is that we are no longer the parent with power and must negotiate with these people we raised around the raising of our grandchildren. These two grandmothers faced two distinctly different situations. The first discovered the line she could not cross when she was confronted by a breach of values that was impossible for her to condone. She chose the only way she could influence the child and did not anticipate the parents' reactions. She has accepted the outcome at least for the moment because she took a stand for a value important to her.

The second grandmother escaped the overt situation in which she would be called upon to make a decision that would cost her the relationship with her grandchildren. My guess is that she continues to carefully thread the needle in managing a sensitive relationship.

Our Parents, Our Selves, Last Call

Surprisingly to me, most likely because my mother died when she was 65 years old, many of the women I talked with had a living parent or had just lost their remaining parent. They are or were in process of losing the longest and most formative relationships of their lives. We often are the caretaker or the one whom our aging parent turns to in time of declining health and ability. I have seen many women who are faced with the decision of moving a parent out of the home into a more supervised setting. I believe it is one of the most difficult life decisions. We are deeply saddened when we no longer recognize them for who they were. We feel like the parent in the relationship.

When the parent dies, we feel a mix of relief and sorrow. It doesn't seem to matter how old you are and how expected it is, the loss of a parent is felt at some primal level of being. Our parents stopped actively protecting us decades ago, but now they have removed the final line of protection and have left us next in line. We are touched by that fact and more touched by the nostalgia of what they meant to us.

Some Things Will Never Change

All these examples could be part of any family story, past, present and future. They are about us being complex human beings. They are about us being women who are hands down best at relationships. Aging doesn't change our intentions around relationships, but it does change our capacity and our priorities.

We turn next to those all-important love relationships.

13

Old and New Partners In Love

"Men have more access to women than women do to men."

—Aging women survey

The life expectancy of a woman at birth exceeds that of a man at birth by about five years according to the 2017 Social Security Period Life Table. Aging improves the outlook for women and men according to the same table. A woman who reaches age 65 is expected to live five years more than she was expected to live at birth. The life expectancy of a man who survives to age 65 improves by nearly seven years (Social Security Administration, 2017).

That's good news for the 65-year-old woman who married a 65-year-old man. The chances are that if you have married or partnered with a man older than you, you will have a few years without him if you both manage to avoid premature death. If you have married or partnered with a woman your age or a bit older, the statistical chances are you will not have many if any years alone. What we do know is that more women end their lives alone than men, some widowed, some divorced and many by choosing to remain single.

In fact, according to "A Profile of Older Americans: 2016" (Administration on Aging, 2016), American women 65 years and older can expect to be widowed, divorced or single. These data show the following:

- Older men were much more likely to be married than older women—70 percent of men, 45 percent of women.
- In 2016, 34 percent of older women were widows.
- About 29 percent (13.6 million) of non-institutionalized older persons live alone (9.3 million women, 4.3 million men).
- Almost half of older women (46 percent) age 75+ live alone.

Various studies tell us that many women chose to live alone. Older women are more likely the one initiating divorce according to a Bowling Green State University study (Brown & Lin, 2014) and psychologists speaking on divorce trends (Ellin, 2015). Divorce is becoming more prevalent after 50 years of age. Increasing life expectancies plays a role when one or both partners want something different in their remaining years. More women have the option to divorce because they have or can expect economic independence following the divorce. The rate of divorce is higher among those 50 year plus who are in second marriages according to the Bowling Green study related to difficulties in blending families and financial issues,

Ending a marriage doesn't mean a woman is ending any interest in having a love partner; although, some women may want to experience a life on their own for the short- or long-term. Other women may want to seek out love relationships sooner or later but find themselves filled with apprehension over being "old" and in the dating scene.

Older men to older women ratios may seem bleak for women looking for the companionship of the right male but are not impossible. We've all read the stories of women and men coming together later or late in life. In that spirit this chapter explores the romantic lives of women growing older. We start by remembering it's never too late.

My single friend and I took a colleague to lunch to recognize her recent accomplishment. During one of the conversations that didn't require much of me, I became aware of a man staring intently at my attractive and vibrant 60-ish friend. I was reasonably sure the man and she didn't know each other, or else my friend would have acknowledged him.

What captured my attention was his apparent attraction to her. He appeared to be in his 60s and clearly was captivated by her. Nothing came of the moment except to remind me that the power of attraction exists at all ages.

Choice

We only can hope that by now we carry a mature understanding of who we are and what we want out of relationships. Partners we love inextricably affect the quality of our living. We are rewarded the most when these relationships work and suffer the most when they don't work. The first days of attraction are as heady for old men and old women as they are for younger couples. Attraction and falling in love continue to be a powerful experience although, as you will read in the next chapter, our sexual chemistry changes with aging. Throughout our lives we have looked, found, lost, and looked again in order to fulfill this very human attraction. Our selection processes are as unique as we are.

Growing older brings less choice and more complexity. One choice it brings for many women is the opportunity to stop the dance of romance. After years of marriage, hook-ups, breakups, mating, children, taking care, loving, running and everything that means, some women are ready to simply be with themselves. It isn't necessarily a decision based on bad experiences although it might be. Some women told me that they had come to enjoy their independence and the opportunity to pursue their interests. Love or romantic relationships take energy and time and complexity that many women don't want in their lives.

Then there are women who long for companionship or serious relationships. Our society has come to grips at last with the understanding that some men are attracted to and in love with other men and some women are attracted to and love other women. A revolution in acceptance has taken place over the past two decades. The Supreme Court legalized same-sex marriage in a 2015 decision. As of early 2019, 38 states have legalized marriages between same sex people.

Seeking romance could be as simple as seeking companionship of a person you can talk with about the details of your lives and sharing your thoughts and emotions. It could be seeking someone with common interests who will share the joy you feel in activities you love. Too many stories of marriage among older people tell us that romance among the aging isn't always the old guy wanting a younger woman although it happens; however, it could be the old woman with the younger guy.

Young Trophy Wives and Aging Cougar Women

Even though it stung, I admired the directness of the women in the interviews who opined that older men wanted younger women, left their middle-aged wives, married the younger woman, and in some cases started a second family. These young wives have come to be known as trophy wives. Depending on the time of year, my husband is either 16 or 17 years older than I am, which was true when we married over 47 years ago. I shudder each time I have been called a trophy wife because I don't think we fit that description, but I understand it. This older man picked a much younger mate.

Trophy wives are so designated because they are prized for their youth and beauty; a prize earned by successful older men often at the expense of their former wife of their same age. Whatever the motivation of the partners, culturally we are more accepting of older men marrying younger women than the opposite, which puts older women at a disadvantage.

We see occasional bursts of like activity on the part of older women, although usually those younger than 50, marrying or hooking up with younger men. These older women are referred to as "cougars" for reasons that escape me, but I've heard the term has to do with wanting to hunt instead of being hunted. One of my interviews was with a woman who married a man 15 years younger than she 25 years earlier. She and he securely go through the joys and trials of marriage and, like my husband and I, adjust to the age difference. I forgot to ask her if he was called a trophy husband, but I think not. Another woman has been in a long-term relationship with a man six years younger than herself for over 25 years. Despite his entreaties, she decided not to marry him.

These marriages or partnerships of older women and younger men or between women are unusual and unexpected. In many ways, it makes more sense for a younger man and older woman to, like the couple in the second example above, because they are more likely to die around the same time. In this first example, however, the young husband likely will outlive his wife by six years (Social Security Administration, 2017). Large age differences typically result in the younger partner being alone for a few years.

It remains far less likely for a woman over 65 to date a significantly younger man. I admit that I would be suspicious of any man younger than 60 who sought my attention for anything other than taking a survey or selling me a cane. This is, of course, if I were single. I had what could have been a perfectly good sexual dream go bad when the man pursuing me turned out to be 40 years younger than me! Even in my dream state, I couldn't comprehend the attraction a young man would have for me. We read about men older by 30, 40, or more years than the 25-year-old women they marry. Young women can bear children, but somehow, I don't think that's the attraction.

Older women are challenged in finding a partner in the face of competition, but there is romance to be found for the older woman with those men who are looking for women in their age range. The wide acceptance of Internet dating with sites specializing in older people is encouraging us to try it.

Finding a Partner or a Friend for the Short- or Long-Term

Not all women want to marry or cohabit. In fact, some decidedly don't, but they do want dating and friendship. Women no longer must depend on social gatherings and volunteer work to make contacts although those activities continue to be good places to meet friends with similar interests. Our modern technological age has brought us online dating that can uncover potential dates with similar interests.

Five decades ago, I met the first couple I knew to meet through an online dating service, and they were wondrously happy. I thrilled for them, and through them I came to realize early on that couples can meet through internet dating.

Since older women outnumber older men, the odds of making an Internet match favor older man. Men receive multiple online inquiries compared to those received by older women. A close former colleague and her current partner, about five years older than she, met online. She made it through the jungle of his responses when she took the initiative to email him several weeks after their coffee date about something that she thought would interest him. They met again and have been together ever since They both view the relationship as long term although at this point she is not ready to marry despite his asking.

Sure, some women have met creeps online. Most women know the difference between lecherous and flirtatious behavior no matter what age. We have an internal response system that informs us of predatory danger—when we are not under the influence of alcohol or drugs. We tend not to trust flirtatious behavior the older we get. If a woman is not confident about her creep identification skills, she needs to have some serious conversations with her women friends who do.

Friends also are those who want to introduce you to someone "just right for you." They probably are right; besides, you will know when it's wrong. What's evident is that a woman won't find a relationship without engaging with others whether through friends, online dating services, or volunteer work.

Choosing a Date or Partner

Some women are cautious for another reason. They are determined not to get into a relationship, partnership, or marriage like the one that ended in divorce. Thirteen percent of women over 65 are listed as divorced; in other words, no longer married and not widowed. Researchers report that the divorce rate of 28 percent for couples over 50 has doubled since 1990, which means many older women are newly divorced, some for the second time from a marriage of shorter duration (Brown & Lin, 2014).

Statistics don't tell us the whole story because a divorced woman could be in a long-term living relationship like some of the women I interviewed who made the decision to cohabit rather than marry. Living together without marrying represents a sea change for my generation and some older boomers.

"I don't think I would be living with him if my mother were alive," said a 64-year-old woman who chose to live with her lover.

Many older women who come out of a difficult marriage and worse divorce said they had gotten used to the independence and didn't want to do marriage again. But that doesn't mean they are not interested in forming love partnerships or dating relationships.

Certain that I did not know the issues around finding the right person, I turned to a savvy divorced woman, "Gloria," who easily talked about her single life and what she looked for in a live-out companion. Over time, she developed a set of criteria that she considered when dating one man became more serious. With her permission, I tell her story.

Gloria started our conversation about men by telling me about her friendship relationships with women. "I cultivate relationships with women. Women will be my support system as I age and I will be theirs," she said, describing a realistic and thought-out vision of her life as an older woman. She had no plans to give up her independence through marriage or live-in companionship.

Gloria's marriage ended in divorce over a decade ago and at the time she had little desire to enter into a partnership for a long time, if ever. She's had several relationships since that she enjoyed as well as learning more about herself. She is quite clear on what she expects from a relationship which she tells men that seem to want longer-term relationships. At the time I interviewed her, she was in a relationship which seemed to work for both and those conversations were taking place. Her criteria or expectations are generic enough that they could apply to any of us. She starts with building and maintaining open and forthright communication.

"We talk about anything we need to in our relationship," she said of her current relationship. "We are continually discovering each other through clarifying conversations." To Gloria, those conversations are part of learning the true values of each other and whether they match, something she sees as essential in a good relationship. She predicts that failure to have alignment of values will end in a failed relationship.

Gloria's wisdom was gained though her own process of growth following her divorce. She took the time and made the effort, which she recommends to all women in the same position so they will not only learn from their mistakes but come to understand who they are. She realized in a profound way that above all she always must be herself and if there were any indication that she was not what the other person needed or wanted; she would end the relationship.

This bit of wisdom is shared by many women who at one time subordinated their needs and desires to their mate's interests or ego. The fact that more older women than older men initiate divorce is not unrelated.

Women Loving Women

For some women who married in their 20s and had children only to divorce as their children grew into independence, their divorce may have surprised even them. They left their husbands for the love of another woman or they left their husband and discovered love with another woman. When I first met Janet, she had been in a committed relationship with her woman partner for over 25 years. They legalized their same-sex relationship by entering into an agreement called a domestic partnership. Domestic partnerships are available to opposite sex couples in a relationship who do not wish to marry but want some legal protection and sharing of assets. Although Janet and her partner were pleased with the new freedom to marry, they hadn't decided whether to marry at the time of the interview.

Janet was in her late 60s and agreed to talk with me about her life as a partner in a lesbian relationship. It is only now at her age that she can feel totally free to talk about her home, partner, and family just as women married to or partnering with men do. She kept silent for years because she was a teacher of small children in a public school. She knew that at any time a parent could take issue with her suitability and, even though unfounded, could drive her from her chosen profession.

"I've lived in both married worlds," she said about a prior marriage that produced children. "The difference I see is that my partner now and I have no defined roles (unlike my husband and me). Neither of us is expected to do the laundry or chop the wood because of our gender." All those things got sorted out by interests and skill in most instances. "We don't need a man to carve a turkey." Janet notes, too, that both women work outside the home, true of most lesbian couples, which may be as much a financial necessity as it is for marriages between men and women.

Janet did not view herself as a lesbian; she never thought about it. When her marriage failed, she met her partner and fell in love. She says it was as simple as that. Her partner and she talked, and she discovered a person who seemed to know her and her strengths and frailties better than anyone ever did. Her partner cared that she became the person she was intended to be. Janet soon returned that love in an age-old story of finding the right person with whom to share your life.

Lesbians in long-term love relationships deal with their relationships as any other couple would. Sexual orientation is only one part of each of them in a not-so-mysterious way. Isn't that the case with all of us?

To Caretake or Not to Caretake

We are aging women dating aging men or women, and there is a greater chance because of our ages that one of us has or is going to develop a chronic disease. One of the risks of any aging relationship is that it will turn into a caregiver situation; that potential should be part of our decision in considering forming a long-term relationship. For Gloria, it's part of the pre-screening process.

For example, Gloria pays careful attention to what her dates say about their health and their overall approach to taking care of their health. She says with conviction:

- "I'm not knowingly going into a relationship in which I am likely to end up being a caretaker."

- "I also don't want to be with someone who won't go to the doctor when he should,"

- "I don't want a partner who won't get his hearing checked when he clearly isn't hearing well."

Not all women feel as strongly about avoiding the caregiver role even in a new relationship. Most, though, would like a partner who cared enough to hear what she has to say.

A different woman with whom I spent considerable time talking took an opposite view in that she married into a relationship in which she likely will become a caregiver. She married a man with existing and compromising chronic disease. She is at peace with the knowledge that she likely will have caregiving responsibilities and that he will die well before her. She loves her husband and the moments they have together. Marriage to her is the public statement of the enduring deep psychological bond they share—so great that it triumphs over the certain knowledge that she has only a short time with him.

Women in long-term partnerships may find themselves heading for the role of caretaker much earlier than they ever anticipated or wanted. As noted in Chapter 10, the baby boomer generation is experiencing chronic disease at a higher rate than any generation that preceded them. A woman (or a man) contemplates the fate of her marriage when she sees her partner's body showing the effects of years of overeating, overdrinking, sedentary work, or a combination of those things. She has talked about the habits to no avail in the past and has given up, that is, until she begins to realize if it continues, she and he never will realize their dreams of retirement. Everything will become more difficult.

Women I know in this situation struggle because they love this person and know that nagging doesn't work well. One of the most difficult tasks we have is to be direct with people who are being harmed by their own choices. Yet, we wish good health for them and for us. Clear-eyed recognition of the risks of having an unhealthy partner who is making bad choices that affect enjoying life together may result in the determination needed to have the talk, the counseling, and ultimately, the change.

If we are the long-term partner or wife who is continuing to make choices that are putting us on the sure path to chronic illness and dysfunction, then we are the ones who must consider what we are doing to our important other. Change of this magnitude is difficult and requires a commitment and support. Who better to share it with than the person whose remaining life will be diminished if we don't?

Many of us are pleasantly surprised that we continue to have an interest in touching, intimacy, and sex, an area we explore next for the aging woman.

14

Aging Women and Sexuality

"I miss the spontaneity."

—*Aging women survey*

We all are fascinated by the ads for enabling products for men "to be there and ready when the time is right" and who inevitably are accompanied by the smiling woman ready and willing by his side. Never mind that most of the couples appear to be in their 40s. How stunning it would be to see an ad that features a couple in their 60s or 70s or 80s lying in bed talking, touching and building their passion while Viagra or its generic, Sildenafil, brings blood to the needed organ.

Female menopause signals the end of reproduction as a reason for sexual intercourse. For most of us, that particular purpose ended much earlier and our bodies cooperated by becoming less fertile. Unless surgically removed, our ovaries slow down and eventually stop the production of eggs to await the squirming sperm whereas men continue to produce sperm although at a much lower rate.

Aging women's bodies slow the production of estrogen, progesterone, and testosterone. Aging men's bodies slow the production of testosterone as anyone within earshot of television or computers knows. I would guess now that most teenagers know about erectile dysfunction and low testosterone than in any time in human history, certainly more than I knew at

Bertha D. Cooper

twice their age. Women's issues haven't merited the same product development for our unique issues of vaginal dryness and declining libido although more ads are surfacing about vaginal lubricants that claim to stimulate both partners.

We Don't Talk about Sex

My generation, now aging, doesn't talk about the intimate details of our sex lives despite being pioneers of cohabitation without benefit of marriage and other free love practices. I did not ask the women I interviewed about any details of their personal lives; it was theirs to offer in response to the broader questions. Most didn't bring up their intimate sexual lives, but a few did. Since I don't talk about my husband's and my sexual activities, I have no idea if younger generations talk about theirs any more than we do or did.

Sure, there are mentions of "hook-ups" and "friends with benefits" but these mentions do not include the details of this most intimate coming together. My husband of an older generation than mine wouldn't talk about it with anyone except me so imagine my astonishment when he sagely understood that our intimacy had to be part of this book.

Obviously, women have differing attitudes, experiences, and desires when it comes to sex. Attitudes and desires change over time and experience. One size does not fit all or even one woman throughout her lifetime. This discussion of sex simply acknowledges that sexuality is a continuing part of our lives and that we will experience changes as we grow older.

Missing Something

Several women I interviewed said that they missed being looked at by men who clearly admired their beauty or figure. They missed being desired or simply being thought of as attractive or pleasant to look at and the spontaneity of that desire. And, they bemoaned that older men check out younger women.

In "Making Appearances," I wrote of our first experience of being "invisible" to younger generations. No longer being noticed by men is another form of invisibility and certainly a loss if enjoyed by women.

These women I interviewed missed the chemical connection that can occur with a stranger even though fleeting or never meant to be fulfilled. Sexual tension is or was a part of our younger lives whether or not we acted on it. As we age, there is simply less chemistry and what's there takes longer to surface. As I aged out farther from menopause, I realized that I

174

wasn't thinking about sex as often as I did before. It came as a revelation because I never realized how much I thought about sex until the thoughts disappeared.

Spontaneity of sex disappeared along with the fleeting thoughts, and there were ever-declining episodes of quickies or sex on the stairwell. My husband and I who always have mutually enjoyed our sexual intimacy realized that what was once spontaneous, we now had to plan. We still wanted the heady closeness of sexual intimacy, but our bodies no longer drove us to it.

Sheryl A. Kingsberg, Ph.D. (2002), explains the difference between desire and drive:

> "... it is age much more than menopausal status that is related to decreased sexual drive. In fact, one of the most significant and universal changes that occur with age is a decline in the drive component of sexual desire (p. 434).

She says women begin to lose their drive as biological mechanisms that involuntarily give us those desirous feelings diminish. She goes on to say that women who are in regular sexual relationships may experience diminished drive but continue to be motivated to have sexual intimacy. They continue to want it.

Kingsberg's important distinction tells us that in general we continue to want intimacy as we grow older; we are just no longer driven to it. Not all women want their intimacy in the form of sexual intercourse, and those that do generally want it as one part of an experience of intimacy.

Use It or Lose It

In an interview I conducted with Carole Kalahar, OB/GYN nurse practitioner with certification as a menopausal practitioner, she stated, "sexual changes are a function of aging; it doesn't mean you are broken" (personal interview, December 12, 2013).

By now, no one should be surprised that any part of our aging bodies can avoid physiological changes that occur due to aging. Membranes get thinner and lose resiliency. Glands don't produce the same moisturizing protection. Our vaginas are less receptive. Change occurs in our sexual response. Like just about every part of our body and mind, if we don't use it, we will lose and have a problem getting it back if we change our mind.

After years of providing health care to women in the areas of obstetrics and gynecology, Carole Kalahar has a way with words for women. Her health evaluations include questions about her patients' sexual activity, such as.

- "How often do you engage in sexual activity?"
- "Do you have penetration during sexual activity?"
- "Do you have pain during sexual activity?"

Listening to her, I realized the only question I ever had been asked about sex by a physician was if I had pain during intercourse. Kalahar's manner is direct, warm, and confident; her questions about sexual intimacy as part of a comprehensive health assessment let her patients know that she treats them as multidimensional beings. "I treat the whole woman," she explains.

What Kalahar helps her menopausal patients understand is that changes in sexual drive and response do result from normal aging but those changes do not mean that sexual life is over. She describes the change noted by Kingsberg as an important shift in the way we practiced sex in our younger years. The usual sexual dance steps are desire followed by stimulation, then lubrication, and climax. That order changes in that we women don't tingle in desire or drive until we are stimulated. Once stimulated, we feel it, want it, and lubrication follows although not necessarily at the former flow over our now-less-elastic vaginal walls.

Our lubrication and vaginal receptivity response are influenced by factors such as our age, the newness of our partner and the heady passion of a new relationship, the skill of our long-term lover, and, important, how long it's been since we had intercourse. The moist working membranes of our vagina will atrophy without use. The vaginal walls thin. The vagina shrinks and becomes less elastic.

If a woman continues having sexual intimacy and intercourse, she produces lubrication, and her vagina maintains enough flexibility to respond although she will probably require more stimulation. If her own lubrication is insufficient, she can apply vaginal lubricant or moisturizer to her vagina.

It's Never Too Late

Our vaginas begin to atrophy following menopause and continue atrophying the more years that pass for most women. Kalahar points out there is a small number of women who do not experience vaginal atrophy, possibly due to genetic predisposition, but the reason is not known.

Kalahar describes a typical situation in which a woman who has been widowed for several years, sometimes many, decides she is ready for an intimate relationship. Kalahar tells women choosing to participate in intercourse again that they will regain vaginal receptivity, but it will take time and treatment.

Options for Vaginal Dryness

Vaginal moisturizers are non-estrogen products and relatively new on the market. More brands are being developed by more companies. Kalahar advises women that vaginal moisturizers can be applied every day as a routine much like a woman applies moisturizer to her face to maintain a less dry vaginal environment.

If estrogen is used, treatment options are to insert an estrogen tablet, apply a topical cream or insert an estradiol ring. The time needed to restore vaginal receptivity varies by individual women. If a woman feels treatment is not effective in a few months, she can see a skilled health care provider for an opinion.[19]

Some women have found vaginal dilators to be useful. Dilators can be purchased in specialty stores or online.

A woman also can use something called an estradiol ring which the woman inserts inside her vagina. The ring releases minute amounts of estradiol, a form of estrogen, over a period of three months. Some women use the ring because it is more convenient and less time consuming although it is more expensive than other measures.

Exercising Our Vagina

We often don't think of our vaginas as needing strengthening exercises, but indeed there are sound reasons to exercise our pelvic floor muscles in the area that is home to pelvic organs such as our intestines, uterus, bladders, and their respective openings: rectum, vagina, and the urethra. Pelvic floor muscles can weaken for a variety of reasons including childbirth, obesity, excessive straining, and the effect of aging muscles. Weak muscles

---

19 She should look for someone who has been certified through the NAMS Certified Menopause Practitioner program
The North American Menopause Society has developed an opportunity for licensed healthcare providers to demonstrate their expertise by passing a competency exam and becoming credentialed as a NAMS Certified Menopause Practitioner or NCMP. NAMS provides a listing of NCMP-credentialed clinicians on its public website.

and relaxed connective tissue can lead to urine leakage, incontinence, and prolapse of bladder and uterus. In the context of sexual intercourse, vaginal muscle strength is important to both partners to achieve satisfaction. There are remedies where muscles are weak.

A certain kind of exercise called Kegel exercises (named after the physician who developed the technique) can be done any time and place in complete privacy because no one knows when a woman is doing the exercise. The convenience helps because regular exercising strengthens and maintains the muscles of the pelvic floor (The North American Menopause Society, 2020). Once a woman performs Kegel exercises, she realizes the sensation also mimics a vaginal response and can appreciate the value in performing sexual intercourse.

The Society and Mayo Clinic has an easy-to-use guide to doing Kegel exercises (Mayo Clinic 2011).[20] The technique for identifying the pelvic floor muscles that require exercise is to be aware of the muscles used when stopping urination midstream. These are the muscles that we want to target; however, and this is a warning, we should not make a practice of stopping urine midstream which can result in urine retention and infection, possibly other problems over time.

Kegel exercises, in order to be effective, must be practiced correctly, regularly and indefinitely, not unlike the exercises recommended to maintain the strength of our legs. The contraction results in the contraction of all the muscles, which is exercising the muscles just as flexing our arm exercises our biceps. Kegel exercises often are recommended as one of the treatments of episodes of urinary incontinence during which small amounts of urine are leaked, often referred to as stress incontinence.

Women can also benefit from therapy to strengthen the muscles of the pelvic floor. Therapy and exercise are performed and taught by specially trained physical therapists. Women who have urinary incontinence or prolapses and for whom Kegel exercises are not effective might explore pelvic floor muscle therapy as an option

Pelvic floor muscle therapy is a specialized form of physical therapy in which the focus is strengthening the muscles of the pelvic floor (International Society of Sexual Medicine, 2020). These muscles function in bowel and bladder control and contribute to sexual arousal and orgasm. The therapy should only be practiced by therapists who have received specialized training. Pelvic floor muscle therapy is available to men and women.

---

20   This guide can be obtained here: https://www.mayoclinic.org/healthy-lifestyle/womens-health/in-depth/kegel-exercises/art-20045283.

Sexual Intimacy in Aging Lesbians

Of course, lesbian women have the same physical issues of decreasing lubrication, vaginal atrophy, and desire following stimulation instead of preceding it. Stimulation becomes more important and may take longer, but couples who wish to continue sexual intimacy will adjust accordingly. Depending on their intimacy preferences, they may seek the same remedies described above to regain vaginal flexibility, especially if seeking a new relationship.

As we learned from Janet in the last chapter, lesbians in long-term love relationships deal with their relationship as any other couple does. The stages are the same, the resolutions are as varied as couples are, and the outcomes are what is right for the couple.

Sexual Adjusting throughout Aging with a Long-Term Partner

Many of us have had and may be fortunate to still have a long-term partner. We have gone through many love life transitions, starting with first-stage romantic ecstasy, to marriage, to children, to being tired after work, to empty nests, to growing older. We know each other very well. I have the vantage point of a long marriage with a man 16 years my senior, so we arrived at old age twice in the past two decades.

Over the past 15 years, my husband and I have gone through sexual adjustment as he went from 75 to early 90s and I went from 60 to 75 years of age. It may have been a time when our age difference really worked for us. Although I am not sure either of us imagined that our parents had sex at the same ages we were, we easily overcame any tendency to give up sex.

I am among many women who have lovers whose satisfaction is tied to theirs. Touching and holding to mutually stimulate each other is an enjoyable part of intimacy between aging men and women, but it begins to take on a somewhat worried aspect when the results aren't as certain anymore. As we grow older, a man's erection and a women's lubrication are no longer as automatic. As we learned, those physical sensors that opened the doors are no longer functioning as well.

When my husband turned 80, he talked with his physician about Viagra and got his first prescriptions. Viagra was expensive but is much better entertainment than a movie with popcorn.[21] We were back!

Then, there was my aging. Two years later, I completely stopped hormone replacement therapy after my gynecologist presented me with the

---

21 The generic version of Viagra became more available during the past few years, which reduced the expense and increased access for men who could otherwise not afford it.

choice of hot flashes or a hysterectomy. The estrogen/progesterone re-placement apparently had been serving some purpose other than stopping hot flashes because I produced even less spontaneous vaginal lubrication for intercourse when I stopped. The friction of a penis on a dry vaginal wall is a real mood killer. It wasn't comfortable, and I began shopping for vaginal lubricant.

What I noticed in my search for over the counter lubricant is a myriad of products that not only lubricate but promise increased sexual pleasure for your male partner as well as yourself. Almost certainly, I think that most women do want their partner to have a great experience and are in-clined to want to add to it. Extra lubrication is inexpensive, easy to use, and a necessity for an aging woman. If the lubricant proves to enhance the man's experience, it's a wonderful bonus.

Difference with Viagra (Sildenafil)

Viagra has proven beneficial to many couples. The quality of sexual re-sponses increases. Gone is the nervousness that intimacy might not end in climax. There is the concern for women that men on Viagra will want more sexual intercourse than they would without the benefit of a pharmaceuti-cal aid. One of the interviewed women who talked about sex, who said that she is frankly concerned about Viagra, was worried because it could mean sex more often that would be more difficult and less intimate. Kalahar also had a few words for her male provider colleagues who prescribe Viagra for male patients without mentioning that their wives' vagina may not be as receptive as the husbands' expectations.

Viagra is short-acting so there is necessarily premeditation to have sex. If ads for some of the other drugs are true, they are long-acting, and he "is ready when she is." I believe that most men are concerned about the readi-ness of their partner. It seems to me that successful sexual intimacy has always been dependent on the mutual desire and readiness of each partner. My husband says that Viagra is a drug that doesn't deal with a partner's readiness so we keep date times. We gave up on spontaneity more than a decade ago. Just happening just didn't happen enough.

Sexual Adjusting with Short-Term Partners

Aging women who are choosing to have sexual intercourse with men without being in a long-term or committed relationship are likely to have intercourse with some older men who are taking short- or long-term drugs for erectile dysfunction. The women also are using lubricant for their own enjoyment. New lovers don't have the advantage of intimate knowledge of their partners, but they are both advantaged by the power of seduction and conquest. Our bodies haven't forgotten how to respond to the chemistry of infatuation.

What should help deal with any insecurity women feel about their aging bodies is that many men are turned on by them and their bodies, sags and all. Funny, how all those concerns disappear in the "moment!"

If we choose sexual partners in our old age, especially if we are starting late after a late divorce or death of a partner, we need to remember that the risks or consequences of sex while dating have increased. We may no longer fear pregnancy, but we must be wary of other things.

Aging Women and Sexually Transmitted Diseases

In February 2012, news media was abuzz over a recently released report from researchers at King's College, London, that stated that the rate of sexually transmitted diseases (STDs) among the middle-aged and elderly had doubled in the United States, Canada, and Britain over the past 10 years (von Simson, 2012).

The US Centers for Disease Control reports almost triple the reported cases of syphilis and chlamydia in the age group 46-65 over the same time period. The American Association of Retired Persons reported in 2017, that the STD infection rate of adults 45 years and older increased by 20 percent between 2015 and 2016 (Lilleston, 2017).

These studies and reports don't tell us the reason for the increase but do offer explanations, the most significant one being that more older people are engaging in sexual intercourse with someone other than a long-term partner. Online dating and erectile dysfunction drugs are increasing opportunities for older Americans. All the excitement of dating, anticipation, and sexual tension are born again in an age of technological and pharmaceutical advancement.

There was a time long ago we thought of condoms as mainly a way to prevent pregnancy. Today, the informed man or woman who engages in sexual intercourse with someone other than a long-term partner insists on the use of a condom. No one wants to get a disease along with all that excitement and adventure. We at our age are long past being a shy young woman about to embark on a first relationship. We have no excuse not to know better.

Kalahar says with concern that she treats older women who are having their first sexually transmitted infection. She says she knows that some will start the relationship with condoms and then inexplicably stop as if growing closer eliminates the possibility of catching something. She points out the same risks and consequences exist for women in new lesbian relationships.

Celebrate Being a Sexual Being

Older women can celebrate being sexual human beings secure in the knowledge that there is still opportunity and we are smart enough to protect our bodies from unwanted disease. We also have the words and experience to be more assertive about what we want from sexual intimacy. We have far less to worry about exposing the lives we live as lesbian women in part because our society is more accepting and less discriminatory and in part because we are older. All of us can look at romance with the wise eye of knowledge gained and life lived.

A reality for women who engage sexually with men is that as we age, there are more of us than there are of them. The odds for women attracted to women are better. We do know what to do when there is not a partner for us out there. As we age, we notice catalogs picturing a variety of anti-aging products and devices. Near the end of these catalogs appear 2-3 pages of devices made to look like and simulate a penis. The number of such products has increased over time, which is a healthy indicator for aging women and sexuality.

Romancing the Old Stone

Men and, in a few cases, women behaving badly has resulted in near zero tolerance of perceived or real flirting behavior. Rules of good behavior are in place that have rendered some people, mostly men, immobilized in speaking with someone of the opposite sex. Men can no longer compliment a woman on her appearance, and a woman can no long reach up to touch a new proud beard. It does take some of the fun out of it, but, as mentioned before, men and women as well as women and women find ways. All things considered, sexual attraction and games can be a lot of fun, which is why some older women miss it.

Not all older women miss the sexual tension or sexual games or youth. Not all had good experiences. Some had painful experiences, and some simply don't care at this point in their lives.

Women and couples together express their love in many ways. One size does not fit all. Let's not forget those couples who have chosen to forego sexual intercourse but continue to enjoy holding and touching each other.

There is no right or wrong way to enjoy each other as long as both are in on the decision.

What we know is that we older women don't have to give up intimacy and sex unless that's what we want. We just don't have the same level of hormones that ruled the romantic fantasies and passions of our younger years. Older women grow to be satisfied in the mirror of nostalgic reflection that some things will not be quite the same. Many of us intend to find out just how long the pleasure of sensual intimacy and sexual fulfillment lasts given opportunity.

Our sexual lives as women growing older are as varied, simple and complicated as we are and represent just one facet of our journey into old age. Next, we explore other challenges and opportunities around our lives as older women.

Bertha D. Cooper

Part Four
Aging Women Becoming
What They Are

Part Four concludes with those events and experiences that lead us to our deeper selves, especially as we contemplate purpose, the finality of major losses, and the finality of our lives. Necessarily, a spiritual search has ensued or is beginning that will likely bring reconciliation if not satisfaction in the finality of this one life or the future beyond this one to other states of being.

15

A Woman's Work (And Play) Is Never Done

"Every age has its beautiful moments"

—Albert Einstein (cited in Calaprice, 1996)

We are making our way through the journey of growing old, packing, unpacking, leaving some things along the path, picking up other things, the most being the growing sense of self in the newness of old age. We've quit fighting what has turned out to be a mirage of relevance. It's not that we give up purpose. We still must have a place, but it will be a place of our own.

It's one of those curious ironies of retirement that some of us don't seem to have enough time. Some of us may be just driven to fill empty space, but I believe it is more about necessity, purpose, and who we are. Women are used to being involved. Women will respond to their family in need. Women will respond to other families in need. Women will crusade for a cause, especially if it's good for children.

So, we wonder. What will fill our time? What is it we want to do? What must we do? What will our growing older years be like? Will it be what we expected? It's time to give ourselves permission to find our own space.

Time of Our Own in a Space of Our Own

We hope that we have the health, the means, and the opportunity to pursue whatever dream suits us about our life growing old. In other words, we hope we have choice and the luxury of contemplating what will fulfill us in these years. Many of us think of doing things we never have done before because we didn't have the time. Given the means, there is a myriad of activities from which to choose, depending on the communities in which we reside.

For some women, their older years are more of the same. They continue working, not necessarily because they need the money but more because they can't imagine life without their passion. More than one woman artist told me that she never would give up her art. Writers don't stop writing. Women continue working because they thrive on their work. One woman in my town operated her restaurant well into her 70s because she loved it and all those who came did so because they loved the food she prepared.

More of us are looking beyond our work or careers. Traveling and exploring land and cultures new to us is high on the list of many women. A fair number of women develop their competitive skills in sports like golf, triathlons, and chess. Others are dipping into their creative inclinations that were subordinated to working for a living and raising a family. Many women view retirement years as the time to give back through community volunteering, whether it is a food bank, a cause, a church, a political party, an organization of interest, or all the above. Women find they are busy and are surprised that they are not experiencing the retirement vision in which they are reading a good book by the fire on a rainy day or in the sun on the beach.

Volunteer work is nearly always undertaken by older women who are either no longer working or working a schedule that allows for volunteering. I am hard pressed to name a retired woman who is not active in some civic or charitable work. Older women are involved in considerable fundraising for health care institutions such as staffing volunteer hospital thrift shops or holding annual Christmas bazaars. Other women support local services by tutoring school children or serving on citizen patrols for the local police department. Food banks and clothes drives are year-around activities. These are quiet unsung workers giving every day in communities.

Many women expand their involvement in the religion of their choice. Many are the cogs that make the Saturday or Sunday or daily service possible through organizing the supplies, room, after-gathering, and, more recently, by being participants in the service.

Many women join or continue membership in service clubs such as Rotary, Lions, and Soroptimists. They organize, hold office, and do service work along with men who only recently have allowed women members into some of these clubs.

Many women choose to broaden their education. Some are attending college for the first time or returning to complete their education. Newspapers feature women in their 70s or 80s who are graduating, often on the same stage as a grandchild. Other women choose to go to classes in areas of study that interest them. I know several older women who are learning a new language.

A Different Kind of Creating

If a woman is able to decrease her work hours or retire completely, she often turns to long-desired artistic pursuits. Unless one is a writer that requires only pen, paper, and a computer, art can be expensive so a woman must have the needed resources. The setup for painting, print-making, and other crafts is a significant cost, including classes since most of us require instruction before we can even start.

Several of the women I spoke with already were fixed in the profession of art, meaning they made a living or a fair amount of money on their art. Others dabbled in found moments of leisure during their work and child-rearing years. Most were just beginning to discover their creative art. One woman related the experience of selling a piece of her art; she was flabbergasted that she didn't know the buyer and somewhat guilt-ridden about the price she put on the piece. Clearly, she wasn't in it for the money.

Another woman was rewarded early in her efforts and came to believe that she produced marketable art and began showing in galleries and exhibitions. It was only when she retired that she could put enough time into producing her craft for profit.

Most older women would-be artists are like the former woman in that they enjoy the experience of creating that seems to come from some newly discovered part of themselves. One artist has adopted a Zen-like attitude about her art; she gives each new piece away.

Other women join or form groups and gatherings around their art. They learn new techniques from each other and receive needed encouragement. Writing groups offer an opportunity to ready one's work and have it praised and critiqued by others whereas other groups are more for the experience of listening to the work of others.

Women are inherently creative; it's part of our very being. Creating visual or written art is a labor of love without the 20-plus-year commitment. We are creating our life as an older woman, a world is open to us if we have our health, the means to accommodate our desires, and are free of obligations that consume our time, resources and energy.

Not All Have Choice

Not all women growing old have the means to step into retirement or the means to satisfy their creative interests following retirement. We will continue to work because we don't have enough savings and Social Security is not enough. We may have family obligations that fill our time and use our resources, such as women taking care of grandchildren while their children work or because their own child has gone missing in some manner. Some have disabled adult children living at home and dependent upon them. Others have become caretakers of their partner and for others, their aging parent. These circumstances leave little time and energy for other pursuits.

Living within Our Means

We can expect to live years longer than our predecessors, requiring the making of financial provisions necessary for a long life. In many instances, women have not had the earning power to adequately save for their future old age. More than likely, our income is fixed, and we can't expect any more than cost-of-living increases to our Social Security or pensions. For some women, the sad reality is that women caught in this situation never will afford the choices available to many women because they don't have the means to support choices.

Women over 60 and facing limited income have lessons to share, most involving choices made earlier in their life. One woman shared a story of a woman whose marriage ended in divorce around the time she was turning 50. She received alimony for life as part of the settlement which worked until statistics caught up with her. Her former husband died, taking her alimony with him and leaving her with only a small Social Security benefit for the remainder of her life which could be as long as 30 more years.

Some women make clear-eyed choices to live on a limited income by choosing or switching to a career that offers little chance for savings. Going into ministerial work or preschool education are examples of career choices that are chronically low-paid careers. Women who depend on Social Security learn quickly that they will receive benefits based on the amount earned in their lifetime. Women more often than men receive lower monthly benefits.

The median annual income for a woman over 65 was $20,431 in 2018 compared to $34,267 for men (Pension Rights Center, 2020). Several factors explain the difference, one being the difference in lower wages or salary paid to women and another being the amount of time worked due to career choices and/or family timeouts. Both are significant factors in determining pension or Social Security benefits.

Social Security benefits are based on a person's earnings throughout 35 years of their working life. A person must have worked and paid into social security along with self and/or employer payroll taxes at least 40 quarters over the course of their working life to be eligible for social security benefits.

The maximum Social Security benefit in 2019 for a new retiree is $3,011 at full retirement age and $3,770 a month at age 70. To receive the maximum amount, recipients must have had income at or above the maximum taxable limit throughout their career ($132,900 in 2019) (Brandon 2019). Not many men or women will achieve the maximum amount, and those that do often are able to save and invest more for their retirement from a higher income.

According to a July 2019 Social Security Fact Sheet related to women:

- In 2017, the average annual Social Security income received by women 65 years and older was $14,353, compared to $18,041 for men.

- In 2017, for unmarried women—including widows—age 65 and older, Social Security comprised 45 percent of their total income. In contrast, Social Security benefits comprised only 32 percent of unmarried elderly men's income.

- In 2017, 48 percent of all elderly unmarried females receiving Social Security benefits relied on Social Security for 90 percent or more of their income.

The National Women's Law Center reports the 2018 poverty rate for women 65 and older was 11 percent, 3 percentage points higher than the poverty rate for men 65 and older (8 percent) (Fins 2019). The poverty rate for women 65 and older living alone was 18 percent, compared to 15 percent of men 65 land older living alone. Only one in 11 women in poverty are white/non-Hispanic; the remaining 91 percent are Black, Latino, Native American and Asian. Many more elderly women of all ethnic groups would be poor without Social Security benefits.

The statistics tell us the situation for some was not good in 2009. The deep economic recession of 2009 and following years worsened or brought more women into economic hardship since small savings were lost to increasing costs of daily living and dreams were lost to financially underwater houses valued below their buying price.[22]

Boom or bust

The seemingly unending upward trajectory that characterized the baby boomer generation ended with the economic downturn of 2008. The impact had long-term effects for some that still were being felt 10 years later. The deep recession resulted in a substantial number of boomers losing meaningful well-paid work. The retirement financial security of so-called late boomers born 1956-1965 was significantly threatened in that both net worth and lifetime earning capacity were reduced, given their age and fewer years left for productive work.

Some boomers, along with anyone else who bought a home at the top of the market, experienced a rapid deceleration of their home's value. Homes often are the fall back for retirement savings in that many couples plan to sell their home and downsize; the outsized decline in value took away a sizable equity for old age for those counting on the equity for retirement funds.

Fifty-year-old people faced the prospect of living off unemployment and eroding any retirement savings they had. Standards of living fell overnight, and many had to turn to aging parents for financial assistance, that is if their parents were alive and able to help. Losing income, investment savings, and home values was a triple whammy for many women, married or single.

PEW Charitable Trusts measured the financial loss that occurred from 2007-2010 for different generations: "War babies" like me, early boomers, and late boomers. War babies lost 20 percent of their net worth compared

---

22   2020 and we find ourselves in another world crisis, the COVID-19 pandemic that's required business slowdowns, in some cases shutdowns to slow the spread of the coronavirus. Unless a working women is in an essential occupation such as medical professionals and grocery clerks, she is depending on unemployment/ other government support to provide for needs and, once again, may need to dip into savings to see herself through the time of restriction. Retired women may fare better financially depending on their current ability to meet any additional expenses. A larger issue may be the isolation required of people 65 and over to stay safe from contacting COVID-19. (Cooper 2020)

to 28 percent by late boomers and 25 percent by early boomers. The loss was due to the plunging market effect on retirement savings and withdrawals taken to make up for lost employment income. High-paying jobs were lost, and many have not been replaced by the same. Many boomers continued to work past the usual retirement age (Fry, 2018).

PEW Charitable Trusts also measured the return to 2018 and found that Gen Xers (born 1961-1979) were the only ones to recover lost wealth. Some boomers recovered nicely and had enough savings to benefit from a subsequent rise in the market. Some boomers were not in the market to begin with and found themselves without retirement savings or pensions. Others lost some or all their pensions when companies reduced or dropped their pensions through bankruptcy negotiations (Fry, 2018).

Fortunately, our society has looked out for the elderly in the form of Social Security and Medicare. Most of us enjoy discounted rates for bus travel, fast food, and theater tickets among other things. Discounted senior housing is available in most communities. Those discounts help women with limited resources participate more than they otherwise would be able.

Somewhat ironically, given the number of women in poverty, women control more than 51 percent of the nation's wealth (Gorman, 2015). Some accumulation of wealth is explained by the fact that women live longer and are the ones who receive the inheritance of their less long-lived husband. Women are likely the ones who pass inheritance on to the next generation. Another reason is that women are becoming more economically independent. Women held 52 percent of management, professional, and related positions and owned 30 percent of businesses in 2015, a trend that is continuing (Gorman, 2015).

Actually, women inhabit both sides of the wealth gap. Most are in the middle somewhere. Yet, the fact remains that women also continued to earn 82 cents for every $1 earned by a man in 2018 (Institute for Women's Policy Research, n.d.).

Most of the women I interviewed were being impacted by the unanticipated 2009 economic downturn. The younger the woman I interviewed, the more concerned she was because the family income had taken direct hits from the recession and retirement funds were being used for today's needs. The older women were more settled but, since they also knew that future unexpected financial issues could easily surface, were cautious in their spending until some of the losses were recouped.

Still Being Mom

Women in all the interview age groupings found themselves more worried about their children's economic situation than their own. Some of their fixed resources were being sent to children. No one I talked with anticipated having to financially help adult children for the basic needs of survival instead of helping with the down payment on the first home. It seems that, just like in the past, the baby boomer generation was forging new territory in both being and parenting adult children.

"I never thought we would have to help our children once they were in their 40s (or 50s)," lamented one mother. "Most of us thought our children would do better than we did." Parents in their mid- to late 50s who held off having children until in their thirties were experiencing the return to the nest of young adult children who were unable to find employment that paid enough to allow them to afford a place of their own. Seven percent of children under 18 lived in households headed by a grandparent in 2009; the economic downturn moved adult children with their families into their parents' home (Goyer, 2010).

More grandmothers are raising grandchildren, not as part of one big extended family but on their own or with a grandfather. A variety of factors influences this trend. Adult children have become lost to addiction, crime, depression, divorce, death, and/or bad luck. Once again, and even while aging, the woman typically chooses children over financial security. The newly formed family unit, unless wealthy, takes a toll on retirement income and savings.

Some women knew shortly after the birth of their child that they would be caring for that child for the rest of their lives. We all greatly admire the extraordinary women and men who meet the challenge of having a disabled child nearly every day. It is our own relief that informs us of the challenge they face. One woman I interviewed said she came to terms early with that reality when she and her husband birthed a child with Down syndrome. They grieved as many parents do for their child's limited potential and how the course of their lives had changed. Yet, they loved their child and moved on to become advocates, not only for their child but also for other disabled children. They had another child and worked to balance the needs of an abled child with a disabled child. The mother still sighs when she tells of the medical or emotional crisis surrounding her disabled child, now an adult. She grows weary but is always present for her child. Now as she and her husband enter old age, their thoughts are the security and well-being of their child who cannot manage the future, which takes so much more than money.

These issues of children, health, poverty, income inequality, children safety, among many choices that affect our daily lives always will be women's issues regardless of age. So will advocacy.

Legacy of Wisdom from and for Generations of Women

Women continue to be active in public policies that affect women. There always will be a group of us, even while growing old, keeping a watchful eye on those decisions that affect the quality of women's, children's, and families' lives. Women are known to bring issues of humanity to public discourse.

Albert Einstein (cited in Calaprice, 1996) stated, "I believe that older people who have scarcely anything to lose ought to be willing to speak out on behalf of those who are young and who are subject to much greater restraint" (p. 191[23]).

However, not all women have an interest in political issues. I know many who avoid discussions around controversial issues. It's not that they are without opinions; they simply choose not to participate in the debates. We know that there can be costs in time, money, or relationships to those debates that require us to pay too high a price for some women. On the other hand, there are women who are out and about in their communities, running for school board, orchestrating a debate about public education, or otherwise participating in public life.

I belong to a loosely formed group of women between the ages of 40 and 75 who are making their voices known, if only to each other, in the unrelenting economic and social crises occurring in our country. We have been angry; we have been sad; we have become discouraged; we have cast blame; we have been made incredulous. But with all that, we have stayed true to a non-violent approach to these matters. We don't toss around sports and war metaphors. We don't talk about beloved grandchildren. We don't swear—much. We celebrate possibility.

Each of us seem to have our own cause related to public policy, but we all support each other in our interests. Mine is health. Another's is education. Another's is gay and lesbian rights. Another's is environmental issues. We are old enough to know we won't be personally affected by many of the issues. We are looking out for future generations who will suffer the

---

23   From a letter to Queen Elizabeth of Belgium, March 28, 1054, Einstein Archive 32-411

consequence of our failure to speak out and act. In this somewhat rarefied atmosphere of civic discourse, we find our voice and often our courage.

We all share in the understanding that women must continue their struggle to maintain gains and promote additional freedom and choice for women. We can view this moment as the moment women of age take their place in speaking wisdom to power. We have a stake in it for ourselves, but especially for our daughters and granddaughters. History tells us we can make a difference, and that difference can change lives for the better.

Many choose to join the local League of Women Voters which provides a nonpartisan platform for many issues and a front row seat through candidate forums to get to know our elected officials. Many women join the local political party of their choice to actively campaign for those candidates that represent the views they hold.

Not surprisingly, women don't share the same positions or passions about issues. Given the history of women's struggle for equality, most of us share understanding that women must continue their struggle to maintain gains and promote additional freedom and choice for women. We can view this moment as the moment women of age take their place in speaking wisdom to power. We have a stake in it if not for ourselves, but for our daughters, granddaughters and future generations of women. History tells us we can make a difference and that difference can change lives for the better.

Transformation of Our Vision of Aging

The strong sense that we, whether a neighborhood or country, have yet to see the magnitude and beauty of the lives of aging people prompted me to embark on writing this book. We are many and providing good examples of women's aging experience in later years, elucidating choices that let us live quality lives, regardless of the natural decline of aging. We may well transform general views and biases about aging women.

Aging in itself doesn't change the things that interest us but it does begin to limit what we do because by now we know we can't do it all. We may be limited by poor health, scarce resources, or family obligations. We may be limited by our declining energy, which tells us at some point it's time to stop hosting family Christmas or time to move to a smaller place with a smaller or no yard.

We hope we will be the woman who turns outside herself for connection and inside herself for prudent management of her most valuable resources: her body, mind, and, if you believe, her soul. We are the only ones who can stall our own growth.

As long as there is a day in front of us, we have some sort of work to do, not the least of which is learning the art of aging with grace and purpose. Part of that purpose is coming to terms with and growing through losses that matter.

Bertha D. Cooper

16

Losses That Matter

"Any natural, normal human being, when faced with any kind of loss, will go from shock all the way through acceptance."

—*Kubler-Ross (1969)*

We sat in the sunlight-filled café eating lunch, our tears spilling on our split order of Eggs Benedict. She, whom I am calling Mrs. Tango, was telling me the story of her husband's death in their home during the darkest part of night three months earlier. Both she and he knew that Mr. Tango was going to die, but they didn't know when. I listened intently as a friend who cared deeply about her sorrow while she relayed their story. I also listened as a woman who likely would lose her husband before she lost herself. We had much in common and I knew that I likely would live her experience as my own.

We both married older men after unsuccessful first marriages and celebrated marriages lasting well over 30 years. Neither of us had our own children, but we did have stepchildren. We had separate careers and interests from our husbands, but we both viewed our husbands as the person with whom we most wanted to be, whether we traveled or spent an evening at home. Our marriages were worlds of profound intimacy, without secrets and with many shared joys and hurts, whether from the past or a single day at work. The whole of us was never thought of without the other.

It was impossible to imagine days without the connected and intertwined activities, opinions, thoughts and being of each other or nights of sleeping in the safety of the presence of the other. We, as couples, are living organisms, so much so that when one dies, the organism suffers an irreparable loss. What remains goes into shock and is struck by the confusion of being alive and dying at the same time.

Loss of Self When Someone Dies

Husbands or partners die or leave in emotional trysts with others taking part of us with them. Children grow up through alternating love/hate relationships with their mother, then leave to their own homes, happy or not, taking part of us with them. Careers lost or left somehow take part of us with them.

"He was the wind in my sails and now I feel like I am a sailboat with no wind," says Mrs. Tango. Mr. Tango is so named for this writing because he spent the last year and a half of his life learning the tango. He became obsessed with the dance of romance and researched everything he could. They attended regular dance events devoted to tango.

Mr. Tango felt the "Tau of Tango" brought him a depth like nothing else at the end although, greater than even that, the tango expressed his deep love for his wife. He told her that he regretted that they stopped dancing during their lives together. He knew how much she loved to dance, and the tango obsession seemed to be his final gift to her. He and she had their last dance just two weeks before his death.

Mr. Tango died at home in their bed with Mrs. Tango by his side. His last words were to, for, and with her and, in the end, he sank into peace as if he had accomplished his goal. She sat with him for hours until daybreak. She could not let him be taken in the dark.

Such beauty, such importance, such a profound loss, and such a love lived for Mr. and Mrs. Tango. But now Mrs. Tango continues her work with a sense of missing not only her Mr. Tango but something important in herself. As Mrs. Tango said, "I know that a lot of my identity has come from my 'work self' but I was surprised by the loss of my 'wife' role. I think that my comfort and refuge from too much work focus happened through the steady loving place I had with (Mr. Tango). No matter how rocky or draining the jobs, I had a solid love to give me balance. I was the other half of a couple much longer and steadier than any career role I ever had. I can feel that loss, and my identity in 'job' now seems more out of balance. I have found new awareness of my identity and need for real balance that won't come by just working less. It is a daily learning process."

Mrs. Tango knows that the total loss is greater and more important than the loss of a single person; it is her way of life, her identity, her balance, and her future. She knows the answers must come without Mr. Tango and knows that she must grieve first.

There are greater and lesser losses. Those losses that take a part of us with them are the hardest and most enduring. They are the topic of this chapter. Loss of love and relationships are the poignant lessons of our lives. A hierarchy exists for each of us, and always near the top is the death of a loved one. The longer the relationship, the greater sense of loss for those of us who know that there isn't enough time left for us to establish the same intimacy of connection again. Earlier, I mentioned my dear friend who died suddenly and how that experience was my first realization that I never could achieve the same level of friendship with another. I wouldn't live long enough. That fact alone erased the opportunity for building relationships over decades as I had with this dear person.

New relationships and new roles are now set in the backdrop of our aging selves. Loss of close husbands, partners, or friends who have been organic parts of our daily lives seems the most life-altering and one we never would choose.

Loss of Self in Retirement

In other arenas of our lives, there are important changes that we choose to make and often fail to account for the accompanying important losses. Think of the woman moving into retirement after a long career that dominated her adult life even if she had children. She differs little from her male counterpart who retires. Both have a general sense of relief that they have accomplished a productive life and sense of anticipation that they no longer have the pressure of meeting the expectations of others.

When asked what they didn't miss about their younger years, the women I interviewed most commonly said they didn't miss having to be what they thought someone else wanted them to be. They didn't have to care as much what someone else thinks of them. They expressed powerful feelings of freedom brought on by an adequately funded retirement.

Yet, there is another side to retirement. Earlier, we talked about the thrust into our 60s that leave us stunned into thinking we have disappeared. There is no question that leaving our work lives behind, even by our own volition, takes a coliseum-sized chunk out of our identity although less in the eyes of others than our own idea of ourselves. I couldn't say the word retirement for two years, which could be excused because I continued to do some consulting. I could not think of what I was without working. My career was a large part of who I was: my mission, my cause, my contribution, and my value. Loss of career equaling loss of identity meant this was a loss that I had to manage. It was a loss I had to grieve just as I had the other major losses in my life. In all ways physical, emotional and mental, I was affected by leaving my career.

I fought the sense of loss with self-talk about my continuing expertise, skill, knowledge, and related experience. I stifled a sense of betrayal or being out of touch when others took my work in what I thought a misguided direction. I struggled to replace my validation with new skills which, much to my dismay, I realized I had to learn before I could even think about being good at it. I stepped in and out of community volunteer work being fearful that my time would be swallowed by meaningless activity.

I began to experience health problems that required attention. I developed an idiopathic condition I had never heard of called frozen shoulder and lost the substantial use of one arm. I often thought when I was working that I was too busy to get sick and now I wondered if that was indeed true. Choice and circumstance were driving me into a complete redefinition of myself. I started writing a book about aging.

One of the women I interviewed retired from a work life that lasted 55 years, the last being in a demanding small business that she owned and, for all practical purposes, was her. I asked to interview her about her retirement early on because I could not imagine that retirement would be easy for her. For the present and foreseeable future, Tracy has financially secured the future and stopped an exhausting pace of operating her business. Yet, for all her achievement and chance for rest after years of work, she is more adrift than secure.

"I feel stagnant," she lamented. "I feel a void. What am I going to do? The light went out! I was going to spend a lot of time gardening and I can't do it." She realizes she must condition her body that lost so much in the last years of her work.

"I was going to read more, but when I read, I feel guilty. I find no purpose in reading," she added. Tracy has no sense that she has reached a point in life that she deserves to relax and rest a bit. She cannot do so, not even for a short time. She says she still has a strong sense that she has more to do. It is too early to tell whether she is still in high gear from many years of hard work or still seeks purpose or both. My guess is a bit of both but mostly the second in that hitting 65 or 70 or retiring does not end a very human drive for meaning and purpose.

I asked her if having children and grandchildren was some compensation. She said no, that they always were part of her life although she thought she might be worrying about them more. She also said that having her children grow up and live their own lives was nowhere near as traumatic as retirement.

Tracy is flailing a bit just like I did. She is experiencing a major loss of self that will require attention and effort to regain and develop. There is every reason to believe that the things that made her successful in her work and family will get her through this.

She has her priorities straight, having lived through the accidental death of one of her grandchildren. "He is totally irreplaceable," she said. His was the unimaginable loss that mattered more than all the others.

The women most at peace with retirement were those who retired from a paying job that they did not see as a big part of their identity. They saw themselves more as something unrelated to their work, like an artist or grandmother. Their purpose was intact and would live beyond them in their legacies of interests and/or family. One woman is a learned astrologer and gives professional readings. Her career provided her livelihood, but 30 years in the study and practice of astrology is her identity. She describes her time now as being infused with an urgency to expand and delve deeper into cosmic knowledge. She says, "No matter what lies ahead, I am and will be an astrologer."

Some women went immediately into volunteer work that suited them and that, for some, became their identity. Some have or are developing a creative side so intrinsic as not to need the recognition of others or better said, not needing to sell it. Not all of us are so lucky to find that fit or have latent artistic talent. One of our tasks is to find our place.

Loss of a Retirement Dream

One of the lessons that came out of the interviews that I think the women would like shared with others is the importance of planning the time after retirement, to develop a greater view than reading good fiction or going out to lunch with friends. Many women envision the time after retirement when both they and their partners would do something together, travel being a frequently mentioned activity. Two women were taken by surprise when they discovered that their husbands had no such interest.

Their husbands' interests were to stay around the house, work in the yard, and do activities that didn't involve planes, trains, or other people. Both women realized that staying with their husbands and still enjoying the activities they want meant they had to find ways to do them without their husbands. One woman is set on finding a woman companion who travels, and the other is very active in the local Red Hat Society club.[24]

Retirement mismatches may or may not be avoided through planning and more communication, but at least communication would challenge our assumptions and help prepare us. We may even enter negotiation with our partners about our shared lives.

Retirement and losses associated with it cannot pass mention without recognizing the change in the role of a woman whose husband retires after years of work, comes home, and doesn't know what to do or the ever-interesting life change when the man who has organized work every day of his work life decides he can help his wife organize her work. In either case, it is head-banging time for the woman whose well-established role is being blown up for the sake of her man's failure to have a plan of his own. No doubt he is going through the same restless search that Tracy and I have, but it never occurred to me to take over the yard work or fix the plumbing.

One woman I interviewed got fed up enough with her husband acting like the CEO of the kitchen that she gave it to him. He has been fixing meals ever since and enjoying it. Women often will accommodate their husband's retirement wishes, especially if he has been the main wage earner. I know several cases in my community in which the husband and wife moved here, and the woman hated it. A friend told me of one situation in which the woman complained about living here at every opportunity. When her husband died, my friend saw the wife a week later, and the woman was smiling and happy. She said she was packing!

In all these cases, solutions likely mirrored the problem-solving of their lives, but none of them resulted in divorce. No one in these instances wanted to go through that important loss.

Loss of Physical Function and Loss of Control

Among our greatest fears is the fear of becoming disabled in a way that results in a loss of independence and control. Still, we know we lose a little or some of both and we must and do adjust. Earlier, I mentioned the remarkable 101-year-old woman who had by this age lost substantial hear-

---

24   The Red Hat Society is an international women's social society targeted to women approaching 50 and beyond. It maintains an Internet presence at https://www. redhatsociety.com/.

ing and substantial vision and was living in a world isolated from sound and sight. Yet, she had peaceful countenance. She was fortunate to have a caring family and a remarkable piece of equipment that allowed her to see words on paper. For her, it was a gradual decline, she successfully adjusted.

None of us know if we will be that fortunate. A discussion of losses that matter is not complete without talking about the permanent or threat of permanent loss of a vital function. If inevitable, we hope it is delayed and say, "the older, the better." Unfortunately, it doesn't always work that way. Such is the case of Melody who is faced with losing her eyesight long before her 100th birthday.

Melody, in her early 60s, still works and lives alone in a home she designed to accommodate her many interests. She has worn glasses to improve her sight since she was in elementary school. When I spoke with her, she recently had been told that she had Drusen disease, a condition of the eye or eyes in which deposits occur that block the retina and can cause the loss of central vision (Porter 2020) At the same time, she was diagnosed with macular degeneration of her left eye. Her eye doctor told her she "had the eyes of a 70-year-old" and eyes that would worsen over time.

Melody was faced with the prospect of losing her vision and anxiously contemplated life without sight or enough sight to do things she does now with ease. Everything else about her is healthy, something she strived to be so she could avoid developing chronic disease.

Now she had to contemplate a life without being able to drive. What would she do in a town so small that public transportation was limited? Even if it weren't, how would she get her easel, canvases, and paints on a bus? Would she be able to enjoy the nature that surrounded her home on the hill? How would she paint? How would she know the difference between purple and black?

Melody finds herself grappling with these questions for a moment, then returning to denial, much like we do in the phases of grieving. She never thought loss of vision would be her issue; it seems impossible to live without her sight. She is a strong resilient woman and will adjust, but at this moment she must just feel the loss that could happen soon or in years. She swings between resolve and despair.

Loss of a Love for and from a Pet

One woman's story prompted me to include the loss of a pet in "Losses that Matter." In responding to the question around significant changes in her life, she began by saying that she and her partner were taking more trips. Her eyes clouded, and she paused in her explanation. I waited. "Our kitty died two years ago." She reached over and softly ran her hand around an area next to her, "she used to lay here." The loss of "Kitty" was the reason they were able to travel more.

Her grief filled the room and seemed as profound as any I had heard or felt. She relayed the story of "Kitty" who died by being put down at 20 years of age. She told the story of "Kitty's" decline and the vigilance she and her partner provided as they cared for their beloved cat. The woman still wondered if they had done everything they could. I believe she never will stop missing and longing for "Kitty."

All of us who have lost a beloved pet know the grief felt over the loss of a pet that was an integral part of our lives, our security, and our identity. A 2011 article, fittingly called "Friends with Benefits: On the Positive Consequences of Pet Ownership" (McConnell et al., 2011), described pet value as measured in recent studies." These studies concluded that people with pets faced significant life stressors better, felt better about themselves, and were less affected by social rejection.

No one really needs a study to tell us the value of our pets; we feel it in our bones and in our grief when they are gone. It could happen during any time of our life, but it is an especially important loss as we age. Sometimes, pets are the closest caring relationship we have.

We also know that when we are old, we must carefully consider whether to get another pet because we may die before the pet does. Arrangements for our dependent companions must be made and included in our wills or last written wishes if we choose another pet. We also must consider whether we have the energy for or want to spend it on a puppy that is going to need walks and playtime. Overall, if we like them to begin with, pets give us purpose, comfort, and love without a lot of questions, and that's all they ask from us.

Unresolved Losses That Matter

Certain losses hold us back because we hang on to them like sticky paper. Most of these preoccupations fall into the category of emotional trauma from past events that we can't seem to do anything about now. They hang around much like the slacks we bought but never wear because they either don't fit or we don't like them. Yet, they stay in our closet because we are afraid of making mistakes or think someday, we will turn around our thinking or bodies so they work for us. The best hope is that somewhere during our lives we receive the counseling or caring that moves us through the difficulty and gives us a perspective that relegates the trauma to the past and truly ends our obsession, however warranted. Often, we don't do the work of resolving significant trauma while we are young, and so it shows up when we are reflecting in our later years.

I managed my own closet by compartmentalizing, a not uncommon method we humans use to keep going in the face of great problems. We are "too busy," and we seem to be doing OK. I was so good at compartmentalizing that I only rehearsed the trauma at night in the form of "night terrors," events that occur shortly after falling asleep and literally cause terror to a waking mind. Hearts pound, and it take a few minutes to come to full wakefulness and even more for the heart to slow. Experts have called this a symptom of Post-Traumatic Stress Disorder or PTSD.

I began to experience night terrors more often following the prolonged death of my brother from alcoholism. I knew then it was emotional baggage from our shared "messy" childhoods, now enhanced by his lingering painful death. I did not seek to resolve the terrible dreams until the balance of my life changed when I retired and the night terrors began to move into a compartment that no longer kept them at bay. I knew I had to have help to face whatever it was.

Strangely enough, when I focused on understanding, as suggested, I saw that the night terrors were a habit of past pain. I decided to seek treatment for a habit and arranged to consult with a certified hypnotherapist who helped me work within myself. I knew that only I could interrupt the habit and with the skillful guidance of the hypnotherapist it was not nearly as difficult as I thought it would be. I was compelled by the stronger desire to live well, as a wise old lady.

I heard from some of the women I interviewed the same desire to come to peace with difficult parts of their pasts. Several were very frank about the issues that confronted them and which they wanted to resolve. They did not compartmentalize. Many had done much better than I at confrontation and resolution.

A few women spoke of the death of a parent or sibling when they were children. These were unbearable losses. The loss of an important figure early in our lives leaves a void indescribable and incomprehensible to a child. If bereft of understanding, comfort, and explanation from a caring adult, the child is left only with imagination which is often a feeling of guilt or abandonment.

The wounded child takes up space in our lives until healed; most women understood this when they pointed to past pains and the significance of those pains in their lives to this day. One woman interviewed spoke of her lifelong struggle to overcome a shockingly evil childhood incomprehensible in its scope and the failure of the adults in her life. She has trouble even after years of counseling believing that anyone would believe her story. Now on the cusp of old age, she is courageously putting her childhood on paper with the intention of putting a face on child abuse victims.

A different woman spoke of being left afraid of physical intimacy after she was molested at the age of seven. She described her struggle with the consequences to her sense of self, which was only put to rest when she came at last to trust the love of her second husband.

Another woman easily spoke of being raised by a "narcissistic" mother and that influence on her sense of self and her life. She says she still carries feelings of low self-worth imprinted by her mother. She is a confident woman in a happy marriage and recently retired from an active professional life. She visits her parents regularly, sets limits, and can return home with the relationship and herself intact.

Reconciling the loss of identity, whether resulting from early life traumas like those described in the stories of these women or through loss of someone or something that took with it a piece of our very being, is a task of every age. It seems relentless and requires us to sharpen our insights to survive and use them when the old sense of shamed self comes up even as we are growing old. We may have less stamina for the work of navigating losses as we age but we are armed with experience and wisdom.

Navigating Losses That Matter

Interviewees each had their own way of navigating losses that matter. They made statements such as:

- "Loss becomes an aspect of who we are; I carry loss as a part of me.
- "Keep going. Put one foot in front of the other."
- "I am comforted by my God."
- "Loss is a natural process. I meditate."
- "I cry. I want to be alone."

We test or develop ways to meet the challenges of significant loss as we grow older. Our ability to adjust and manage will be mirrored by how we adjusted and managed in the past. Some of the women I interviewed who were in their 50s or early 60s said they didn't know how they handled important losses. They felt that they had yet to be tested. If my interviews are any indication, our ability to navigate losses increases with age, no doubt due to an increase in the number of significant losses we have, which should surprise no one. Most of us go on because we must. We grieve, and we adapt.

Prayer, meditation, contemplation, and time move most of us forward. We turn to family and friends who often share the loss. One woman memorably put it about the family gathering after the death of her mother, "I walked into the roomful of family—it was like walking into a hug."

Kiss the Joy As It Flies

As we grow older, we relentlessly learn about important losses, chosen or not. We learn what we must do to honor the losses that matter. We learn to honor our remaining time. We learn to spend our time in true love and friendship or spend it alone in true love and friendship with ourselves.

I live with my beloved aging husband, and each day as he loses something of himself, I lose something of him. His essence and his deep love for me remain. My deep love for him remains, and in many ways, it seems deeper and more profound if that is possible.

I have periodic meltdowns in which I cry in his comforting arms and tell him how much I worry about him. He tells me not to worry, that he is fine. He says in his most loving way that he will tell me when it is time to worry and then we will cry together. We both know that I worry about life without him. I can't imagine it except in the starkest terms of living alone in a smaller place and talking to empty spaces. He cannot be replaced any more than the nearly 50 years that we have spent together.

As we head toward old age, we live and learn challenges that take our breath away or leave us momentarily stumbling in place. Sometimes, we feel too weary to stretch, too tired to cope with one more life gone from ours. We open a set of eyes that begins to see more of what we can do and what we can be even if our eyes don't work as well. We become covetous of our remaining time and leave old baggage at the curbside.

Mostly, we do our best to stay in the moment and kiss the joy as it flies.

Bertha D. Cooper

17

Aging Women and Spirituality

"I believe that love is what we are really here to learn. It is likely the only thing we can take with us on the last journey."

—*Aging women survey*

We in America spend time, effort and money on denying aging and the finality of death. Americans may be the most proficient deniers. We live in a conglomerate of multiple religions, ethnic backgrounds, cultures, and economic status. We know too much—and we know too little. Despite all our pretenses and our best efforts to deny death or maybe because of them, we have taken on the search for meaning. Turning old brings into sharp focus questions about the meaning of our lives and meaning far greater than our single life.

Search for Meaning

The time has come to talk about death. Our death is the period at the end of the sentence of our life. Is death so close we think we can almost sense it? Since we can no longer escape the reality that we will die and leave this life, most of us want to leave feeling that our life had meaning. Or maybe it is that we want a greater meaning, a greater sense of belonging to a larger whole that sees our tiny contribution as a necessary part. This is not our first search for meaning, but it will be our final search, at least in this life.

We are very good at turning tragedies like premature deaths into meaning. We turn them into causes helping others, such as the creation of MADD, Mothers Against Drunk Drivers. Through the sorrow and anger at the senseless nature of their loss, women came together to become a loud voice in preventing and deterring more loss due to people who drank, got behind the wheel, and killed others with their automobiles. MADD created the legacy, meaning, and significance of the short lives of their dead children. The same is happening around mass shootings and the death of children at the end of an assault rifle as people gather to give meaning to these lost young lives.

Death is not a tragedy when one is old and it is expected. Yet, the same human instincts that give birth to creating causes from tragedy rise and send us searching for relevance in our lives and our deaths.

We examine our lives and what we will do next. We assess our successes, failures, contributions, and selfish leanings. As discussed in "What Happened to My Life" and "Losses that Matter," we process the past in order to find our place in a life now old. We think and decide about how we will use our remaining years. Folded into all our thinking is the sometimes cautious, sometimes bold confrontation with our death, including the practical and divine.

Exploration and Making Friends with Death

We are first practical. With small exception, the women I interviewed at all ages had made some plan for their death in that they had wills, living and material, and had told someone what they wanted done with their remains. When I asked if they had contemplated their own deaths, most responded that they hoped to die quickly and not suffer. Once again, they emphasized how much they did not want to be a burden to someone. The practical considerations of death were dealt with much easier than the spiritual questions, which were begging for answers.

It is not uncommon to turn more toward spiritual questions the older we get and the closer we get to death. The questions belong to us, not just philosophers and clerics. We begin to feel a greater inclination to sort through our answers because we realize that we have less remaining time for coming to terms with our death. Somewhat ironically, we find that we have more time for serious spiritual contemplation if we are so inclined. The resolution of our own death becomes an imperative and, typically, we have more opportunity to consider the resolution because we are not working or raising children. Also, we must.

Once I had the time, I found myself deep into spiritual exploration. Like many other women, spirituality always was part of my life. I had a spiritual experience in my 20s that greatly influenced me and set the tone for the rest of my life. It wasn't that I started wearing robes and wandering the desert. In fact, I continued to look normal and navigate through life's ups and downs. What I had that I didn't have before was a "knowing" of love and unity of being. I was totally surprised that someone like me would have such an experience. I told only one person the first five years following the experience and since then only a handful more mainly because, even to me, it all sounded a bit crazy.

I was raised in one of the Lutheran religions and became disillusioned soon after confirmation. The church didn't seem to like my family, which I later learned was because my father was a member of the Fraternal Order of Masons. I didn't think there would be much acceptance or help for me in putting the experience in perspective. I learned I was right when 20 years later I told a Lutheran pastor about my experience and he kindly told me that his humble experience of conversion, which occurred when he was mowing a lawn, was a much truer experience than mine. I kept the "knowing" but put any overt expression of it into hibernation. I knew the experience had made me much stronger.

Having the "knowing" didn't particularly help me when I reached my early 50s when the fact of my mortality dawned on me. Certainly, I thought about my death early in my life, but I always had the comfort of the many years stretched before me. Even then, I remember the anxiety the thought of infinity engendered. As I grew older, anxieties morphed into a yearning to resurface the bliss of the "knowing" experience. I also began to feel curiosity and confidence in exploring differing points of view.

I wanted to know what other women thought about death and how it fit into their spiritual lives. Did they have the same questions? Did they search? How did they develop spiritual fitness that worked for them? I included the question "How has your spiritual life changed, if at all, in the last (20) years of your life?" in the interviews. The question was deliberately general in order to elicit the participant's definition of spirituality, not mine. Most responses were contemplative and were fascinatingly diverse in perspective.

Several women cited experiences that led them to or away from a spiritual path as one of the three events or experiences that led them to what they are today.

Peace with or without Answers

I heard among the younger (ages 55-62) women a similar spiritual evolution occurring from middle to old age. In general, they expressed more anxiety in their questions about death than older participants, who by the time they reached 70 or beyond, were content either with the search for answers or the answers they had. The search became more serene and, if resolved, didn't necessarily end in a belief in God or afterlife.

One woman said she was struggling through a dry spiritual period brought on by a family circumstance that seemed to darken her spirit. Earlier in life, she had spiritual experiences that put her in touch with a deeper, positive way of knowing that now eluded her. She was not the only woman who experienced something unexplainable.

Through my interviews, reading, and explorations, I learned that many people have spiritual experiences that are unexplainable but nonetheless sustaining. Several of the women I interviewed mentioned the influence of an "other worldly experience" that informed them that something existed that was greater than the immediate world in which they lived.

One woman described a vivid dream when she was younger in which she talked with God. When she woke, she recalled the words and wrote as if she had no other option. The result was a profound message conveyed in beautiful poem.

One woman described an experience in which her uncle came to her in a dream, asking her forgiveness. She learned the next day that he had died during the night of her dream. Yet another described herself as a born-again Christian and stated emphatically that her spiritual peace resulted from strong faith in Jesus throughout her life and had little to do with aging.

One of the women I interviewed decided early in her life that she was agnostic and was very comfortable in her belief. She expressed herself serenely and went on to say that she believed in humans helping each other as if to say one doesn't need outside motivation to be a good person.

Still another woman backed away from religion when her son died of cancer in his 20s. "All religion felt like fantasy." Now over 25 years later and older, she says she is open to spirituality. Still another woman saw herself as leaning more toward Buddhism. She saw and felt spiritual meaning in nature, especially animals.

I came to confirm in my fashion what wiser women knew already; there is little homogeneity in spiritual direction of our lives, at least in terms of being identified with one religion or belief system among many. Few women mentioned the importance of their chosen religion, even those that belonged to a church. Religious affiliation no longer seems to be a coalescing factor in a country as diverse as America and communities in which there are at least one or two or more organizations for each religion.

Most of the women interviewed that held belief in something greater described themselves as spiritual rather than religious even if they had a strong religious affiliation. Those who attended church regularly were confident in their faith although most mentioned reservations about their church's expression of faith. They did not hesitate to express conflicts with the priorities of the church. One woman who is clearly devoted and practices her religion daily opined that she was frustrated with her church because it was "not progressive enough." Another thought her church was becoming too "political."

Even though we may be on different paths, most of us share the desire for spiritual meaning in our lives as we age and approach death. Selfishly, it may be the need to quell the fear of our own non-existence or to feel we have spent our time wisely, or if we haven't, to be forgiven if only by ourselves. For some of us, the search has been long, starting at an early age. For others, the question was asked and answered early in life, whether through strong religious faith and guidance, a spiritual experience, or some inner wisdom not possessed by most of us. Some women pursue the study of spirituality and life's meaning.

Hanna described her lifelong search for understanding as culminating in the study of esoteric philosophies that align one's life mission with the soul within rather than the personality. Esoteric philosophy believes in the evolution of life through many lifetimes over thousands of years. She is not propelled by fear or anxiety but rather, in her words, a quest for truth about her reason for being. Hers has become an unselfish endeavor driven by her desire to serve others in the way she was destined to serve. I gleaned in listening to her that this large complicated question will have a simple answer even if never revealed to us.

I learned from another woman I interviewed that yoga is more than positions and breathing; it is a way of living and a path to enlightenment. She shared with me the phases put forth in her yoga practice that describe different stages of life that coincide with the movement of the sun. They are the sunrise or youth of our lives that is developmental and the middle age of our lives that is stabilization. Fittingly to aging, she described the sunset of our lives as an emphasis on moving away from the external material world toward the interior of the mind and heart in preparation for death.

Prayer and meditation each were mentioned by more than one woman. Each involves solitary contemplation between the doer and her God or spirit by whatever label provides her the most connection. As silent as each is, it can be done any place at any time.

Have you ever contemplated your own death?

This is a question I asked of interviewees. Their answers were easily grouped by age.

Interviewees ages 55-59 stated such things as:

- "I do not want to suffer."
- "I hope to die before my husband dies."
- "I worry more about it. I want to go fast."
- "I am preoccupied with death. It could happen because I am old enough." "I am afraid of (the) process (of dying)."

Interviewees ages 60-64 stated such things as:

- "I hope I would go quickly; I am not afraid of (death)."
- "It struck me that a dying person is still something alive."
- "Yes, my life was threatened when I was a child."
- "What does death mean—still coming to an idea."

Interviewees ages 65-69 stated such things as:

- "People should be able take control of own death if warranted and person wants to. Take self out of suffering."
- "Yes, I am designing my own funeral service. I want (my death) to be a conscious process."
- "I have thought more about widowhood than my own death. I hope (my death) is not prolonged; I don't want to be a burden. I don't fear death."

- "Yes, I do not want to die as long as I have relatively good mind and health."

- "Not a lot."

Interviewees ages 70-78 stated such things as:

- "So abstract."

- "I don't want to die first."

- "I think I will die and life will go on without me."

- "Sometimes I'm frightened. I wonder if people will miss me or I will be forgotten."

"I'm fine; I know where I am going," were words spoken by the father of two sisters I interviewed. I interviewed them separately and both responded to the question "Have you ever contemplated your own death?" with the same answer. They described the gathering that occurred around their father before and when he died. He asked for family, and he asked for food for everyone. He was cheerful and confident, putting everyone at ease. He talked freely about leaving them and this life. He left these two daughters and the other family members in the room a beautiful memory and a legacy of no longer fearing death.

Touching Beauty of Our Search

The search is teaching me that spirituality is more than knowing or fearing our deaths and ascribing meaning to our lives; it is about how we live our lives. At the core of religious teachings, Eastern or Western, and New Age teachings are compassion, understanding, tolerance of failings, charity, service and, among many other attributes, relief of suffering.

I still am on the spiritual search. For me, the search is as meaningful as any answer I will reach, if any. I have concluded that with or without revelatory experience, the spiritual road we take is our road full of detours, freeways, and destinations. The common thread is all that I have learned so far is love. It is no longer servicing our pride, ego, personality, and image at the expense of the desire or capacity to fully engage with someone else, to appreciate and to love if they are not busy servicing their own pride, ego, personality, and image, which renders them incapable of accepting love.

Most spiritual teachers tell us to let go of these images of ourselves, get out of ourselves, and see, really see, what is around in the moment. Most tell us to be of service to ideas or causes greater than ourselves. When we are young, we are not formed enough to really know what that means although youth is often a time of causes. When we are old, we learn the meaning unless our path led us into places of pain, suffering, and bitterness so much that we are not ready.

We know these latter people. They are unhappy and complaining. They only think of themselves. They are the ones my sample unanimously said had not, did not, and would not age successfully. We wish we knew more about how to help them, more than intending not to be one of them.

The experience of the two sisters who received the gift of peaceful dying and death from their father should remind us that we, too, leave a legacy to those who witness our death. My own mother died a fearful death when I was in my 30s. Her death followed a long decline into disability. I was filled with sorrow for her and for me in that I would carry her grief as well as mine for a long time.

Should anyone be around at the time of my death, I want them to know peace from me and for them. Most of us do. We don't want to be a burden after life, either. If no one witnesses my death, I want to leave the legacy of living in peace at the end of my life. I hope I do it; I hope you do it, too. To do so is a sublime gift that truly keeps on giving.

Some searches led to belief in reincarnation and many lives lived before and to be lived after this one. I find the idea of reincarnation curious and exciting; it's also comforting. I often have wanted to have experiences that I knew just weren't possible to have in the one life I had.

For now, this is the only life I know, and I intend to make the most of it. Our life and this moment won't come again, whether we move on to another life or the energy of being takes a place among stars. This life won't happen again. Neither will this old age come again.

After all, we're only old once.

We are coming of old age.

18

Coming of Old Age

"Be the change you wish to see in the world."

—*Mahatma Gandhi*

An Old Lady's Sweater

I picked the sweater out with careful attention to detail. It had to open in the front, reach nearly to my knees, have long sleeves, and fit slightly large so that at any moment I could wrap it around me like a security blanket. The color had to be subtle enough to blend into the background, taking me with it. Most important, it had to be on sale!

Then, eleven years ago I saw it in a spring catalog sent out to sell off winter inventory. Perfect in every way, it was indeed my old lady's sweater. I eagerly ordered it, and the sweater arrived to take its honored space in our closet. I easily could imagine wearing it for the next 20 or so years as it and I age in place. It would end as I, worn and raggedy but always comfortable in our own being.

My sweater may be one of the few opportunities for certainty of feeling cared for in my old age. I know enough about aging through my work in health care and my own experience to know that certain things are inevitable, like I am going to feel cold when others are warm.

When I bought my sweater and shortly thereafter started my book, I was entering what I call the young of old age. Now I leave it to be just old, but with a bit of time before I reach the old of old age.

I have reached the point of confidence in my understanding of aging, enough to bring this book to women yearning to understand what's happening to them as they age and what the future holds. I've learned that women want to know how to treat aging as a natural phase of life in a culture that continues to deny aging.

So, here I am with a book I believe in and offer for all the women like the women I interviewed who are ready to use their wisdom to move into a quality life of old age.

We all reach for something certain at a time when so much is uncertain. Still, we learn to live with the certainty of accelerated impermanence. We learn too often about loss, and we wonder or wander in our thoughts about our life now, our relevance, and our death. It helps to remember that we are in yet another phase of life, one we only will see once, like being a child or being a teenager. The only difference is that this phase is followed by no other. Our lives will end, and the planet will move on without us.

Embracing Growing Old

I am 77 years now. I have arrived at being old. I don't know what and when an illness or infirmity will strike me but I am not going to wait around for it to happen any more than I waited for it when I was 20, 30, or 50 years old. I will do my best to control what I can to avoid the pathologies of aging while doing my best to embrace the natural process of aging.

Being old is different. I happen to like different. Being old is change. I like change. Right now, I wouldn't have it any other way.

There are days when I lament the loss of endurance, flexibility, and consistent ability to retrieve words still in my brain. I always grieve the loss of people in my life, whether through moving, failed friendships, dementia, or death. Then, I am fine and adjusting to yet another change. All the while, I am alive and in love with my life and my old lady's sweater.

Being old isn't easy but neither was being a teenager or the first day of a new job. Somehow, I, although not good, am better at aging than I was at those other things probably because I have learned that everything is impermanent and not to get overly excited about any one thing. We are many. We are coming of old age.

When I started writing this book I was apprehensive and curious. I felt driven to understand and put words to the human importance of this phase of life and value of all us who will and have lived it. I felt compelled to confront our fears and our prejudice. The writing became the teacher of discipline and focus, the mentor that guided me to questions and answers.

I was and still am bothered that our society denies and fears aging and is unable to find a place of honor for those who have made their contribution and continue to do more if able. Of late, more seem to feel that the so-called elderly are a drain on society, a cost not balanced by prior contributions or wisdom gained. Since women live longer and old women are encouraged to look young, aging women suffer more under the weight of society's dishonor.

We who worked for women's rights to equal pay, equal job opportunity, and access to birth control are horrified that these hard-won things still are not institutionalized in our country or culture. Dishonor of women and their value as human beings still is threaded through the daily lives of all women. It is a hard reality for many of us. The collective shame is something we will carry to our graves or to the wind.

Now, we must come to terms with the irony that not all things are impermanent as much as we want, at least not in our lifetime. Still, we participated in moving women's place into the light when younger and now, we will do the same for aging.

I knew when I started my journey into aging I was not alone in my desire to understand this part of my life as much as I understood the years before now. The women I interviewed and talked with over four years were willing cohorts. I discovered varying levels of curiosity, comfort, and anxiety. They and I are as unique as autumn leaves with some things in common and some not. We share a common interest in elevating the view of growing old in the minds of our culture that seeks to deny aging and shun wrinkled faces. We share a common interest in aging with health and wisdom. We wish to die without being a burden.

I met many wonderful women who inhabit this book. I have selected two for this final chapter because they are now nearing 90 years of age and are good examples of women who embrace their old age. They walk the path of natural aging and are the beauty of aging. They are my heroines.

Small and Mighty, Ginny Embraces Life and Death

"I look 10 years younger than I am. My friends said I was 78 going on 68," Ginny said with a mix of modesty and pride. Indeed, this petite woman appeared engaged and strong both physically and mentally. I hadn't intended to interview anyone over 75, but when two of the women I interviewed independently insisted on it, I couldn't resist meeting this woman.

When Ginny welcomed me into her immaculate but comfortable home, she treated me with much more deference than I deserved. Turned out she thought I already had written my book, an impression I quickly corrected, and she and I both relaxed. Her husband was home at the time and came to meet me. It was easy to feel the love and comfort this couple felt for each other in their 59th year of marriage. He, too, looked fit and 10 years younger than his 81 years.

The reason the two women thought Ginny should be interviewed for the book became apparent early in the interview. Here was a determined, intelligent, engaged, reflective, and disciplined woman. She walked with strength and purpose. She talked modestly about herself, being careful to be completely honest. She also had a certain beauty of presence seemingly totally without pretense or guile.

As our interview progressed, I began to see her as a woman who was committed to her truth. Several times, she expressed sorrow that she was not a better person in certain situations. She derived considerable strength from her religion and sought counsel through attending daily services. Still, she wondered about her own value and if she had done and was doing enough.

She describes herself, the second of ten children, as a farmer's daughter. She wanted to go to college but didn't when she knew the cost would create hardship for her family. She regrets not having a "title," something that would have given her credibility if only for her own sense of value. Instead, she went into retail and learned that she indeed had a gift of giving to others a reflection of their own self-worth.

Ginny demonstrated remarkably strong discipline in habits that support good health, and she was evidence that it was worth the effort. She exercised for strength and endurance at the community gym three times a week and walked with friends the other days. She is careful about what she eats. Her only medication is for cholesterol management. She describes her health as excellent.

Ginny, like many older women, is active in volunteer work in her community. She is part of a group that welcomes newcomers to the area. Her fondest activity is giving her gift of support and dignity to those under hospice care.

Ginny is not without strong opinions and the voice to express them. As devoted as she is to her church, she says she hasn't found her niche. She wishes for a more progressive faith environment.

Commenting on women who try to look younger, she says, "Women who try to look younger don't have a good self-image to begin with."

Ginny says she is the more emotional one in her marriage, which seems just fine with her husband. She describes him as the most important person or thing in her life that made her what she is. The next time we talked, this important man was gone from her life.

We met again close to the one-year anniversary of his death. Ginny's husband developed a serious condition and died from it within six months of the diagnosis. I wondered how she would cope. Characteristically, she wondered if she should feel more or differently than she did. She readily reached out for pastoral and professional counseling and her family to help her through her grieving process. I told her I didn't think she needed to worry because their feelings for each other were alive in the room with us. She dabbed a tear and said she felt his presence in many places.

Ginny lives one of those lives that will never see great public recognition however deserved. She demonstrates all the attributes of one who lives responsibly, fully, graciously and in touch with the worth of others. She was and is not afraid to need. She is as authentic as one can be. She is the true beauty of aging and my heroine.

Planning Ahead, Caroline Lives in the Moment

I never interviewed Caroline for this book; at least not until this final chapter. I observed her from afar and with great admiration. Someone said she was near 80 which I just didn't believe. It was less how she looked, although she presented quite well, than how and what she thought and talked about. In fact, I was somewhat careful to keep my distance because I knew it would be difficult for me to say no to her. She is a natural at the art of persuasion.

I wasn't alone in that thinking. I learned that Caroline had inspired many women to become involved in issues of our day, particularly those around human rights and equal access to services. Despite my inclination to stay out of her field of vision, she kept track of me, which was both a source of delight and trepidation for me. When I at last came to the completion of this book, I dared to risk the encounter and asked if I could interview her.

Caroline is reluctant to talk about herself but agreed to help me in completing my book. Over the phone as in person, she exudes kindness, wisdom, competence, and confidence. She truly is a person whom one wants to be around.

She moved from our area several years ago when she finally got tired of ferry trips and driving home in dark rainy nights at one in the morning. She was about 77 years old at the time.

Caroline is a woman fully engaged in life. She enjoys the symphony, opera, plays and concerts and has every intention of participating in the arts as long as possible. Arts aren't her only interest. She is fully involved in the activities of the retirement community to which she moved. In fact, she chose this particular community because it was bustling with activities that she enjoyed and located so that she could walk to nearly all the events she liked.

Caroline's innate persuasive manner and charm quickly placed her in positions of leadership in her community. She was instrumental in the development of a program to involve active residents in bringing the more disabled residents into programs. Now she is part of the resident governance. She has a prominent role in a political action group intended to pass legislation that will increase access to affordable health care in our state.

"Busy, yes," she says, and she looks forward to every day and every minute of it. When she wakes in the morning, she begins her list for fully living the day.

"What is it," I asked her. "Where does this spirit and dedication come from?"

Caroline was the fourth daughter out of five and had one brother. The third daughter was born with cerebral palsy and has required help throughout her life. Caroline explains her penchant for "fixing things" to the sense of responsibility she felt for her older sister. Caroline related an incident that occurred when she was about five years old that she believes put her in touch with appreciating what she had and the desire to make things better. That day she grew impatient with her sister who required a walking device and told her to get out of it. The sister did and fell down, and their mother was very annoyed with Caroline.

Caroline credits her relationship with her sister as influencing her world view in a positive and productive way. She became a nurse and practiced until she moved with her husband to a foreign country in order to save her marriage.

Not only did she save her marriage, she learned that she liked adventures and meeting new friends. Like many of the women I interviewed for this book, she broadened her life view through living in another culture and acquired the sense of confidence that she could live just about anywhere.

Everything about Caroline seems relaxed. She walks every day and eats the right foods to nourish her body. She has no diagnosed health issues. She takes care of herself and seeks medical attention if she needs it, like the time she broke her arm when she slipped on the ice. Much to my surprise she said she refuses preventative tests such as colonoscopies and mammograms. She reasons that she doesn't want to go through the "stuff" to stay alive. "I'm not concerned about the future," she says with her brand of calm and sincerity.

"I don't want to be resuscitated. I've had a good life and would prefer to just die without intervention," Caroline says. Upon reflection and following my comment on people wanting to die in their sleep, she added, "I would like to have a short illness so I could say goodbye to my close friends and family." Her love for people and her joy in life would be her final words if she has her way. She is the true beauty of aging and my heroine.

Final Thoughts

My heroines are examples of living well into their 70s, and I would not be surprised if I found the same if I had the honor of interviewing them again a decade from now.[25] They represent much of what is in this book. They are examples of women who have chosen wisely on their aging path. We see bits of ourselves in their stories.

---

25   I caught up with Ginny and Caroline the summer of 2020:
Ginny is now 89 years old and sounds every bit like the Ginny I interviewed ten years ago and again eight years ago following the death of her husband. In the interim, she developed one health condition which is fully under control. The pandemic has meant she cannot have visits from family and also put a crimp in her usual active self but she continues long walks on her own. Her understanding and determination prevail. She describes losing relationships as people die and groups dissolve as "losing things bit by bit." She continues to seek replacement for her own wellbeing and to do meaningful volunteer work.
Caroline is now 87 years old and continues being who she is and making the most of life. She shared her thoughts on the pandemic and aging. "The pandemic is another version of life I didn›t expect but I have my books, telephone, internet, family, and friends. What more does an 87-year-old desire? Well, how about an interesting 87-year-old guy? I am lucky because I tend to enjoy what I have instead of missing what I don›t have."

We are all heroines of our own life. Today we are the result of everything we've been, done, and chosen. Growing old doesn't end us and what more we will and can become. As a refresher, I follow *Women, We're Only Old Once!* with notes for quick study or long contemplation.

I end the last chapter with something I wrote over eleven years ago at the beginning of this journey. At the time, I seemed to write from a deep sense of joy at the very act of being old, more a poetic sense than anything I really knew. It is about the old woman whom we cannot help but love.

- She has a deep love of young children and animals and is often seen feeding the birds in winter.

- She laughs with great energy and has knowing eyes, sometimes sad, that view life around her with hard-won patience and wisdom.

- Her face is lined, and her hands are worn from a life lived. Her body softens as if it knows she no longer needs to battle for primacy.

- She daily expresses her gratitude for her friends and family who cherish her and hopes she will be able and there for them as long as she can.

- She is apprehensive born from fear for others when cultures and countries seem to be on the wrong path.

- Still, she relaxes on thoughts, reflection and memories and the ability to be lost in all of them.

- She has reconciled her place, her meaning, her spirituality, her very being. She will be all that she is, using all her energy until there is none.

We women are complicated beings in the expression of ourselves and what we do throughout our lives, but in essence we are profoundly caring for others. We who can tap into our love for others are the most fortunate and have responsibility to serve others with what talent and skill we have been given.

As years slip by, life becomes more about quality than quantity. We give in moments instead of years and do the best when we are true to ourselves, the best when we accept and walk the path of aging, the best when we are the expression of the beauty of aging.

Let us choose wisely. This is the only old age we will have.

Notes for Quick Study or Contemplation

Aging Attitude Adjustment

- Aging is not a disease.
- Anti-aging is a business, not an option.
- A positive, engaged attitude is beautiful.
- People engaged in life with a passion and commitment for something or for other people, or both, age the most successfully.
- Chronic disease is not inevitable in old age.
- Death is inevitable, but healthy choices significantly improve the quality of life as we grow into old age.
- Energy and endurance naturally decline; we must choose how to expend what we have.
- We are in control: we pick our stresses, and we pick our joys.
- Use it, or lose it.
- It's never too late!

Navigating the Transition to Old Age

- Work through denial.
- Understand growing old is another transition to a new phase of life.
- Realize the rate of change and awareness of impermanence accelerates in aging.
- Put our life until now in order and acquire perspective on what we have become.
- Envision the possibilities; realize what we must do and can do.
- Grieve for the losses, and move on to the joys.
- Complete wills and lists for legacy, health care decisions, and remains early so it's done.

Chose a Life Well Lived

- Learn and listen to what is happening to your body.
- Learn what is natural and what is not.
- Learn what choices result in prevention of disease and dysfunction.
- Move and strengthen our body for safety, health and presence.
- Nourish our bodies with the foods important to a healthy old age.
- Maintain a healthy weight as a tool to prevent disease and dysfunction.
- Conserve our energy for what we must do and want to do; pick our stresses.
- Follow recommended guidelines for preventative screening and see a health care professional on a regular basis.
- Seek professional advice from a health care provider for all unexplained symptoms and when taking on new physical activities that stress the body.

- Seek support from friends, counselors, and groups for our endeavors; the chance for success improves with support and decreases for those who chose to "go it alone".

Managing Life As an Older Woman

- Choose what is and isn't important to us in presentation.
- Keep and chose relationships with care.
- Old and new love relationships go on if it matters.
- Dating is not dead, and sex is not over.
- Many of us are still mothers.
- Many of us have become caretakers of grandchildren, aging parents, or an infirm partner.
- Many of us live on limited means.
- Many of us continue to advocate for causes that concern women and families.

Coming of Age and the Meaning of Us

- We are only old once and should live this final phase with all the wisdom gained and remaining energy we have.
- Losses of self, identity, and purpose are the most challenging to work through.
- We search for the meaning of our place in time and mostly find peace and resolution.
- We can bring in a new age for aging women in America.
- We are role models for generations of women to follow.
- Kiss the joy as it flies!

Bertha D. Cooper

References

Administration on Aging. (2016). *A profile of older Americans: 2016.*

Allen, L., (2008, February 1). How common is vitamin B-12 deficiency? *The American Journal of Clinical Nutrition* 89(2): 693S–696S.

Alzheimer's Association. (2018). *Alzheimer's disease facts and figures.* p17.

Arnold, C. (2013, August/September). Eating disorders and women over 50. *AARP The Magazine.* Retrieved 07/15/20 from https://www.aarp.org/health/conditions-treatments/info-08-2013/midlife-eating-disorders.html.

Barbour, K. Helmick, C. Boring, M., & Brady, T. (2017, March 10). Vital signs: prevalence of doctor-diagnosed arthritis and arthritis-attributable activity limitation—United States, 2013–2015. *Morbidity and Mortality Weekly Report*: 66(9);246–253.

Bortz, W. (1982, September 10). Disuse and aging. *JAMA* 248(10):1203-1208.

Burns E., & Kakara R. (2011, May 11). *Deaths from Falls Among Adults Aged ≥65 Years—United States, 2007–2016. Morbidity and Mortality Weekly Report* 67(18): 509-514.

Brandon, E. (2018, August 5). What Is the maximum possible Social Security benefit in 2019? *US News and World* Report. Retrieved 7/02/20 from https://money.usnews.com/money/retirement/social-security/articles/what-is-the-maximum-possible-social-security-benefit

Brown, S.L., & Lin, I.-F. (2012). The gray divorce revolution: Rising divorce among middle-aged and older adults, 1990–2010. *Journals of Gerontology* Series B: Psychological Sciences and Social Sciences 67(6): 731–741.

Calaprice, A. (1996) *The Quotable Einstein.* Princeton, NJ: Princeton University Press.

Center for Disease Control and Prevention. (2020). *National diabetes statistics report.* Retrieved 7/30/20 from https://www.cdc.gov/diabetes/pdfs/data/statistics/national-diabetes-statistics-report.pdf

Center for Disease Control and Prevention. (2020). *Important facts about falls.* Retrieved 7/23/20 from https://www.cdc.gov/HomeandRecreationalSafety/Falls/adultfalls.html

Center for Disease Control and Prevention. (2013, July 19). *State-specific healthy life expectancy at age 65 years — United States, 2007–2009.* Morbidity and Mortality Weekly Report 62(28): 561-566 Retrieved 07/09/20 from https://www.cdc.gov/mmwr/preview/mmwrhtml/mm6228a1.htm?s_cid=mm6228a1_w#fig3

Center for Disease Control and Prevention. (2011) *Falls among older adults: an overview.* Retrieved from the Internet 2/21/11 (no long available online)

Center for Disease Control and Prevention. (2008). *Percent of US adults 55 and over with chronic conditions.* Retrieved 7/26/20 from https://www.cdc.gov/nchs/health_policy/adult_chronic_conditions.htm\

Cooper, B. D. (2020). *Old and on hold.* Hollister, CA: MSI Press.

Crane, B. (2011, June 27). Pickles [comic strip]. *The Seattle Times.*

DeBey, S. (2011, July 20). Issues of Faith. *Peninsula Daily News.*

Eich, J.M. (1980) The cue-dependent nature of state-dependent retrieval. *Memory & Cognition* 8: 157-173.

Elin, A. (2015, October 31). After full lives together, more older couples are divorcing. *New York Times:* B4.

Epigee Women's Health. (2020). *Menopause and weight gain.* Retrieved 07/13/20 from http://www.epigee.org/menopause/weight_gain.html

Erickson, E. (1993). *Childhood and Society.* New York: W. Norton & Company.

Felitti, J., Anda, R., Nordenberg, D., Williamson, D., Spitz, A., Edwards, V., Koss, M., & Marks, J. (1998, May 1). Relationship of childhood abuse and household dysfunction to many of the leading causes of death in adults, the adverse childhood experiences (ACE) study. *American Journal of Preventative Medicine* 14 (4): 245-258.

Fins, A. (*2019*). *National snapshot: poverty among women & families fact sheet.* National Women's Law Center. Retrieved 7/2/20 from https://nwlcciw49tixgw5lbab.stackpathdns.com/wpcontent/uploads/2019/10/PovertySnapshot2019-1.pdf

Fogoros, R. (2018). *Reflux disease (GERD).* Very Well Health. Retrieved 7/29/20 from https://www.verywellhealth.com/gastroesophageal-reflux-disease-overview-4013146

Fry, R. (2018). *Gen X rebounds as the only generation to recover the wealth lost after the housing crash.* PEW Research Center Fact Tank. Retrieved 7/16/20 from http://www.pewresearch.org/fact-tank/2018/07/23/gen-x-rebounds-as-the-only-generation-to-recover-the-wealth-lost-after-the-housing-crash/

Gagne, D. A., Von Holle, A., Brownley, K. A., Runfola, C. D., Hofmeier, S., Branch, K. E., & Bulik, C. M. (2012). Eating disorder symptoms and weight and shape concerns in a large web⊠based convenience sample of women ages 50 and above: results of the gender and body image (GABI) study. *International Journal of Eating Disorders* 45(7): 832-844.

Gambert, S., & Pinkstaff, S. (2006.) Emerging epidemic: diabetes in older adults: demography, economic impact and pathophysiology. *Diabetes Spectrum* 19(4).

Gawande, A. (2007, April 30). Annals of medicine: The way we age now. *The New Yorker 2007*: 2.

Giorgi, A. (2016). *Presbyopia*. Healthline, Retrieved 3/20/20 from https://www. healthline.com/health/presbyopia

Gorman, R. (2015, April 7). Women now control more than half of US personal wealth, which will only increase in years to come. *Business Insider*. Retrieved 7/16/20 from https://www.businessinsider.com/women-now-control-more-than-half-of-us-personal-wealth-2015-4

Goyer, A. (2010, December 20). More grandparents raising grandkids. *AARP Real Possibilities*. Retrieved 7/16/20 from https://www.aarp.org/ relationships/grandparenting/info-12-2010/more_grandparents_raising_grandchildren.html

Hayflick, L. (1994/1996). *How and why we age*. New York: Ballantine.

Hayes, K. (February 12, 2018). *How much protein do you need after 50*? Healthy Living, AARP. Retrieved 3/18/20 from https://www.aarp.org/health/healthy-living/info-2018/protein-needs-fd.html

Heron, M. (2019, June 24). Deaths: leading causes for 2017. *National Vital Statistics Report* 68 (6): 1-77.

Institute for Women's Policy Research. (n.d.). Pay equity & discrimination. Retrieved 7/16/20 from https://iwpr.org/issue/employment-education-economic-change/pay-equity-discrimination/

International Society of Sexual Medicine. (n.d.). What is pelvic floor physical therapy? Retrieved July1, 2020 from https://www.issm.info/sexual-health-qa/what-is-pelvic-floor-physical-therapy/

Kingsberg, S. (2002, October) The impact of aging on sexual function in women and their partners. *Archives of Sexual Behavior* 31 (5).

Kubler-E. (2014/1969). *On death and dying*. New York: Scribner.

Infoplease. (n.d.). Life expectancy by age. 1850–2011. *Infoplease*. Retrieved 7/29/20 from https://www.infoplease.com/us/mortality/life-expectancy-age-1850-2011.

Lilleston, R. (2017). STD rates keep rising for older adults. *AARP Real Possibilities*. Retrieved 07/27/20 from https://www.aarp.org/health/conditions-treatments/info-2017/std-exposure-rises-older-adults-fd.html

Lizcano, F., & Guzman, G. (2014, Mar 6). *Estrogen deficiency and the origin of obesity during menopause. Biomed Research International* 2014: 757461. https://www.ncbi.nlm.nih.gov/pmc/articles/PMC3964739/

Lunden, J. (2020). *Why did I come into this room? A candid conversation about aging*. Manila: Forefront Books.

Mahak, J. (2019, March 7). *Why do you never forget how to ride a bike? Science ABC*. Retrieved 08/03/20 from https://www.scienceabc.com/eyeopeners/what-is-muscle-memory.html

Marcin, A. (2019). *Height in girls: When do they stop growing, what's the median height, and more. Healthline.* Retrieved 3/12/20 from https://www. healthline.com/health/when-do-girls-stop-growing.

Marian, V., & Neisser, U. (2000). Language-dependent recall of autobiographical memories. *Journal of Experimental Psychology: General.* 129(3): 361–368.

Mayo Clinic. (2020). Metabolic syndrome. Retrieved 08/3/20 from https://www. mayoclinic.org/diseases-conditions/metabolic-syndrome/symptoms-causes/ syc-20351916.

Mayo Clinic. (2020) *Patient care and health information, osteoarthritis.* Retrieved 07/13/20 from https://www.mayoclinic.org/diseases-conditions/ osteoarthritis/symptoms-causes/syc-20351925

Mayo Clinic. (2019). Daily aspirin therapy: Understand the benefits and risks. Retrieved 7/17/20 from https://www.mayoclinic.org/diseases-conditions/ heart-disease/in-depth/daily-aspirin-therapy/art-20046797

Mayo Clinic. (2018). *Kegel exercises: A how-to guide for women.* Retrieved 7/16/20 from https://www.mayoclinic.org/healthy-lifestyle/womens-health/ in-depth/kegel-exercises/art

Mazzeo, R., Cavanagh, P., Evans, W., Fiatarone, M., Hagberg, J., McAuley, E., & Startzell, J. (1998, June). Position stand on exercise and physical activity for older adults. *Medicine & Sports & Exercise* 30(6): 975-991.

Mempowered. (2020). Word-finding problems. *Mempowered!* Retrieved April 20, 2020 from http://www.memory-key.com/problems/everyday_problems/ word-finding.

McConnell, A., Brown, C., Shoda, T., Stayton, L., & Martin, C. (2011, December). Friends with benefits: On the positive consequences of pet ownership. *Journal of Personality and Social Psychology* 101(6): 1239-1252.

Myss, C. (1996). *Anatomy of spirit, the seven stages of power and healing.* New York: Random House.

Nall, R. (2017). *10 types of dementia. Healthline.* Retrieved 07/16/20 from https://www.healthline.com/health/types-dementia.

National Council on Aging. (2017, February 2). Top 10 chronic conditions in adults 65+ and what you can do to prevent or manage them. *NCOA Blog.* Retrieved 07/29/20 from https://www.ncoa.org/blog/10-common-chronic-diseases-prevention-tips/

National Institute of Aging (June 2007). Unexplained fatigue in the elderly, mechanisms and modifiers of fatigue. Workshop.

National Institute of Diabetes and Digestive and Kidney Diseases. (2017). Diabetes Overview. Retrieved 7/29/20 https://www.niddk.nih.gov/health-information/diabetes/overview and https://www.niddk.nih.gov/health-information/diabetes/overview/preventing-problems/heart-disease-stroke

National Heart, Lung, and Blood Institute. (n.d.). According to waist circumference. guidelines on overweight and obesity: electronic textbook. Retrieved 7/14/20 from https://www.nhlbi.nih.gov/health-pro/guidelines/current/obesity-guidelines/e_textbook/txgd/4142.htm

Nursing Home Diaries. (2016, January 6). *How many seniors really end up In nursing homes?* Retrieved 07/09/20 https://nursinghomediaries.com/howmany/#:~:text -

Parker P. T. (2012, January 1). The Fat Trap. *New York Time Sunday Magazine* 2012: 22.

Parkkari J., Kannus P., Palvanen M., Natri A., Vainio J, Aho H., Vuori I., & Järvinen M. (1999). Majority of hip fractures occur as a result of a fall and impact on the greater trochanter of the femur: a prospective controlled hip fracture study with 206 consecutive patients. *Calcified Tissue International* 65:183–7.

Peery A., Keku T. & Martin C. F., Swathi, E., Runge, T., Galanko, J. A., & Sandler. R. S. (2016). Distribution and characteristics of colonic diverticula in a United States screening population. *Clinical Gastroenterology and Hepatology.* Epub ahead of print. Retrieved 7/14/20 from https://pubmed.ncbi.nlm.nih.gov/26872402/

Pension Rights Center. (n.d.). *Income received by different groups.* Retrieved 07/01/20 from http://www.pensionrights.org/publications/statistic/income-received-different-groups.

Pillemer, K. (2012, February 11). *Parents of estranged children offer advice. Huffington Post Blog.* Retrieved 7/16/20 from https://www.huffpost.com/entry/estranged-children_b_1267734

Poppink, J. (n.d.). Anorexia nervosa-associated laboratory findings. *Eating Disorder Recovery. 307.1.* Retrieved 07/15/20 from https://www.eatingdisorderrecovery.net/getting-help/the-dsm/440-3071-anorexia-nervosa-associated-laboratory-findings.

Porter, D, (2020, March 25). *What are Drusen. American Academy of Ophthalmology.* Retrieved 7/16/20 from https://www.aao.org/eye-health/diseases/what-are-drusen

Potter, J. V. (2020). *Harnessing the power of grief.* Hollister, CA: MSI Press.

Reynolds, G. (2020, March 31). How 'muscle memory' may help keep us fit. *New York Times:* D6

Roubenoff, R. (2004). Sarcopenic obesity: the confluence of two epidemics. *Obesity Research.* 12, 887–888.

Santos-Longhurst, A. (2018). Diaphragm overview. *Healthline.* Retrieved 07/14/20 from https://www.healthline.com/human-body-maps/diaphragm?source=post_page

Shahedi, K., Fuller, G., & Bolus, R., Cohen, C., Vu, M., Shah, R., Agarwal, N., Kaneshir, M., Atia, M., Sheen, V., Kurzbard,. N., Van Oijen, M. G. H., Ye, L., Hodgkins, P., Erder, M. H., & Spiegel, B. (2013) Long-term risk of acute diverticulitis among patients with incidental diverticulosis found during colonoscopy. *Clinical Gastroenterology and Hepatology* 11(12):1609–1613.

Shafto, M., Burke, D., Stamatakis, E., Tam, P., & Tyler, L (2007, December). On the tip-of-the-tongue: neural correlates of increased word-finding failures in normal aging. *Journal of Cognitive Neuroscience* 19 (12): 2060-2070.

Social Security Administration. (2019). *Fact Sheet: Social Security Is Important to Women.* Retrieved 7/1/20 from https://www.ssa.gov/news/press/factsheets/women-alt.pdf

Social Security Administration. (2017). Actuarial life table. *Period Life Table,* 2017. Retrieved 07/31/20 from https://www.ssa.gov/oact/STATS/table4c6.html

Taylor, M. (2019, March 14). Getting enough protein may be the key to healthy aging. *Prevention.* Retrieved 07/15/20 from https://www.prevention.com/food-nutrition/healthy-eating/a26390479/protein-for-older-adults/

Tierney, J. (2013, July 8). What is nostalgia good for? Quite a bit, research shows. *New York Times.*

Temple University. (2008, October 5). Mental barriers hamper obese women's efforts to get exercise. *Science Daily.* Retrieved 08/06/20 from https://www.sciencedaily.com/releases/2008/10/081005203055.htm

The North American Menopause Society. (2020). Yoga, Kegel exercises, pelvic floor physical therapy. Retrieved 07/16/20 from https://www.menopause.org/for-women/sexual-health-menopause-online/effective-treatments-for-sexual-problems/yoga-kegel-exercises-pelvic-floor-physical-therapy.

Van Cauter, E., Knutson, K., Leproult, R., & Spiegel, K. (2005). The impact of sleep deprivation on hormones and metabolism. *Medscape Neurology* 7(1): n.p.

Villareal, D., Banks, M., Siener, C., Sinacore, D., & Klein, A. (2004). Physical frailty and body composition in obese elderly men and women. *Obesity Research* 12: 913–920.

von Simson, R. (2012, February 2). Sexual health and the older adult, trends show that doctors must be more vigilant. *Student BMJ* Kings College.

Web MD. (2020). Vitamin B12: What to know. Retrieved 7/17/20 from https://www.webmd.com/diet/vitamin-b12-deficiency-symptoms-causes#2-6.

Wempen, K. (2016). *Are you getting too much protein? Mayo Clinic.* Retrieved 07/15/20 from https://www.mayoclinichealthsystem.org/hometown-health/speaking-of-health/are-you-getting-too-much-protein

West, H. (2017). 9 signs and symptoms of vitamin B12 deficiency. *Healthline.* Retrieved 3/22/20 from https://www.healthline.com/nutrition/vitamin-b12-deficiency-symptoms

Wildschut, T. Sedikides, C. Arndt, J. & Routledge, C. (2006). Nostalgia: Content, triggers, functions. *Journal of Personality and Social Psychology* 91(5): 975-993.

Worldometer. (2020). Life expectancy of the world population. Retrieved 07/23/20 from https://www.worldometers.info/demographics/life-expectancy/#countries-ranked-by-life-expectancy

Also by Bertha Cooper

Old and On Hold
Aging in Place during a Pandemic

Bertha D. Cooper, BSN

Written for active vulnerable elders by a vulnerable elder, this book provides unique perspective on the meaning, adjustment, and management of "stay at home." Others made vulnerable by a pandemic will find support, practical guides and relevance in managing life disrupted by an invisible threat and a nation struggling to save itself.

Select MSI Books

Health & Fitness

108 Yoga and Self-Care Practices for Busy Mommas (Gentile)

Girl, You Got This! (Renz)

Living Well with Chronic Illness (Charnas)

Survival of the Caregiver (Snyder)

The Optimistic Food Addict (Fisanick)

Pandemic Series

!0 Quick Homework Tips (Alder & Trombly)

Choice and Structure for Children with Autism (McNeil)

Exercising in a Pandemic (Young)

God Speaks into Darkness (Easterling)

How to Stay Calm in Chaos (Gentile)

Old and On Hold (Cooper)

Parenting in a Pandemic (Bayardelle)

Porn and the Pandemic (Shea)

Seeking Balance in an Unbalanced Time (Greenebaum)

Staying Safe While Sheltering in Place (Schnuelle, Adams, & Henderson)

The Pandemic and Hope (Ortman)

Tips, Tools, and Anecdotes to Help during a Pandemic (Charnas)

Self-Help Books

100 Tips and Tools for Managing Chronic Illness (Charnas)

A Woman's Guide to Self-Nurturing (Romer)

Creative Aging: A Baby Boomer's Guide to Successful Living (Vassiliadis & Romer)

Divorced! Survival Techniques for Singles over Forty (Romer)

Harnessing the Power of Grief (Potter)

Healing from Incest (Henderson & Emerton)

Helping the Disabled Veteran (Romer)

How My Cat Made Me a Better Man (Feig)

How to Get Happy and Stay That Way: Practical Techniques for Putting Joy into Your Life (Romer)

How to Live from Your Heart (Hucknall) (Book of the Year Finalist)

Life after Losing a Child (Young & Romer)

Passing On (Romer)

Publishing for Smarties: Finding a Publisher (Ham)

Recovering from Domestic Violence, Abuse, and Stalking (Romer)

RV Oopsies (MacDonald)The Widower's Guide to a New Life (Romer)(Book of the Year Finalist)

The Rose and the Sword (Bach & Hucknall)

The Widower's Guide to a New Life (Romer)

Widow: A Survival Guide for the First Year (Romer)

Widow: How to Survive (and Thrive!) in Your 2d, 3d, and 4th Years (Romer)

CPSIA information can be obtained
at www.ICGtesting.com
Printed in the USA
FSHW021155121020
74640FS